Crime
Scene

Crime Scene

On the Streets with a Rookie Police Reporter

Mitch Gelman

TIMES BOOKS

Grateful acknowledgment is made to the following for permission to reprint previously published material:
EMI MUSIC PUBLISHING: Excerpts from "Talkin' Bout a Revolution" and "Behind the Wall" by Tracy Chapman. Copyright © 1988 by EMI April Music Inc./Purple Rabbit Music. All rights controlled and administered by EMI April Music Inc. All rights reserved. International copyright secured. Reprinted by permission.
MCA MUSIC PUBLISHING: Excerpts from "What I Am" by Edie Brickell, Kenneth Withrow, John Houser, John Rush, and Alan Aly. Copyright © 1988 by Geffen Music, Edie Brickell Songs, Withrow Publishing, Enlightened Kitty, and Strange Mind Productions. All rights administered by MCA Music Publishing, a division of MCA, Inc., New York, N.Y. 10019. All rights reserved. Reprinted by permission.

Library of Congress Cataloging-in-Publication Data
Gelman, Mitch.
    Crime scene: on the streets with a rookie police reporter/ Mitch Gelman.—1st ed.
    p. cm.
    ISBN 0-8129-2084-8
    1. Crime and the press—New York (N.Y.) 2. Police and the press—New York (N.Y.) 3. New York (N.Y.)—Social conditions. 4. Gelman, Mitch. I. Title.
PN4899.N41G45 1992
070.4′49364′097471—dc20   92-5139

Manufactured in the United States of America

9 8 7 6 5 4 3 2

First Edition

*In memory of Al Golden
and Abe Korman*

Contents

Prologue   3

Byline   11

Breaking In   17

Probation   28

New Year   44

Shoe Leather   59

Living Dead   77

Little Italy   96

Keeping Faith   120

The Wild Thing   146

Joys of Summer   166

Getting On   181

"They Got the Wrong Niggers"   201

"To Me, He Sounded Like an American"   218

Never Say Die   232

Another Record   255

Epilogue   271

Acknowledgments   276

Crime
Scene

Prologue

On Christmas Eve, I was counting homicides.

The city was closing in on a new murder record, and my job was to be there as soon as possible after it happened. Most of the radio stations were playing Christmas carols, but I stayed tuned to WINS, the all-news station, where the announcer was keeping up with the city's run for the record. Every time he mentioned it, it sounded like a sports score, except the numbers were too high. In 1988, someone was murdered every five hours in New York City; the next homicide victim would be number 1,842, making it the bloodiest year in city history. That's big news in my business.

I had been a cop reporter for nearly six months and was almost finished with my probationary period. But I was still out to prove that I could do the job. My check-in and check-out times were set by criminals, so I never knew what I would be doing the next day (or hour) or where I'd be going. Some crackhead with a gun had more influence over my life than any parent, teacher, boss or lover ever had. When he shot somebody, a chain reaction began. My beeper would go off. I'd call one of the editors, find out what happened and off I'd go. *Bang! Beep! Hello. Goodbye.* Just like that, my evening would end and the next news story would begin.

Some people live day-to-day, but police reporters live story-to-story. And with all the robberies, rapes and murders in this town, that can be

3

a wicked, wonderful, spontaneous pace. Police reporting is a young person's game, competitive and all-consuming. It's hard to imagine being a good police reporter and a good father or husband. You rise with the sirens and eat and sleep between beeps. Crime occasionally tapers off, but the old cliché about it never taking a holiday is true. Not even on Christmas.

So on the night before, I was stopped at a red light somewhere around 66th Street and Second Avenue. The radiocaster announced that the cops had made it official: the record had fallen sometime during the afternoon. Adrenaline pumped into my neck and shoulders, and as soon as the light turned green, my foot pressed a little harder than usual on the accelerator.

I checked the passenger seat to make sure I had my thin spiral notebook and a ballpoint pen. I wove the car through traffic, down Second Avenue, eager to get an early start on this one. For six months I'd been doing legwork, gathering quotes for other people's stories, covering press conferences and writing two-paragraph shorts on minor killings. This could be my first front-page story.

The top floors of the Citicorp building were lit up in an electronic red, white and green Christmas tree. Usually you could see the tree from miles away, but the night was so cold and wet that the lights just glowed through the damp haze. This was one of Manhattan's newest and most handsome buildings, but it seemed ironic that a monument to such power and wealth stood fifty-nine stories above a city that seemed to be dying from crime. What diabolical timing, too, for the murder record to be set. It was as if a devious God wanted to say, Merry Christmas, New York.

I pulled over, bought a carton of eggnog and then steered the car along the East River, down the FDR Drive to Police Headquarters. I rode the elevator to the thirteenth floor and banged on the door of the deputy commissioner of public information's office. Sergeant Ed Burns was on duty. During the day, Burns ran his own public relations firm, but at night he worked as a cop. When it was slow, Burns usually put most of the phone lines on hold and lay down on the couch in the back office, getting the work done as effortlessly as possible. He came to the door wearing pajamas and slippers. I offered him a cup of the eggnog, and as he wiped sleep from his eyes, we toasted the holidays. Burns was polite, but I had interrupted his rest and he was not happy to see me. After the proper cordial exchange, I asked him about the murder record.

"All you want to do is hype the death toll. There's a million other stories, but all you want is a cheap headline. Don't you understand—except to you and your fucking editors, these numbers don't mean a thing," Burns said.

I started to debate with him. "If we identify this record victim, we can make him a symbol. And that'll make people mad."

"Write about something important, like all the guns out there," he said. "Or the way the cops are making thousands of arrests and these scumbags are being released because the jails are packed like sardine cans. This murder-rate stuff is crap. It's just a bunch of fucking numbers."

"It's more than that," I began, but Burns had clearly given up. He had better things to do than preach to me. He just shook his head, marveling at how naïve and ridiculous I sounded. Then he pointed toward the sheets.

"They're there if you want 'em," he said.

The crime sheets gave the who, what, when and where of unusual crimes, murders, rapes and big arrests. A dozen homicides from the last forty-eight hours were still on the clipboard. I paged through them, trying to pick out the record-breaker. The mark had been passed sometime that afternoon, but Burns said there was no way to know exactly who the 1,842nd victim was. After all, next week the cops could find a body that had been stuffed in a closet, or the medical examiner's office might determine that a guy the police thought had been killed had actually died from natural causes. That gave me a bit of latitude.

I wanted to find one killing that would dramatize the entire surge of wasted minds, bodies, even bullets. I wanted readers to take a minute from Christmas Day to mourn this death and all the others. I wanted them to cry over this story and feel the loss. I was also looking for a murder that was provocative enough to make the front page. In New

York, not every murder even got in the paper. This was not some small town or even a mid-size city. A killing had to have an angle or a hook to get good play. I noticed one on the sheets that might work.

Michael Evans had been stabbed with a bayonet at 1:40 P.M., a few blocks away from his house on Union Street in the Brownsville–East New York section of Brooklyn. I kept picturing some guy lying on the ground with a bayonet sticking out of his chest. The only other time I'd heard about someone being killed with a bayonet was a German soldier in the movie version of *All Quiet on the Western Front.* Evans's neighborhood in Brooklyn was six square miles of the most drug-ravaged, murderous terrain in the city. Historically, this area had bred crime. During the 1940s it was the base of the old Jewish Mafia in New York, headquarters to Murder Inc. Twenty years later, the lower end of the Italian mob—the goodfellas and wiseguys who hijacked trucks and rubbed each other out—made it their home. By the late 1980s, years after the last middle-class whites and blacks had moved to finer neighborhoods in Queens or on Long Island, homicide detectives were calling it the Wild, Wild East. Now Michael Evans had died on these streets.

I arrived at the Evans home at twelve-thirty A.M. on Christmas morning. He had lived on the top floor of a two-story row house with his wife and three children. The house had heat and running hot and cold water, which was more than could be said about a lot of places in the neighborhood. At both ends of the block, homeless men and women and crack addicts huddled beside fires in vacant lots like stray animals drawn to the warmth. I climbed the Evanses' stoop and rang the bell, but no one was home. A neighbor heard my clatter and said Evans's wife, Brenda, was staying with friends and was too upset to talk. He suggested I return later, when she might feel a little better.

I was disappointed she wasn't around, because an early interview would have given me a real edge on the story. I'd also wanted to get this part over with quickly. The initial contact with grieving relatives was like jumping into a cold pool of water; it was best to just do it and not think about it too much. This time I'd have to wait.

So much of this part of the city was depressed by people's poverty, fear and anger, and covering this death amid this desolation didn't leave much to be hopeful about. Driving back to Manhattan, I was feeling down and looking for a way to capture some of the holiday spirit when, about half a mile from the Evans home, I was drawn to a church on top of a hill.

Almost all of the people packed inside for midnight mass were black. The pews were filled, and the sanctuary had standing room only. Pinned chest to back in a tangle of arms and legs, dark suits and bright dresses, the worshipers reached out for a place where there were no thieves or killers. I leaned against a wall by the door and joined in as they sang "Silent Night." The melody rose into the steeple and bounced off the stained-glass windows. *"Silent night, holy night. All is calm, all is bright."* So powerful. So rich, warm and innocent. *"Round yon virgin mother and child. Holy infant, so tender and mild."* The words and music penetrated deeply. It seemed odd I would end up there that night; it also seemed appropriate. In that church, among the Bibles and away from the bullets and bayonets, the spirit was greater than the suffering.

The minister ended the service with a prayer for peace, and as the parishioners filed out, an usher distributed calendars for the new year. I prayed silently that 1989 would be a year without any records like that night's, but something inside nagged at my sincerity: I also wanted page-one stories.

In my car, I turned the radio to Christmas music and drove home to get a few hours' sleep.

A few minutes after ten the next morning, I showed up at the Evans house carrying books, rubber balls and bubble gum for the children. Maurice Evans, the four-month-old, was asleep, but the other two were up. Michael Brandon, Jr., two, was scampering along the linoleum kitchen floor, playing with a space shuttle toy he'd received a few hours earlier. Millie, who was six, was outside with friends, asking her grandmother for money to go to the deli. Millie was delighted with the red bicycle she had found under the tree, but her grandmother said the girl knew why her father wasn't there to see her open the gift.

"Jesus didn't take Daddy," Millie had said after ripping wrapping paper from the bike. "Someone stabbed him."

Brenda Evans had gone to the morgue, and still wasn't home when I arrived. The Brooklyn morgue is in the basement of a building behind the borough's busiest hospital, connected by a tunnel and an elevator to the emergency room. On Christmas morning, an attendant pulled a white sheet off her husband, who lay on a steel tray in one of 190 freezer compartments. Brenda saw only his face, his thin nose, broad forehead and walnut skin. It was Michael.

Around noon, she returned home in a brown sedan. Her eyes were still heavy and tired, weighed down by what she had witnessed the day before. I didn't know how to approach her. The only reason I was covering her husband's murder was that its timing made it important. He was a statistic, like a dozen other people killed in his neighborhood every month, but his number happened to be more significant than the rest. That was not something I could tell Brenda Evans. She had to believe I was there because Michael Evans's life deserved to be remembered. Fortunately, she never asked why I had come, so I did not have to lie to her. She washed her face, toweled off the tears and began talking.

Brenda had been with her husband when he was killed, so she could not only tell me about him as a person, she could also give me plenty of details about his murder. Get the *details*; every editor I ever had had drummed that into my head. Details made a story good.

Brenda and Michael Evans were on their way home with the last of their Christmas shopping. Evans was an assistant manager at a Key Food supermarket warehouse, and Brenda was an auditor with the Board of Education. Their salaries added up nicely, and if all continued going well, they planned to move to a better neighborhood soon. Evans wore a thick gray overcoat and carried the bulk of the bundles, which included the red bicycle for his pride and joy, his little ballerina, Millie, and two bags filled with presents for his young sons. He had lugged the packages from downtown Brooklyn on the subway and was almost home when the man with the bayonet leaped from a doorway.

In this part of Brooklyn, where there were perhaps more guns per capita than anywhere that wasn't an army base, it seemed nuts to kill someone with a bayonet. This was the late 1980s in New York, not a feudal hamlet in eighteenth-century France.

Evans, armed only with his packages, tried to defend himself, but the man plunged the bayonet through Evans's overcoat, pulled it out and fled. As Michael Evans fell, the gifts scattered on the sidewalk.

"C'mon Brenda," he said, stumbling to his feet. "Get the presents. The children have to have Christmas."

He did not know he had been stabbed until he opened his overcoat and his blood spilled on his wife and on the gifts. Evans fell back down again. He was dead.

Cops say most homicides are caused by love, drugs or money. In Michael Evans's case, it was another woman. Brenda Evans and her mother-in-law had been receiving notes and cards from a man who lived down the street. His name was Gregory Phillips, and he was very much in love with the woman he lived with. But Phillips's girlfriend had "this thing" with Evans, according to the letters. Phillips wrote that if "this thing" didn't end, he would stop it himself. Earlier in the week, the two had had a fight on Evans's stoop. Like the letters, it ended with a death threat.

Detectives learned all of this within a few hours of the stabbing. This case was what they call a "ground ball," easy to solve. When detectives went to Phillips's apartment, he was waiting for them at his kitchen table. The bayonet, covered with Evans's burnt-red dried blood, was lying in front of him.

"I think I'm the guy you're looking for," he said.

They arrested Phillips, took the bayonet as evidence and charged him with second-degree murder.

Before I could go back to the office to write, I had to wait for a *Newsday* photographer to get some art for the story. Out the window, I watched two kids playing with their new Christmas toys, imitation Uzi machine guns. The taller boy also clutched a plastic pistol. He ducked into an alley and then peeked around a wall. Slowly, he crept out and fired; the smaller boy returned half-a-dozen make-believe rounds. Both called out the sounds of their gunshots. *Terrat-a-trrat-trrat. Terrat-a-trrat-trrat.* As I waited, they traded shots and shouts.

When Lee Romero, the photographer, arrived, I suggested he take a portrait of the Evans family around their Christmas tree with the red bicycle in the foreground. It showed the stark horror written in deep lines on their faces; the presents at their feet underscored the tragic timing of their loss. For a police reporter, the Evanses' misery was the perfect Christmas story, and Romero's portrait illustrated it perfectly.

"This is terrific," I told Romero when he showed me the print back at the office. My voice betrayed too much of my excitement.

"You're a ghoul," he snapped back, his voice getting louder as he walked away. "You know that? You're a ghoul. All you care about is seeing your story on the front page."

I tried to laugh it off, but his comment stung. He brought me back to the reality that those kids and that woman in front of that tree were not just a front-page story. They were feeling the monstrous, haunting pain of death, the shock of murder. The children had lost a father, and Brenda Evans had lost her husband. Something she'd said earlier in the day, tears in her tired eyes, came back to me. "Christmas will never be good again. It is ruined for us forever."

Romero was halfway across the room by then, but he glanced back. I pretended not to see him. We both knew that the next morning his picture and my story would lead the paper. The headline: CHRISTMAS MURDER 1988.

Byline

I was introduced to journalism early. My father was a magazine editor, and when I was old enough to read, my parents showed me a copy of *The New York Times* they'd saved from March 21, 1962, the day I was born. Nothing very important had happened, but it was the first newspaper I looked at with any interest.

Opposite a story on page forty-one about a hike in the dog licensing fee was a little police news. Mayor Robert Wagner had asked a Police Academy graduating class to pay special attention to people who were trying to corrupt the city's youth with narcotics. It was a short story about a problem that would still be exploding more than a quarter century later.

When I was in fourth grade, my parents came to a school bazaar. The kids were selling cakes, clothes and games to raise money, and a band was playing the Rolling Stones' "Jumpin' Jack Flash." I was hobbling around on crutches, the result of knee ligaments I'd torn while skiing. I remember seeing my dad stuff a five-dollar bill into a coffee can for the school paper. To a nine-year-old, five dollars was a lot of money, and I was astonished my dad had just given it away like that. But he proudly said, "You have to support the press."

Until then, most of my interest had been in sneaking out of class to play basketball, cops and robbers or poker with my friends, but I soon discovered reporting could be fun, too. I made a press pass out of orange construction paper and used a shoelace to hang it around my neck. A few weeks later, a big fire raged at a Hudson River pier near the school. When I heard the trucks roaring past the school at lunchtime, I snuck out of the building and ran toward the river. Firefighters lugged thick canvas hoses and aimed them at flames jumping through the smoke. Police cars screeched up, sirens blaring, and cops stretched crime scene tape around the fire's perimeter. Excitedly, I flipped my handmade press pass, and an officer let me slip under the tape as long as I promised to stay behind the fire trucks.

I started asking one of the battalion chiefs questions: Was there anybody inside? How many firemen had come? My class had been making conservation posters about the water shortage. I wanted to know if he'd noticed any decrease in pressure or problems in fighting the blaze? "Not so far," the chief said. I headed back to school with a piece of paper scribbled with quotes from the chief, whose name I hadn't bothered to write down.

I went to junior high school in Chelsea. Like many of the city schools back then, it was integrated, about equal parts black, Puerto Rican and white. The school was named after O. Henry, the writer who lived much of his life in the neighborhood, and the newspaper was called the *O. Henry Short Story*. I joined the paper in sixth grade and wrote mostly on sports. We didn't have a lot of editions, but every few months, we helped our faculty adviser carry a thousand copies back to school, hot off the presses. There was nothing greater than seeing my name published on top of an article, and I fantasized that someday I'd write for one of the real New York papers. There was only one thing I wanted to do more: play professional baseball.

In the mid-1970s, New York City was struck by a fiscal crisis. The quality of life there began to erode. Libraries closed, cops were fired and the school system decided that things like newspapers were luxuries it couldn't afford. My family decided it was time to join the flight to the Sun Belt, and moved to Los Angeles. At first, I felt like a deserter. Leaving the city just when it fell on tough times seemed to contradict the liberal social values I'd been raised on. But New York's problems were easier to forget after a little while in L.A. I didn't have a lot of trouble adjusting to the eighty-degree weather or our swimming pool overlooking the city. Within weeks I had a suntan, and the day I turned sixteen I got a driver's license and all the freedom that came with it.

But one thing I didn't like about the suburbs was having a newspaper delivered to your driveway. It wasn't the same as buying the news from a gruff old man at the green wooden newsstand across from the bagel place on Eighth Street and Sixth Avenue. Also, the *Los Angeles Times* was a cumbersome, multisectioned broadsheet; you practically had to lay it out on a kitchen table to read it. The *Daily News* was a tabloid and had fit right in front of me on the subway. It was the perfect size to roll into a baseball bat for my friends and me to hit aluminum-foil balls with in vacant classrooms at lunchtime. Still, I learned to make do with the real sports fields in Los Angeles and spent most of my high school years playing baseball and football.

It wasn't long, though, before I was back in newspapers. The summer between my junior and senior years, a friend of my father's who worked at the Los Angeles *Herald Examiner* got me a job as a copyboy, clipping and spiking wire copy as it came over the ticker. The next summer, I came back as a city desk clerk, which meant I answered a lot of phones. In addition to taking messages for reporters, I took calls from the psychos who somehow thought the newspaper could either find them a job, get them out of jail or put them in contact with the appropriate agency for stopping UFOs from hovering over their homes. For my third summer at the paper I was a reporter-intern. One of the veterans told me he was glad to see me again. "You roll in every summer," he said. "Like the smog!" That was enough for the *Herald*—and L.A.

California was a great place to do things—to drive, to swim, to jog, to play ball, see movies and all that—but I never felt I could really *live* in Los Angeles. Things seemed less real there. After graduating from the University of California, Berkeley, and spending a year studying politics and economics at the National University of Singapore, I returned to New York. I got part-time work as a stringer reporting stories a few days a week for *Time* magazine's New York bureau. I enjoyed working there, but it seemed to me that weekly newsmagazines spent a lot of time chasing newspaper stories, and I wanted to be closer to the action.

I set my sights on *New York Newsday*, a brash tabloid trying to crack the local newspaper market controlled by the *Daily News, The New York Times* and the *New York Post. New York Newsday* was a spin-off of the paper's Long Island edition, and its reporters covered New York as aggressively as *The New York Times* covered Afghanistan. They were muckrakers in the Lincoln Steffens tradition who wrote about corruption in City Hall, housing discrimination, crack abuse and police brutality—topics that mattered to New Yorkers, more than three million of whom still got their news from newspapers. I thought I could contribute to the community as a reporter and applied for a job at *Newsday* with visions of righting wrongs and having a voice in city affairs.

A friend from the *Herald* called Thomas Plate, the editor of *New York Newsday*'s editorial pages. Plate had been at the *Herald* when I was there, but I knew him only as a pin-striped suit who wrote hip editorials and had covered the 1980 presidential campaign. After several interviews with Plate and his staff, I was hired as a researcher. I sat in on daily meetings and listened to the paper's heavyweights make *Newsday* policy. Occasionally I'd get a chance to throw in an opinion, but mostly I researched issues, wrote memos and ordered croissants and Danish pastries for editorial board meetings. Plate felt it was his duty to knock the yup-pup out of all his young hires, and I was no exception. In the beginning, I resisted his requests that I make coffee, but one day I gave in. All it took was one taste and Plate never wanted me to make coffee again.

To avoid any conflicts of interest, the paper's editorial policy was independent from its news coverage, and we maintained this separation between church and state. The gap between sitting around pontificating about the news and what I wanted to learn how to do—actually be out there covering it—was even greater. This was never clearer than the day I asked police reporter Richie Esposito about a story he'd written on a police-fire feud. His shoes were off and his feet were propped up on his desk. I asked him how he'd gotten a secret memo from a deputy mayor that revealed the gravity of the fighting between the two public safety agencies. Although we had talked in the past—

when I was stringing for *Time*, he helped me chase a story he had broken for *Newsday* on NYPD detectives being loaned to the CIA—Esposito just muttered something about getting the memo from a friend. He wasn't sharing anything about how a reporter gets a leak like that. I slinked away, hurt that he didn't trust me. Only later did I realize that his ability to keep secrets was part of why he'd been able to get the story.

I loved going to the newsroom, seeing and talking to the reporters, and I wanted to work with them. Once I got desperate and sent the paper's editor, Don Forst, a cinnamon-coated brioche in an interoffice envelope to show how frustrated I was that part of my job was ordering pastries. Finally, after almost two years on the editorial pages, Forst called me to his office.

Leaning forward in his chair, Forst, who wears wide ties out of some 1950s newsroom, picked up a toy gavel that squeaked when he banged it on the desk. He told me my days with pastries were about to end. He wanted me to go downtown, to Police Headquarters, to work as a reporter. All right! He wasn't sending me to the style section or the sports department, where reporters covered fluff and went to ball games and movies. He was putting me right into the heart of the city. My father said covering crime was the best way to learn how to be a reporter. I couldn't wait.

Two city desk editors couldn't wait, either. Hap Hairston, who worked directly under Forst, dropped a heavy arm on my shoulders the next time he saw me. "I own you now," he whispered. "I own you." I tried to joke that he might own 65 percent, but Don King handled the rest. Still, I knew he was right, and I didn't care. Tom Curran, the editor who opened in the morning, also staked out his share in a computer message that said, "Looking forward to when you get your sorry self up here so I can chase you after two-dead, six-injured stories!"

On my last day on the editorial pages, the staff went out for drinks and gave me a couple of funny gifts: a hand-held massager to work out the stress from working with jumpy editors, and a travel alarm clock for my first overseas assignments—to Queens and Brooklyn. This was a gag because, unless you count a few Mets games, I hadn't been to

Queens since my grandmother died in 1979, and although my father grew up in Brooklyn, I hardly knew that borough, either. That afternoon we had a lot of fun laughing about my future career, but I wouldn't have been any more excited if the paper were sending me to the Moscow bureau.

Breaking In

My alarm clock went off at six A.M. on July 19, 1988, and I popped out of bed full of energy. It usually took me awhile to get my motor running in the morning, but not today.

I grabbed some white socks, pulled on a pair of shorts and a clean T-shirt, tied the laces on my New Balance joggers and took the elevator down for a run through midtown Manhattan. As I headed out the door of my apartment building, I couldn't help smiling. I was finally going to be a reporter at a newspaper in the city where I grew up.

Around six-twenty A.M., I dashed back into the two-bedroom apartment I shared with a roommate who was still sleeping. I couldn't resist cranking up WINS to hear the morning news while I showered and shaved. I wanted everything to be just right that morning. I picked out a pair of gray flannels, a button-down Oxford shirt and my blue blazer. Then I spent a full three minutes at the mirror getting my tie to slide right up in the center of the collar. I shoveled down a bowl of Raisin Bran, grabbed my brown leather briefcase and nearly tripped over myself getting out the door.

Outside, I threw a dollar-forty down for copies of *Newsday*, the *Times*, *News* and *Post*, and scanned the front pages as I walked down the street on my way to the subway at Grand Central Station. My head in the paper, I nearly bumped into a couple of pedestrians and a parking meter on the way.

It was too early for the Lexington Avenue Express to be crowded yet, so it rocketed two long stops downtown to the Brooklyn Bridge–City Hall station. It was already hot, and I was sweating by the time I climbed the stairs out of the subway. I looked up and everything was there: City Hall, the World Trade Center, the state and federal court-houses on Foley Square and, finally, Police Headquarters, across a long brick plaza to the east.

A stout, fourteen-story redbrick fortress set firmly upon stilts, Head-quarters looked like a lunar module built for a concrete landscape. The building's four corners each pointed toward one of the city's outer boroughs. It was at the center of the stage I was about to enter, and I froze for a moment before crossing the plaza.

The thrill I had when I walked by the uniformed cop guarding the door at Police Headquarters was the same one I had felt twenty years earlier when my father gave me my first baseball glove. Getting that glove had been a rite of passage. The snap of the rawhide hardball against the stiff, unmolded pocket meant that boyhood dreams, wild ones of fame and fortune, of chasing down fly balls like Mickey Mantle, were real possibilities. Those dreams had lasted a long time. Then, during my freshman year of college, about the same time Darryl Straw-berry signed his first contract with the New York Mets, I was cut from my college team. I traded in my glove for the portable Olivetti Lettera 32 typewriter my father had given me for my bar mitzvah. Conceding the green grass to Strawberry, I looked somewhere else.

The presence of writers like Jimmy Breslin and Pete Hamill were etched in my mind every bit as much as Mantle was. Dad used to talk about Breslin and Hamill a lot when he edited their copy at the maga-zines they worked for. Conversation at our dinner table often revolved around their working class, antiwar, pro-city politics. Some sons follow their fathers into steel mills or law firms. I followed mine into our family business.

As a boy, I figured there were two ways I could earn my father's respect and admiration: hit home runs and steal bases like Mantle or write as passionately and insightfully as Breslin and Hamill. Mantle had gotten fat and retired to a bar on Central Park South, but Breslin and Hamill were still writing three columns a week. They continued to feel the city's heartbeat and to write about its politics, education, arts and, of course, crime. They became my heroes. So when I walked into the Cop Shop, a cluster of newspaper offices on the second floor of Headquarters, a press pass in my jacket pocket and a briefcase in my right hand, I could smell the leather of that baseball glove and hear the rawhide snap of the hardball like it was yesterday.

The three desks in *Newsday*'s small office were cluttered with last week's papers, yesterday's phone messages and notes for tomorrow's news. Copies of *Newsday*, the *Post*, *News* and *Times* were stacked in knee-high piles in an industrial steel bookcase. An old typewriter collected dust in a corner, and a black Bearcat police scanner sat on the sill of a window that didn't open. Two desks had computers on them, wide Epsons with keyboards that clicked when you typed. There were five phones in the office: three with regular lines and one with a direct line to the deputy commissioner of public information's office—spin control central—on the building's thirteenth floor. Another was a special line that was kept secret from the police department so they wouldn't tap it.

Over one of the desks, someone had taped up an old Pete Hamill column about reporters drinking and talking and singing folk songs late into the night at the Lion's Head pub as a snowfall dusted Christopher Street outside. The paper had yellowed but the column's spirit remained fresh. I could hardly believe I was sitting beneath a Hamill column and working for the same paper as Breslin. The newsprint in the office smelled as sweet as any newly mowed outfield ever had. I had walked into a tradition, one that linked my own heritage to that of the city. This time, my dream had come true.

I would work Tuesdays through Saturdays, starting at ten A.M., but Richie Esposito, the bureau chief, had told me to come in early the first week. He wanted to give me his own headquarters orientation. As I waited for Esposito to arrive, reading the papers, some guy I couldn't see threw the first high, hard one.

"So, who are ya, kid?"

The voice came from the office next door to *Newsday*'s. I peered around the partition and saw a man leaning his thick arms on a slate-gray desk. The desk was clean except for a couple of rotary dial phones, a slice of unlined paper and a thick lead pencil.

"Joe Cotter of the *New York Post*," he said, introducing himself.

I told him my name and that I'd been promoted from the researcher job on the editorial pages.

"Okay. That's okay," he said. "But the first thing is you have to get a chain to hang that press card on. Then we can worry about making you a real reporter."

Cotter told he me had been working out of the Cop Shop, also known as the Shack, since 1948, when it really was a shack behind the old Police Headquarters on Centre Street. There were eight daily papers in the city back then. In 1988 there were four and the old Headquarters was a co-op apartment building, but Cotter, an Irishman with sparkling eyes, was still around.

"Step inside and relax yourself for a minute," he said.

I walked in and Cotter offered me a cup of tea, which I swallowed too quickly. Listening to him talk was like taking a tour of the city's newspaper past. Cotter was a throwback to the front-page days of big city newspapering, when reporters called the desk and screamed, "Hello, sweetheart! Get me rewrite!" when newsrooms clattered with typewriters and even copyboys wore jackets and ties. During his first few years, Cotter had even carried bets to bookies and brought booze to editors. "There was many a time when I hustled out to some nearby gin mill to get a coffee cup filled with scotch for some suffering soul on the city desk," he said. He remembered when reporters at the original Shack listened to fire bells that dinged out addresses of blazes like the Morse code. Through the decades, Cotter wrote about police scandals, mob murders and disasters, including one when two planes collided, one crashing on Staten Island and the other in Brooklyn. But now, he said, all the fires melted together and the cop stories were one big shooting complicated by an intricate whodunit.

"The news business was more romantic back then," he said. "There were more of us reporters. Not too many had gone to college and we were self-taught writers, and damn good ones. There's still the same sense of camaraderie and competition and the thrill of the chase, but it's not the same."

I must have been a sight for Cotter. I weighed a slim 150 pounds, ate right, ran and went to the gym four times a week. My blond hair and blue eyes made me look a lot more like a Californian than a New Yorker. One colleague said I looked like Joe College and another said I seemed as naïve as a babe tossed into a jungle. I was brimming with idealism that morning. If someone had asked me, I could have given my standard speech about the press being the glue that holds a democracy together, that government could and should work, that people were inherently good and that cops always arrested the ones who went bad. (Thank God, nobody asked.)

I heard a shuffling and a door being flung open. Suddenly, after a whirlwind rustling of air, Esposito burst into the Cop Shop and saw me with Cotter.

"Trying to steal another of my guys, Joe?" he said with a grin. Then, twisting his head in my direction, he lowered his voice: "Yo, kid, just don't forget who's paying your salary."

Richie—and everybody called him that or Espo—was thirty-three years old and had been a police reporter for eight years. He had started out as a copyboy with the *Daily News* and become a reporter both there and at the *Post.* He had covered the NYPD, the FBI and the Drug Enforcement Administration, as well as the Port Authority and Transit and Housing police departments, the United States Marshals and Secret Service. He seemed to like being the paper's police bureau chief, but he also had ambitions to rise further in the paper's hierarchy.

He grew up on Pleasant Avenue in East Harlem, where legend had it more murderers were born during the first half of the century than anyplace except Sicily. Esposito had short, wiry black hair, a rectangular face and olive skin. He wore designer eyeglasses, liked Italian suits and carried himself like he was still a neighborhood guy. Part of him remained a street kid, but he now lived in the West Village, far from Pleasant Avenue. And he was as comfortable talking to editors as to detectives.

In the Cop Shop, Esposito was a highly caffeinated, chain-smoking blur, always doing more than one thing at once. He had three speeds: fast, faster and one that can only be compared to a Ferrari racing around a corner on two wheels, always on the verge of crashing, but never going out of control. Luckily for me, he was also a good teacher.

I stood there gazing as he simultaneously hung his beige summer suit coat on a hanger and opened his leather attaché case, which was filled with manila folders, pens, detectives' business cards and a paper-back copy of *Bonfire of the Vanities.* He picked out his prized posses-sion, a leather-bound loose-leaf address book, and tossed it on his desk. Packed with names and numbers written in pen and pencil up and down the pages, it was the product of eight years of collecting the numbers of cops, district attorneys, defense lawyers, politicians and high-powered public relations men. His phone book was the envy of the daily press corps. After making two quick calls, talking in rapid-fire bursts into the receiver, he turned to me.

"Here's the most important thing to know," Esposito said.

Then he showed me the kitchenette in the Division of Community Affairs, where, for five dollars every two weeks, I could get all the lukewarm, rancid coffee my stomach could handle. (I preferred tea at the time, but coffee was a habit I'd have to pick up if I was going to be a real reporter.)

"C'mon," he said, "I'll introduce you around at DCPI."

The deputy commissioner of public information's office was on the thirteenth floor. We waited an interminably long time for an elevator, and once it arrived, it was crammed, not with the corporate types at the main *Newsday* building uptown, but with men in toupees who were tucking their stomachs under their belts, and women with gaudy lip-stick and flashy gold necklaces clutching purses to their sides. The department brass, who drove in from Long Island, wore identification cards clipped to their suit jacket pockets; the rest of the elevator crowd were civilian employees, the black, white, Asian and Hispanic messengers, custodians and bookkeepers who worked in Headquar-ters.

The public information office took up enough space for a tennis court. It was cleaner and more modern than the Cop Shop. The cops in DCPI had a color television, a fax machine, two scanners and about twenty-five telephones, including special lines to the police commissioner and the top chiefs. The office was staffed by police officers who sat in pods and stayed on top of what was going on all over the city. The higher the officer's rank, the bigger his pod. Deputy Commissioner Alice McGillion had her own office, and her executive officer, Captain Thomas Fahey, had a smaller office next to hers. Esposito moved smoothly among the cops, joking with them and sharing tidbits about what he had done over the weekend. He introduced me first to McGillion and Fahey, and then to the cops who worked for them. Esposito said that was the cop way: Do everything according to rank so nobody gets their nose out of joint.

The first thing I would have to do each morning was take the principal case sheet out of *Newsday*'s mailbox. The typewritten sheet had brief accounts of all murders, bank robberies and suspensions of officers from the day before. Next, Esposito showed me the handwritten crime sheets on a plain wooden clipboard. These were more detailed and had to be checked every forty-five minutes so that we were up on everything that happened. Once I read the sheets, he said I should make follow-up calls to the detectives in the precincts to "get a feel" for the killings that had happened overnight.

Back downstairs, Esposito handed me a police roster that listed the phone numbers of the various divisions and precincts. (It took me a week before I figured out why there were two numbers for every precinct: one was for the patrol cops, the other for the detective squad. I guess I was pretty slow to catch on, but there was a lot to pick up.) The city had seventy-five precincts, and just to be sure that novice reporters would have trouble learning them, they were numbered out of sequence. The numbers, which ranged from one to 123, jumped all around. Manhattan, for example, had eighteen precincts with numbers between one and thirty-four, and three more with names: the Central Park Precinct, Midtown North and Midtown South. I found precincts with numbers between forty and fifty-two in the Bronx and those between sixty and ninety in Brooklyn. The low hundreds were in Queens, and Staten Island was home to the 120th, 122nd, and 123rd precincts, making me wonder if the 121st had been lost under a landfill. As I studied a map of the precincts, I decided it must have been set up by a bunch of drunk cops playing darts in a bar one night.

Esposito also told me to familiarize myself with the organizational chart of the police department that hung on the wall over his desk. It looked like a spider web, with more than fifty little boxes and lines running every which way. I felt like a fly trapped somewhere between the box labeled chief of personnel and the one off to the side of the deputy commissioner for management and budget. And it was only nine-thirty A.M.

While Esposito was showing me how to use the computers and how to send copy uptown, reporters from the *Times*, the *News*, *El Diario* and *Noticias del Mundo* stopped by to say hello. When Ginny Byrne from the Associated Press came in, Esposito introduced her as a very important person.

"Basically," she said, "if I move a story on the wire before you tell the editors uptown, that's not good for you. So, be nice." If a wire service got a story before we did, Esposito added, the editors would think we'd been goofing off. I could tell that a lot of this job would be about constantly trying to stay ahead of the competition.

One way of doing that was by paying attention to the scanner, which sat on a windowsill crackling unintelligible background noise. "What you have to listen for is a series of beeps and the dispatcher calling a 'Ten-thirteen,' cop-code for 'officer in trouble.'" Esposito said a confirmed 10-13 meant a potentially big story, possibly a cop shot, and I was to beep him if he wasn't there and call one of the editors on the desk.

By this point, I was overwhelmed and feeling completely miscast in my new role. Esposito had to meet a source across town, but if anything happened, I should call either Laura Durkin, the cops and courts editor, or Tom Curran, uptown. He wrote down his beeper number and said, "Beep me if you need me." Then he was gone.

I didn't know what to do, so I opened a newspaper. But I was so terrified I'd miss a big story that I couldn't make any sense of what I was reading. I just sat there trying to keep my head up and my ears open.

Laura Durkin called pretty regularly to make sure nothing was going on. She kept close tabs on the bureau. Laura had been a hotshot reporter on Long Island, but she was still new as an editor and was scared something might fall through the cracks. She also must have figured that with me down there alone, green as a sapling, she had good reason to be concerned. Laura had pet names for her reporters and started calling me Snookie or Cookie. Sometimes she used Ferret-face, which I accepted as a term of endearment. She called twice in the first hour after Esposito left, but I didn't have anything to report.

A few minutes before eleven A.M., the DCPI hotline rang and all the papers and the AP picked up. The cops had found an unidentified body in a gutter. If we wanted more on the case, the police spokesman said to call the Brooklyn South Homicide Squad.

I phoned Laura about the story. She told me to gather the information and send up a short slugged cBODY20. A slug is a story's computer name that the editors list on the daily news budget. The "c" stood for city desk and "20" for the date the story would be in the paper.

"Okay, Snookie. Send it up soon. We try to get the junk out of the way early, in case something big happens," Laura said.

"I'll try," I said.

I spoke to a detective at Brooklyn South Homicide and wrote down as much as he had about the killing and the body. This was not a difficult story, but I sat stiffly in front of my terminal trying to craft every sentence as if I were writing the Great American Novel.

Instead, I was creating a mess.

Throughout the day, the bureau's other three reporters, Alison Carper, Elaine Rivera and Chapin Wright, arrived at the Shack. But I didn't talk to them too much because I was nervously working on my unidentified body.

A few minutes before our six P.M. deadline, Esposito made a flurry of changes in my story, shifting a sentence up and adding an attribution in the middle. His touching up seemed more like a rewrite, and with every change a pit in my stomach filled with insecurity. Finally, he said it was ready. We pressed a few computer keys and cBODY20 was gone to the city queue. A night desk editor made the last fixes and moved it to the copy desk on Long Island, where the story was sent electronically to the presses and set to run as a page thirty-seven cop brief in the July 20 early edition.

It would look like this:

> Brooklyn homicide detectives have been unable to identify a woman found shot to death and lying face down in an East Flatbush gutter more than a week ago.
>
> The woman, who did not appear to be a drug user or a prostitute, was found dead on 42nd Street near Clarendon Road on July 11. She was described by Det. Louis Failla, of the Brooklyn South Homicide Squad, as a black woman between twenty-five and thirty years old, 5-feet, 2-inches tall, about 115 pounds with a gold tooth in the front of her mouth. . . .

"Good first day," Esposito said when I was done.

"Thanks," I told him. "See you tomorrow."

I took the subway home and slept restlessly that night waiting to get up and buy the paper in the morning. But before I left for work my phone rang. Tom Curran was making good on his promise to chase my sorry ass all over the city. During the night's thunderstorm, a man waiting at a bus stop in Staten Island had been killed when a bolt of lightning sent a chunk of cement flying from a building façade. The cement split the man's head open, and Curran was sending me out to cover the story.

"Book 'im, Dano," he said on the phone.

I didn't have a car yet, so I had to take a subway to the ferry, then catch a cab to the bus stop where the man had been killed. I found the gnarled spokes of the man's umbrella and bits of his brain interspersed with a dollar's worth of quarters, nickels and dimes—his bus fare— scattered on the pavement.

The cops were not releasing the victim's name, but a woman who lived in a building nearby said he was Mike Clark, and that he was a mentally handicapped man who walked with a limp and worked as a custodian in the athletic department at Wagner College. A *Newsday* photographer arrived with a car, and we drove to the college, where a woman in the public relations office let the photographer copy Clark's

ID picture. I called Curran from a bar with the details, including a description of the brain matter on the sidewalk.

"Good work, Dano. But there's parts of that you may not want to put in the paper," he said.

I left out the brains but tried to include as many other details as I could. The next day, Don Forst told me the stuff about the coins and the umbrella spokes was a nice touch. Pride washed over me. Getting Forst's approval made me feel I might make it as a reporter after all.

When I got home Saturday night, my first week on the beat over, I stared in the mirror at the press pass hanging around my neck from a cheap silver-plated chain I'd bought from a street vendor: 1988 WORKING PRESS NO. 2916. MITCHELL B. GELMAN OF NEW YORK NEWSDAY IS ENTITLED TO PASS POLICE AND FIRE LINES WHEREVER FORMED. I'd had the picture taken at a dollar booth in a drugstore, and I looked like I'd just gotten out of an insane asylum. But the orange press pass, the same color as the one I had made in elementary school, was signed at the bottom by the police and fire commissioners. It was official, and so was I.

As long as I could make it through probation.

Probation

Probation was six months, but it wasn't the kind you get for doing something wrong. The editors described it as a time during which they could see if they liked us and we could see if we liked them, making it sound like both sides had mutual rights of refusal. I guess that was true, but I was worried about their right to refuse me.

During probation, I approached each story as if it were the last I'd ever write. This included the one on August 2 about a deaf man who'd been shot and killed during a robbery outside an East Harlem public housing project. Esposito told me to find out if the man had been shot because he couldn't hear the robbers' demands.

"Can you see it?" he said. "He couldn't hear the guys so they killed him. What a sad story. See if that was it."

It seemed like a stretch to me, but what did I know? I was on probation. Before I left, Esposito told me not to worry about being hassled up in East Harlem.

"We don't get trouble at the projects," he said.

In my suit and tie, I looked like a walking victim, and I turned to Elaine for more reassurance.

"Just be sure to keep your press pass out," she said.

"One more thing," Esposito added. "Get a picture."

I obediently took the subway to 114th Street and found neighbors of

28

the victim, twenty-four-year-old David Jackson. They said he had been minding his own business, drinking a bottle of cheap wine, when three men robbed him for fifteen dollars. There was a lot of crack dealing in the projects, but they said Jackson wasn't involved. Nobody knew why the men had shot him.

Except for the crime scene seal across the threshold, Jackson's apartment door was slightly open. I stepped inside and slinked from one dark and dingy room into another, looking on shelves and inside drawers for a photograph. But I was scared a cop might come, so I left empty-handed almost as quickly as I'd entered. Back at the Cop Shop, I wrote six hundred words about David Jackson's death, but with no photograph. Not only did this story not make the first few pages, in the end, the night desk cut it to a brief. Next time I was going to get a picture.

I rolled into DCPI early that Saturday and saw a sheet on a fifteen-year-old Queens boy who had been killed when a gang chased him in front of a car. In December 1986, a black teen had been fatally hit by a car as he ran to escape a white mob in Howard Beach, a predominantly white Queens neighborhood not far from where the fifteen-year-old had lived. Although both victim and attackers were white this time, the cases had eerie parallels. The Saturday editor, Barbara Strauch, told me to forget everything else and get to the boy's neighborhood. No subways went near Bayside, a suburban section of Queens, so I took a car service the last leg.

Jimmy Ginex had been riding his bicycle with friends when a pack of young toughs pulled up in a Jeep. They tried to take his bike, and Jimmy, trying to get away, ran in front of a speeding car. Jimmy's family lived in a big house with a gate around a yard. An uncle out front told me to get lost when I asked for an interview and to go to hell when I requested a picture. Earlier that morning, however, a woman who used to babysit for Jimmy had given me an out-of-focus photo of him. The picture wasn't publishable, but tears streamed down Jimmy's uncle's cheeks when I showed it to him.

"I really don't want to have to use this one," I said.

"Wait here," he said.

A few minutes later, Jimmy's uncle brought out a better picture. I slid it into my briefcase, promised to mail it back, and split before he could change his mind.

I spent the rest of the afternoon hunting for kids who'd been playing with Jimmy the night before. A curly-headed young woman from the *Daily News* was also nosing around, and I tried to keep my interviews secret from her. As I was leaving in a radio cab, she was with a group on a corner. I told the driver to pull over, saw they were kids I'd already talked to, and sped off.

Esposito woke me with a Sunday morning call from his Long Island beach house. He couldn't buy our New York edition there, but he'd seen Jimmy Ginex's picture on the front page of the *News*.

"Did we get a picture?" he asked.

"Yeah, we had it on page two with the story," I said.

"Okay."

A few days earlier, Esposito had told me to get a beeper from one of the clerks who answered phones and took care of administrative matters on the city desk. Doctors, drug dealers and police reporters all needed beepers, and Esposito, who wasn't shy about using them to wake reporters in the morning or send us out on stories at night, wanted me to have one, too. He asked me if I'd gotten mine yet. The clerks didn't have an extra one, and I hadn't pushed, figuring out of touch was out of trouble. That wouldn't do, Esposito said; he told me to get one even if a clerk had to strip it off a general assignment reporter.

"And," he added, *"don't ever turn it off."*

Before going to the Shack Tuesday, I got a beeper. I turned it on in the newsroom and heard its sound. Then, I moved the switch to the silent, five-second vibrate mode. I touched it to my cheek, thrilled with my new toy.

When I got downtown, Elaine Rivera said the curly-headed *News* reporter, Rose Marie Arce, had called her over the weekend and asked who I was. She told Elaine I'd left her stranded in Bayside. "She wanted to know why you didn't offer her a ride," Elaine said.

Oh, shit, I thought, *all I need is a feud with a competing reporter.* I called Arce that night. Lying back on my bed, doing my best impression of a diplomat, I told her that I'd thought she had a car and was sorry. She accepted my apology.

I probably overreacted to the call Elaine received from her friend, but I was very concerned about what other reporters thought of me. I'd never made friends easily and was afraid I wouldn't be accepted. I was already worried enough that Elaine, Chapin and Alison, who'd all worked for other papers before coming to New York, thought I had used contacts to get hired at *Newsday* pretty much out of school. I tried to conceal this fear by acting as professional and enthusiastic as possible, but some of my efforts—such as leaving memos about the overnight sheets and offering to help make calls on other people's stories—came off much more contrived than genuine.

In early August, the members of the police bureau got together for dinner at the Lion's Head. City editor Hap Hairston (the one who said he owned me) was coming to discuss our crime coverage. Alison, Chapin and Elaine seemed indifferent to the dinner. Their attitude was basically, "What's the big deal about listening to Richie talk and watching Hap eat?" But for me, going to the Lion's Head was special. This was the saloon that my father used to go to, a writer's haunt where Jimmy Breslin once ran around the end of the bar to get a drink for Robert F. Kennedy during his senate campaign in 1964. It had low ceilings and a long oak bar with the hand-carved head of a lion behind the beer taps. The wall across from the bar was covered with framed book jackets by authors who drank at the Head, including Hamill, Breslin, Nick Pileggi, Robert Ward, Jack Newfield and Dennis Smith. And a half-dozen newspaper columns mentioning the pub were posted by the kitchen door.

When I was on the editorial pages, I occasionally came in, scanned the columns and listened to the book covers exhorting me to work harder, read more, learn to write better. The Lion's Head was Greenwich Village's journalism Wall of Fame, and as far as I was concerned, the Nobel Prize was small consolation for writers who would never see their work framed there. It wasn't just a place to come for a drink. It was a watering hole for people whose talents had earned them a spot there. And the night of the bureau dinner, I felt for the first time that I actually belonged.

Alison, Chapin, Elaine, Richie and I took the round table in the dining room and talked for a while. Hap showed up an hour late. He carried a Stolichnaya on the rocks and noted that we were the soberest band of police reporters he'd ever seen. Only Chapin was drinking a beer. Richie and Elaine had diet sodas, Alison sipped a seltzer and I nursed a ginger ale.

Hap, who took pride in his vices, did nothing in moderation. He lived each minute as if his time were running out. Unshaven, overweight and, in wrinkled slacks and a T-shirt, looking more like a homeless person than an editor, he sat down, ordered another Stoli and ripped into the bread basket. Hap had a cinematographer's genius for seeing the potential of a story from its barest elements, but he did lack manners.

"You know, it's okay you guys aren't drinking," Hap said, sounding like a boxing manager giving a prefight talk, gesturing with the bread and pausing only for another sip of vodka. "Because you guys are *awesome*. The best. There's only three things I want from you. That's to kick ass, kick ass and kick ass. The *News*, *Post* and *Times*—kick their asses.

"Richie's in charge. If you guys fuck up—and you won't, but if you do—it's on him.

"There's one more thing," he said, raising a rip of sourdough bread for emphasis. "We have four shifts on the beat, the eight, ten, one and night slots. The morning guy gives us our jump, the ten o'clock guy owns the building, the one o'clock is our best off-the-news writer and the night person covers late-breakers, has to be quick and fast on deadline. You can divide that up, change them around any way you want. I don't care who is there. But be there. Every slot, all the time, must be covered without any gaps."

At the time, Elaine was scheduled to open, I came in at ten, Alison at one, and Chapin did the four-to-midnight shift. Richie worked around the clock. Of course, all of this fluctuated with the flow of news.

When Hap was finished, Esposito said a few words, and the others raised some concerns about the way the paper was playing police stories. I was so amazed to be there that I just picked through the bones in my broiled trout. Esposito noticed my silence and looked over when the coffee came.

"How are you doing? Any problems so far?" he asked.

"No. I'm just happy to be over the wall."

"Yeah. You're in," he said.

That's not what I meant exactly. I was a long way from in, that I knew. But I was off the editorial pages, out of the claustrophobic midtown offices and into the city. What I meant was I had escaped into a job that dealt with what was going on in the real world.

"So far, so good," I said.

"Yeah, wait another eighteen months," he said. "You won't look like Mitch Gelman anymore!"

I smiled. I didn't believe covering cops could change me that much.

Before we left, we made plans to pose for a photograph that would run in an ad promoting the bureau. The next week, we gathered around Esposito's desk. He sat in a chair and Alison, Chapin, Elaine and I stood around him like his court. The ad described *Newsday*'s crime coverage as "arresting." A *Daily News* reporter thought it was so funny he taped it to a Cop Shop wall. I was embarrassed by the ad, but it did make the point that the paper was as serious about covering crime as it was about the courts, politics or entertainment.

In the next few weeks, Chapin and Elaine picked up on Hap's offer to let us fill our own slots. Alison, the most skilled writer in the bureau, liked writing features more than breaking news. She didn't want to change her shift; she wanted to leave the bureau altogether. Chapin and Elaine, however, both asked if I would switch with them.

One evening after work, Chapin asked if I wanted to have a beer. He was a veteran, quiet and generous with advice. He wore V-neck sweaters, had a soft mustache and gentle features, and was married, with a son. His only bad habit was junk food. He started each shift with a Coke and a Twinkie or a slice of pound cake.

We went to a bar across from the office. He said the night desk editors were more nurturing than the day editors so it might be a good place for me to learn the ins and outs of the job. Hap had told him that if I agreed, they'd make the change. I got out of this by telling him that working nights was not my first choice but I would switch if he ever had a family emergency. That was easy enough, but Elaine was another story.

Elaine had an infectious, energetic personality. A colleague once described her as the only person who could turn an elevator into a disco. She lived in Washington Heights, an impoverished Hispanic neighborhood that included many of the people we wrote about. She had a fierce sense of social justice and would bristle with fury at even the slightest hint of bigotry or sexism. Elaine was a beautiful and committed reporter, but she was not a morning person.

When I came in at ten, she'd be sitting at her terminal, a cup of coffee and a half-eaten carrot cake or bran muffin on her desk. Elaine was usually dressed in a black T-shirt and a pair of jeans, and she often looked tired. She liked to stay out late with friends and sources, and didn't get going until the sun was high in the sky.

"I can't do this anymore," she'd say every morning.

Eight or ten times during my first month, she called me at home at seven A.M. to ask if I'd cover for her. She would say she wasn't feeling well, had a doctor's appointment or was on her way to an interview. I was pretty much doing the morning job anyway, so when she convinced Esposito to switch me to her shift, it just made my starting time official.

Working the early shift meant rolling out of bed to WINS and racing down to the Cop Shop by 8 A.M. to find out what was behind the radio's headline crime news. Most days I took the subway, but if I was running late, I'd jump in a cab and read the paper on the way downtown, grudgingly paying the seven-dollar fare, which was more than I could afford.

Getting up earlier also made it more difficult to go to the gym or run before work, and hanging out late at night held its punishments just hours later. Waking up wondering what horrors had happened while I was sleeping was not the best way to start the morning. Before I could even get a first cup of coffee, I had to find out how many people had died overnight—and why. Somehow, fueled either by youth or the fear of missing a story, I managed to get to the sheets before my editors got to me.

In those first few months, I was still learning the fundamentals of news writing. A police story wasn't very complex—only a few facts, details, attribution and a little drama neatly packaged in seven to ten paragraphs—but it was harder than it seemed. The night editors who had to fix my rough copy must have been thrilled that I was getting in my practice on their deadlines.

One day, when I covered a story on a homicide in a luxury Manhattan parking garage, the night desk made their frustration clear. Earlier in the week, I had read a *New Yorker* profile of Pulitzer Prize–winning *Miami Herald* police reporter Edna Buchanan. The piece, by Calvin Trillin, described a writing style called the Miller Chop, named for the editor who taught it to Buchanan. The Miller Chop was an ironic, punchy, one-sentence phrase used to quickly sum up a news story's lead. Buchanan wrote one about a quarrelsome couple that went like this:

> The man she loved slapped her face. Furious, she says she told him never, ever to do that again. "What are you going to do, kill me?" he asked and handed her a gun. "Here, kill me," he challenged. She did.

When I tried the Miller Chop on the garage story, I turned it into the Gelman Ramble. My lead started noplace and went nowhere, and the rest of the story was even worse.

> A luxury Manhattan garage that offers an "Early Bird Special" for people who drop their cars off before 10 A.M. received a visitor yesterday morning who was not interested in storing an automobile.
>
> The night attendant at the parking structure known as the 59th Street Garage was shot to death by someone who apparently slipped in beneath a half-open gate, police said. When a daytime valet arrived for work at around 6 A.M., he found the body lying on the cement floor of the garage's basement. The body was sprawled between two four-door sedans.
>
> The victim, a 43-year-old unidentified

> Hispanic man, had worked at the garage for
> less than six months, said another em-
> ployee. He was wearing his attendant's uni-
> form when he was shot once in the head.

Dee Murphy, a night desk editor, was not impressed. "Mitch: Here's why the story doesn't really lend itself to your approach," her computer message began. "We don't have a victim ID. We don't have a suspect. We don't have any car stolen. Nor do we know what he was killed over. We don't have a series of parking attendant murders we can peg this to. As a result, we're left with a routine first-day killing story. Which requires pretty straightforward, basic inverted pyramid story structure."

> The night attendant at a luxury Manhat-
> tan parking garage was shot to death yes-
> terday morning in what police said
> apparently was a robbery attempt.

I had a lot to learn about writing, while at the same time I was still getting a handle on covering stories on the street.

On August 16, a police officer named Joe Galapo was killed right on deadline. Detectives swarmed all around the front of the Elegante Car Service on Fourth Avenue in Brooklyn, where Galapo had been shot. I saw that Captain Thomas Fahey from DCPI was keeping the press penned into a corner, so I put my press pass in my shirt pocket and went in the other direction. A man on the second floor of the building next door told me he had heard the shots, and he helped make the details of the shooting clearer.

Two cops were driving south on Fourth Avenue when they spotted a drug deal going down. They made a U-turn and jumped out of their unmarked car, drew their guns and threw two suspects against a car. As the cops were about to cuff the suspects, one of them, a young sandy-haired man, spun around, striking one of the officer's arms. The cop's arm jerked up and his gun went off. The bullet, police would later report, hit Galapo in the head.

I left the apartment building and still had to find out what happened to the suspects. One was in custody, but Fahey wasn't saying anything about the other. Deadline for the first edition—"the starter"—was coming fast, and I had to get more information. I walked up behind three men wearing trench coats and gold detective's shields, and tried to eavesdrop, but before I could hear anything Fahey came running across the street.

"What the hell are you doing?" he said.

I played dumb.

"Get the hell over there with the rest of the press," he said, pushing me a step in front of him. "You know you're making me look bad in front of the bosses. You can't do that."

"Sorry," I said.

"Get the hell . . ."

I gave up and called the desk with what I knew. The rewrite guy, Clem Richardson, took my feed and switched me to Esposito, who sent me to the 72nd Precinct. It was nearly nine P.M. when I got there, and dozens of cops were standing out front, some in small circles, others holding hands. Most were in jeans and flannel shirts, sweaters or windbreakers with shields dangling from chains; they were plainclothes cops, members of the Brooklyn South Narcotics Squad, Galapo's unit.

At nine-thirty, a car pulled up. It was an officer just back from the hospital. I couldn't hear what he said. A few heads nodded, and one of the cops, a bearded officer with an anguished look on his face, sat down on a bumper. He put his head in his hands and cried. Twenty minutes later, I called the desk and asked for Clem.

"You know that the officer died," I said.

"No. That's what you're there for. Thanks for calling, man," he said.

"Okay."

It struck me then that I was the one in charge of finding out what happened, and I should have called immediately. Fortunately I had reached Clem before ten P.M., in time for the starter.

The next morning, Esposito sent me back to the 72nd Precinct for a press conference and told me to find out where Galapo had lived and to call with information for a profile. "I want every lick and splatter," he said. But before I left, he wanted to talk about something. He put his feet up and spoke in a casual, almost brotherly tone.

"Heard you had a run-in yesterday," he said.

"Did Fahey tell you?" I said, insulted, surprised and a little bit embarrassed.

"They're like that. In their cop minds, they think I'm like the commanding officer of the bureau so they fill me in on what's doing."

"We were on deadline. I was trying to get what happened for the starter," I said.

"Yeah . . ."

"What did Fahey say I did?"

"That you were doing like I used to do, tucking your press pass in your pocket and running around like you were a detective."

"Something like that. He got really pissed, huh? What should I have done?" I asked.

"Just remember," Esposito said, looking me in the eye, "Italian Rules apply."

"And those are what?"

"Do what it takes. Just don't get caught."

The more I thought about Fahey going around my back to my boss, the madder I got. The cops were actually trying to tell me how to cover stories. I was finding out that dealing with the public information office was the most irritating part of the beat. My father taught me that public relations people were obstacles that journalists were paid to avoid. He used to browbeat them and threaten to cut off their clients when he was an editor at *Life* and, later, at *TV Guide*. P.R. types were the Enemy; their job was to put a good spin on bad news and to promote as much fluff as possible. The cops at Police Headquarters were the same—always restricting, not facilitating, the flow of information. Still, reporters had to go through them to get even routine crime statistics and to set up interviews with chiefs and detectives. Until I had developed good sources—and I had none—I needed the public information officers a lot more than they needed me. I was useless to the paper if I couldn't get news fast. And Fahey had shown they would go over my head in a second.

A few weeks later, Esposito called at dawn. I reached for the phone and answered, groggy and barely coherent. He was wide awake, already at his Ferrari speed. "There's a hostage situation. Two kids being held by their father on Clinton Street. The guy's got a shotgun and is shooting at cops on the FDR Drive. Get down there," he fired off.

"On my way," I said.

All morning, I stood with dozens of other reporters and television cameramen outside the building. The tension built with every hour while the police department's hostage negotiating team tried to talk to Chu Mun Cho, a Taiwanese immigrant upset because he could not pay his phone and rent bills. The cops spoke in Mandarin and English, but Chu only responded in bullets. At three P.M., Police Commissioner Ben Ward somberly announced that Chu had killed his two children, eight-year-old Helen and ten-year-old Warren, and that shots fired by Emergency Service Unit officers had killed Chu. Along with reporters from the *News, Times* and *Post*, I started early the next day to follow up on what happened. For them, it was just another second-day story, but for me it was a chance to show I could deliver.

Using Cole's cross directory, which lists phone numbers by address instead of name, I called the Chus' neighbors and found one of them who knew the family's Chinatown doctor. He worked in a tiny office above a fruit and flower shop. The Chu kids were sick often, he said, and seemed timid and afraid. Later, in Helen Chu's school, her principal said the little girl had told her teacher she was afraid her father might harm her. The teacher had reported this to the city's Human Resources Administration, but whatever HRA did—if anything—wasn't enough to save the children.

Back at the Cop Shop later that afternoon, I was patched into the speaker phone in Forst's office. The editors were in their news meeting, picking the front-page story. Forst wanted to know if Helen Chu had said she thought her father would kill her, "kill" being the word they wanted to use in a headline. I couldn't go that far. The school would only say that Helen's father had threatened the family with violence. I told the editors I'd call them back. After nearly two years ordering pastries, writing memos, bucking for a job on cityside, this was my first real shot at page one. If the editors wanted "kill," I was going to get them "kill."

I phoned Dr. T. C. Tai, of Chinatown. Having lived in Asia, I knew that aggressive questions would intimidate him, so I lowered my voice a few decibels and politely asked if Helen and Warren had seemed scared when he saw them. Did they have bruises? Or express any fear that their father might hurt them? Perhaps kill them? Well, yes, Dr. Tai said, that could be. Yes, it was fair to say that Helen and Warren had appeared afraid for their lives? Yes, he said, afraid of their father. I excitedly called the meeting with what the doctor had said. But Forst and the other editors decided the doctor's quotes were not solid enough to make page one. That was a letdown, but I still had to write six hundred words on the Chus. Staring at the blank screen, I started to panic.

My notebook was filled with lots of information, but getting all of it organized into a story was like putting together a jigsaw puzzle. I had more details than the other papers, but was having trouble weaving them into a narrative. The story I eventually moved from the Shack was filled with convoluted sentences and had too many meandering quotes and isolated facts, but with some helpful editing from the night desk, we got it into the paper.

At the main office the next day, Forst asked to see me. He didn't compliment my subtle touches, as he had with the piece about the man killed by lightning; he wanted to share a piece of advice. A lot of times, he said, young reporters try too hard to write well and end up being too fancy. To make sure I would write short, crisp sentences, he banned me from using conjunctions for a year. No "ands" or "buts" in any of my stories. I sat there in shock. I was never good at taking criticism, even when it was meant to be constructive.

"Huh?" I managed to mutter.

"Look at Breslin. Read Hemingway. Short sentences are how the English language was meant to be written," he said. "Give it some time."

What a commandment! It was like the coach was telling me to play third base without a glove. A year seemed like forever. I knew my writing needed work. But yikes! Was he really trying to tell me I was functionally illiterate? I didn't know if I could do it.

Over the next month I wrote nearly every day, struggling to keep conjunctions out of my short sentences. I wrote about an art student murdered in Brooklyn, a homeless man who killed a priest in St. Patrick's Cathedral, Mike Tyson's doomed marriage and four people killed when a disco was sprayed with gunfire. Some days I wished I could have been in two places at the same time. On a Saturday story in September, I got clobbered by the *News* because I didn't go to a crime scene. The story was about a young girl stabbed and seriously wounded by her father. The sheets told me it had the makings of a good tale, but it was a dreary day, I was tired and the girl wasn't dead. Instead of going to the girl's apartment, a long subway ride away, I reported the story over the phone using the cross directory. The next morning, when I went out to run, I found out how bad a mistake that had been.

The front-page headline of the *Daily News* screamed that the father had tried to kill his daughter to save her from the Devil. It hit me like a roundhouse right to the gut, nearly knocking the wind right out of me on Second Avenue. The byline was Rose Marie Arce, Elaine's friend who I'd stranded in Bayside a month earlier. She had a picture of the girl, an interview with her mother, a psychological history of her father's fanaticism and a description of the blood-stained room where he tried to cut Satan from his daughter's heart.

I swore never to get beat like that for being lazy ever again and decided to buy a car. The next week, I took a cab out to Paragon Honda in Queens, wrote a check for half my life savings and drove home in a 1988 Honda Civic four-door with NYP (New York Press) license plates. With my new car, I was ready for anything.

To establish myself as a reporter, I had to try to immerse myself in whatever horror I had to write about that day. Some nights I would go home and try to forget about the crimes, but they began to take a toll, and I didn't know whether to laugh at how bizarre they were or cry because they were so sad. Either way, I never had much time to dwell on what happened yesterday, because tomorrow came too fast.

By the end of November, my probation was winding down. But I was still concerned about the impression I was making on my editors. I was getting used to grabbing coffee on the way to work, reading the papers, checking the sheets and calling the desk in the same fluid early morning motions. The unpredictable rhythms of the job were starting to settle in.

I expected my beeper to go off at any time and had given up worrying that I wasn't running in the morning. I read every sheet and followed up every homicide, went in early and stayed late. I jumped when Esposito beeped, and I listened to every word Forst said like it was gospel. I was zealous, determined and ambitious, at times to a blinding fault. But nothing showed my desire to prove myself during those first few months better than the story I wrote about the Human Torch.

It started with a hotline call from the DCPI cop who said a man had set himself on fire across the street from the United Nations. The cops didn't know who he was or why he had done it, only that there'd been a case of self-immolation on the northwest corner of 42nd Street and First Avenue. The flames had burned ten feet high for four minutes, enough to give the man third-degree burns over 90 percent of his body.

Now he was in critical condition, likely to die, at New York Hospital–Cornell Burn Center. I went to the corner and saw that a small circle on the sidewalk had been singed gray with ash. The many U.N. flags waved across the street. Next to the fire-mark on the sidewalk was a smoldering valise and a stack of sopping wet personal papers.

On my hands and knees, I sifted through the papers, and the life of the man who killed himself came together. The documents said his name was Mehrdad Imen, a thirty-two-year-old Iranian immigrant. A *Times* reporter was also there, so I stuffed pieces of paper from the pile into my pockets: a carbon copy of a plane ticket that showed he had paid $308 in Sunnyvale, California, for a one-way fare from San Francisco to New York, a letter to U.N. secretary general Javier Pérez de Cuéllar, a business card from an FBI agent in San Francisco, family photographs, a résumé in Russian and a phone number for a brother in San Diego.

I took the papers to the midtown office and spread them out on my desk. They were a puzzle solved, the last chapter in a spy thriller. If it was a reporter's job to get details, here they were. Forst came over to look at charred scraps of the man's life, and I asked if he could do anything with them, maybe a montage or something to illustrate the story. "Don't get cocky," he said. "You're still a short-timer here." I wrote about Mehrdad Imen that day and again the next.

The first story mentioned that police believed he set himself afire in support of an anti-Khomeini demonstration going on nearby. The second, which I wrote after Imen died, included new information from an interview with his brother in California, whose phone number I'd found among the papers in the valise. His brother said many of Imen's friends had been executed by Khomeini, and that he'd been struck in the head with shrapnel during the Iran-Iraq war. "He was interested in politics and hated Khomeini," the brother said. That was as close as anyone would come to know why Imen killed himself.

After that, Esposito told me not to worry anymore about passing probation. My six months were not up yet, but I was relieved. Although he mentioned this in passing, Esposito's confidence in my work took some pressure off. I was pleased he had noticed I was willing to push myself and wasn't looking for an easy way to get by. A few weeks later, he and Laura Durkin wrote my evaluation.

> Mitch Gelman is working very hard to learn the business of reporting. He is enthusiastic as a *bulldog* when launched on a story, works a lot of extra hours and willingly accepts direction.
>
> Gelman has the ability to absorb every bit of information about a story, but he needs to improve his ability to weigh the importance of the facts he has gathered. In the coming months, he also should continue to work on improving his writing skills.

I couldn't ask for more than that. It meant I'd make it! I felt like going out to celebrate. Then I remembered I had to be at the Shack at eight in the morning. I went home, had a glass of wine with dinner and slept well, hoping I'd wake up and feel like a real reporter. I thought other people would maybe take me as seriously as I was taking myself. I'd forgotten I was working in a newsroom, where teasing is part of the game. The next day, the night desk editors were calling me "Bulldog Gelman"!

New Year

On New Year's Eve, I went to a party at a friend's Lower East Side apartment and stayed boringly sober. Halfway into the party, a friend poked me in the ribs. She pointed at the Page Net beeper growing out of my left hip and asked if I planned to turn off the little black box and have fun. That was a nice idea, but I was on call in case anything happened before our deadline.

A few minutes before midnight, I made my final cop call of 1988, checking with DCPI to get the latest crowd estimate in Times Square. Four hundred thousand people, nearly 5 percent of the city's eight million legal and illegal residents plus a few thousand tourists, had gathered to watch the ball come down, but nothing major happened. Still, I had an uneasy feeling that the armistice wouldn't last long, and I was right. Almost as soon as the paper went to bed, the year's killing started among the masses at Times Square. With champagne corks still littering the gutter, Andrew Tringle, a nineteen-year-old resident of Queens, didn't live to see the first hour of 1989. He was struck in the heart with a .25-caliber bullet following an argument.

Tringle was the first of four people slain throughout the city by two-thirty A.M. All the papers had murder roundups on January 2. Charting the killing rate had become the city's latest pastime, like following Jackie Robinson's batting average had been for my father and keeping

44

tabs on Tammany Hall politics had been for a generation before him. Murder was the new way of measuring the state of the city.

On Tuesday morning, Forst sent a message—more like a Papal decree—through Curran to the Cop Shop. Esposito was on vacation, and I was the early guy so his command came to me. He wanted a list of all the men, women and children who'd been killed in the city in 1988. The impact of these deaths was no longer getting through with stories on the murder of the day or overnight wrap-ups. Forst wanted to run the whole list of 1,896 New Yorkers who were no longer with us because of the city's crime wave. It would certainly be powerful. New Yorkers were becoming numb to crime, and the list might jolt them awake and trigger a surge of outrage. Of course, getting this information from the police department would be like prying loose classified documents from the Pentagon. I also knew that fighting for the list would involve paying a price in good relations with DCPI. But this was an order from on high, and I took the thunder straight to the thirteenth floor.

This wasn't going to be easy, because already I wasn't getting along very well with most of the public information officers. My questions were never tactful enough, and I upset them even further by writing what they said instead of what they would later tell me they had meant to say. My relations with DCPI were so strained that one of the cops, Sergeant Diane Kubler, just grunted whenever she saw me. Another, Officer Janice Swinney, would warn the others whenever she saw me getting off the elevator. "Hush! Watch what you say. Mitch is coming," she'd call out so that everyone, including me, could hear.

One exception in that office was Captain Thomas Fahey, who I'd come to like in spite of our little confrontation at the scene of Officer Galapo's killing. Fahey had boxed me around at the beginning, but he was one of the few cops who was still cordial to me. The turning point in our relationship had come one afternoon when I approached him with a potentially embarrassing tip. I had become friendly with one of the headquarters' security guards, a young black man I will call Alex. One morning Alex told me that a high-ranking chief had recently entertained some friends at the shooting range in the basement of Headquarters. The chief had subsidized their fun by authorizing overtime for a range assistant.

When I told Fahey about this, he said he'd find out if it was true. It was. "Isn't there anything we can hide from you guys anymore?" Fahey said, smiling like a child caught with his hand in the cookie jar. The chief's friends were actually members of the nonprofit Police Foundation, big fund-raisers for the department. "Okay," I said. "Maybe this doesn't get in the paper. I'll talk to my editors."

This was my first attempt at playing by Italian Rules. The other guy had gotten caught, but I was willing to forget about it, believing that in return I'd receive a favor or clemency sometime in the future. Unfortunately, around the time I needed to exchange this chit for the homicide list, Fahey was transferred to the Narcotics Division. Rather than running the high-visibility public information office, he'd been placed behind a desk, with less autonomy. He must have pissed off someone.

I had to go to the office's new executive officer. Inspector Richard Mayronne was a husky, barrel-chested man who had previously commanded the Midtown South Precinct, the busiest in the city. He was part of the department's Old Boys Club, its traditional white ethnic backbone. A cigar-chomping, gruff-talking charter member, Mayronne's New Year's resolution was to lose weight. To prove he was serious, he had a blender and a canister of Slim Fast diet formula in his office. But Mayronne was a man of huge appetites who couldn't live off powdered concoctions. He once joked to a group of female reporters that his wife liked him hefty because, as he put it, "you can't drive a telephone pole with a tackhammer." Talking to the guys, he would share other intimacies. When asked what he would do if someone tried to rob him at gunpoint, Mayronne had a ready answer. "Hey, I'm a big guy. I'd give him my money. Whatever he wanted. I'd even suck his dick if he wanted. And I've never done that for anyone. Except that once," he said, pausing to roll his cigar around in his mouth. "But I really needed the ride." Mayronne was what a lot of people thought a New York cop was supposed to be, a swaggering tough guy, his language peppered with gutter humor and his heart made of pure gold.

When Mayronne came to DCPI, I'd been reading *American Caesar*, William Manchester's biography of General Douglas MacArthur. It was a safe book to discuss around the department because it showed that even though I looked and talked like an ACLU member, at least I read military history. Mayronne said the biography was his favorite book, which didn't surprise me because he seemed like a MacArthurite. The part he recalled most vividly, though, was not one of the general's Korean War campaigns or his Pacific theater strategies, but a prayer MacArthur wrote for his son. After that, I knew that there was more to this guy than his reputation as one of the department's colossal ball-busters.

My first official dealing with Mayronne concerned the request for the list. He chewed on his cigar and said he would ask his boss, Commissioner McGillion, what she wanted to do. Once it went to McGillion, I knew I was in trouble.

A few minutes later, our direct line from DCPI rang. It was not Mayronne or McGillion, but John Clifford, the commissioner's right-hand sergeant, her whip and bearer of all bad news. Her answer was no. Before Clifford could go on, I thanked him, but asked to speak to the commissioner in person.

"You can do whatever you want," Clifford said, "but there's no way, no way you are going to get that list."

Alice McGillion is a slim woman with pale skin, wispy blond hair and overcast gray eyes. She was soft-spoken most of the time, something she could afford to be because she had as much power as anyone in the department. Before becoming deputy commissioner of public information eight years earlier, she'd worked in the mayor's press office. Not only did she have the police commissioner's support, she also had the full backing of Mayor Ed Koch, the commissioner's boss.

McGillion was an extremely skilled manipulator of people who exercised her power with Machiavellian precision. She instilled fear in the fiercest department chiefs; mercenary in her loyalties, the only true convictions she seemed to have were those that served her current position. She had been polite to me until one day when the paper ran an editorial criticizing the police department. She asked me who'd written it, but I'd pleaded separation of church and state and told her I no longer had any say in editorial policy. Since then, except for an occasional hello every third or fourth time we passed in a hallway, we hadn't exchanged a word. She had no great need for *Newsday* and even less use for me. If she ever wanted to leak something regarding political policy, she'd go to the *Times,* or if she wanted to reach the city's blue-collar folk, she could do it through the *News* or *Post.* She also had her own contacts at *Newsday,* which meant I was nothing more than chicken feed to her.

When I went up to her office, McGillion coldly waved me in. "Thanks for seeing me, Commissioner," I said, sitting on a cushioned chair in her office.

"If it is about the list of homicide victims you want, we're not going to give it to you," she said without emotion.

Seeing that the direct approach had gotten me nowhere, I argued that the list was public information and that I even knew where it was. It was in the homicide log book in the chief of detective's office, and Anne Murray, a *Post* reporter, had been allowed to go through the book for a story a few weeks back. McGillion said Murray had come to them with a limited, simple request and didn't want the whole list. That would take too much time, and she couldn't assign an officer to copy the book for us. Sensing a point of compromise, I offered to copy the book myself, or get a *Newsday* intern to do it. No, McGillion said, the book had other notations that we could not see because the information might jeopardize cases.

With that, I became enraged. I asked how she could give someone from the *Post* access to the book and not a *Newsday* reporter. This seemed like a double standard, and I was not going to roll over while she played favorites. If McGillion wanted a fight, she'd have a Freedom of Information Law request on her desk in half an hour. She said to go ahead, that we might eventually win access to the book, but she'd stall it as long as possible. I stormed out, and as I was leaving, Sergeant Clifford glowered at me with so much contempt that I dismissed all regard for tact. On my way to the elevator, I declared a secret war against the bastards. For a moment, I hated all cops. I hated the color blue.

I gave Curran the bad news, but swore I'd get the list, and typed up a FOIL request, formally seeking access under the law that allowed access to any information that didn't violate the confidentiality rights of others. However, by then I was having second thoughts about going through with it. The cops understood tempers, and threats were part of the daily dance we did with DCPI. But taking legal action would worsen the stares and taunts I already received on the thirteenth floor.

I wasn't sure if I could afford any more of their wrath. At the same time, if I wanted them to respect me, I had to file that FOIL. I took the letter out of the dusty old typewriter and, without a word, placed it on Sergeant Clifford's desk. He didn't look up. I walked away.

Putting the FOIL out of my mind was not difficult. There were enough new crimes to cover without worrying about old ones. Murder, robbery, rape and assault were out of control. In New York's low-income areas, crack was easier to get than a library card. School kids were more familiar with the deadly force of Tec-9s and Uzis than they were with Steinbeck and Fitzgerald. And with so few well-paying jobs available for working-class teens, many of them began to see violence as the only way to tighten a growing gap between rich and poor. This new wave of crime and violence was accompanied by so many shoot-outs that no one was safe. The shootings gave rise to the stray bullet, a new and truly terrible addition to daily city living. It seemingly came out of nowhere and most often did its damage before the victim knew he'd been hit. Cops called these victims "mushrooms," because they popped up in the middle of gunfire.

At seven A.M. on January 4, I got a wake-up call from Chris Hatch, a photo editor who was always the first person on the desk in the mornings. He had a sixth sense for news and would call a few times a week with big overnight crimes or fires. This time Hatch said a fourteen-year-old Brooklyn boy had been killed by a stray bullet on his way home from church. He had gotten caught in a crossfire between the police and a fleeing suspect.

I pulled on a clean shirt and a tie, clipped on my beeper and hopped into a pair of loafers. No time for a run, and the sink full of dinner dishes would have to wait. As I drove to Flatbush, I heard about the shooting on WINS, but the announcer didn't have the boy's name.

This was not like the Christmas murder I had covered ten days earlier. Michael Evans had met his end by screwing around with his killer's girlfriend. You could explain his death, but this kid (police later reported his name, Jeffrey Vilain) was on his way home from a Jehovah's Witnesses meeting. There was no way his killing ever should have happened.

When I arrived at the Kingdom Hall on Clarkson Avenue, the red front door was locked. I banged on it and rang the buzzer, but no one was in. I rang the buzzer upstairs, and a boy in a blue jogging suit came down. I introduced myself as a reporter, and he invited me in. His name was Frantz Depoux. He was thirteen years old and his eyes were bloodshot. It was clear from the absentminded way he offered me a chair at his kitchen table that he hadn't slept all night. An uneaten bowl of cornflakes sat on the table, the milk pushed to the side. Frantz was Jeffrey Vilain's best friend. I put my arm around his shoulders. Comfort was all I could offer as he recounted what had happened.

Every Sunday, Tuesday and Friday, Jeffrey's family went to the Kingdom Hall for the French-language Jehovah's Witnesses meetings. The night before had been like every other Tuesday night for the family. Jeffrey, his grandfather, aunt and two cousins left their apartment around six-thirty P.M., leaving his mother at home because she was not feeling well.

Jeffrey was beaming with pride after the meeting. The elders had asked him to prepare a special reading, the second time in a month he'd been given this honor. His assignment was Ezekiel, chapter 40, verses 1–16, and he had it written on a white sheet of paper stuck in his black-bound Bible. He had to prepare an analysis of the passage and talk for five minutes about it the next week. The Old Testament book of Ezekiel recounts the exiled prophet's visions of Jerusalem's destruction and his judgment that human sacrifices were needed to save the tribes of Israel from destroying themselves. Jeffrey was eager to learn Ezekiel's message.

The first sound Jeffrey's oldest cousin, Nasmine Aly, remembered hearing, she would later say, was a shot. Then, Jeffrey's aunt screaming: "Get down!" Lying on the pavement, Nasmine, sixteen, who'd been jealous the elders had singled out Jeffrey just moments before, watched him turn briefly to see what was happening. A split second of curiosity later, Jeffrey crumbled to his knees. A bullet had entered his right cheek and exited the back of his head.

The shoot-out was between a cop and a young man who jumped suspiciously out of a livery cab. Of thirteen bullets fired, only one struck a person.

As soon as Frantz Depoux heard the shots, he sprang from his living room window, where he'd been waving goodbye, and ran down the stairs, to Jeffrey's side.

"Jeffrey, don't die. Don't die. Please don't leave me," he pleaded.

No response.

"He never moved. Not once," Frantz recalled at the kitchen table. "I held his head in my hands and saw the blood coming out of his face. I was thinking, it couldn't be. But it was. It was."

By morning, the crime scene tape had been removed from the street, but the pavement was stained with the blood of an innocent child. Something more than the life of a fourteen-year-old boy had slipped away with Jeffrey's last breath. The loss was there in Frantz's face. No dreams could ever be simple again, and no promises would be certain. No relationships could be consummated without the fear that somehow they would end horribly. A firefight had come to Clarkson Avenue, killing Jeffrey Vilain and turning Frantz Depoux into whatever you call a boy who loses his closest friend.

Before I said goodbye, Frantz told me I could find Jeffrey's family at his aunt's apartment. Grieving relatives did not always want to be bothered by reporters, but Jeffrey's aunt, Yanique Aly, let me in. His uncle, Gary Dorvil, talked about Jeffrey as a small boy, and Nasmine talked about the pangs of guilt she felt for her earlier envy. The most poignant moments of distress came from the other side of an ivory white wall. There, in the bedroom, Jeffrey's mother lay on a mattress with her head buried in the pillows. She could not stand or walk, let alone talk about the loss of her son. She could only wail. The anguished belts of her wounded heart sounded from behind the bedroom wall. She thrashed her arms and kicked her legs in the bed. And screamed, sending a chill through my chest.

Jeffrey's father, who had not seen him for three years, also came to the apartment that morning. He pulled up in a truck and immediately went into the bedroom. He sat on a folding chair by a radiator as Jeffrey's mother continued to cry.

Jeffrey's mother and grandfather, a tailor, had emigrated to New York from Haiti. They were among more than 250,000 Haitians who fled to Brooklyn in the late sixties and seventies while Papa Doc Duvalier and his son tortured their homeland. Jeffrey's grandfather arrived in 1967, and his daughter joined him three years later. In 1989, Jeffrey was in the eighth grade, his final year at Mahalia Jackson Intermediate School. The school was surrounded by a wrought-iron fence and built like a fortress, with stone and brick and as few windows as possible. Its one entrance was monitored by a security guard all day.

Jeffrey's principal, Maishe Levitan, had heard on the radio that a fourteen-year-old boy had been killed in Flatbush. He'd hoped it wasn't one of his students. But when I walked into his office with an I'm-sorry-to-have-to-disturb-you-with-this-type-of-thing look on my face, he seemed to know what had happened.

"Which one of mine is it?" he asked.

Twelve of Levitan's kids had been killed since 1980, but all of them had been involved in drugs or belonged to youth gangs. They were self-destructive kids, aged nine to fourteen, who came from troubled homes or had found trouble in the streets. They were destined for jail or a violent end. In their own way, Levitan said, these children's fates were instructive. They showed that bad things befell those who made bad choices. Jeffrey's death was different.

"It shatters the lesson," he said.

As Levitan somberly announced Jeffrey's death over the public address system, I thought about my first year in school. I started kindergarten in 1968, when American soldiers were dying in Southeast Asia and Martin Luther King, Jr., and Robert Kennedy were assassinated at home. We learned about death from newspaper clips, magazine photographs and television. Two decades later, the students at Mahalia Jackson Intermediate School did not have to go to the papers to learn about tragedy. The papers came to them. Death stole students from their classroom, seats filled one day were empty the next. And these students knew why.

Before I left his office, Levitan handed me a copy of the school's yearbook, a white paperback edition with a student's sketch of the jazz singer on the cover. The familiar features included photos of the year-book staff, faculty members, the basketball team and cheerleaders, and a note of inspiration urging the seniors to go into the future with their heads held high, aiming for grand things. It seemed like a typical year-book, except it also contained writings by some of the students. One poem by an eighth grader named Toshua was particularly moving. Called "City Life," it seemed to capture the world Jeffrey's classmates experienced every day.

> City life is just not right,
> Too many people affecting each other's lives.
> The air smells as if no one cares;
> When you walk down the streets, you're always
> scared.
> The sun shines too brightly in your eyes,
> But it stops when someone dies.
> When you know cops should be around,
> People are killing others or beating them down.
> Bums lying across the sidewalk with no life left to live,
> But out there, there's no work to give.
> Just to survive, each day's a fight.
> Just remember—this is city life.

When I got back to the Cop Shop, with the yearbook among my notes, I called the desk and told Laura Durkin what I had. "Okay, Snookie. Okay. Okay," she said, trying to cut me off without killing my energy. "That's all good stuff to try to get into the story, but the one key question you have to get answered is, Whose bullet killed him? Was it the cop or the guy who was running from the car?" She also wanted to know how Jeffrey's family felt about the police officer's decision to open fire. I had gotten so wrapped up in the emotion of the story that I'd missed its key news element.

I grabbed the phone to get the missing information. The police couldn't determine conclusively the bullet's caliber because the fatal shot, which hadn't lodged in Jeffrey's head, was not recovered. Mc-

Gillion had given a copy of a police drawing of the scene to a *Daily News* reporter who shared it with me. According to the angles of the shots indicated by the sketch, it seemed more likely that Jeffrey had been killed by the crook's copper-jacketed 9-mm. slug than by the cop's .38-caliber bullet. But there was no way to be absolutely certain.

I was angry that McGillion hadn't given me the sketch, but I figured she was still upset about the FOIL I'd filed, and I couldn't exactly expect too many favors for a while. Anyway, getting a leak like the sketch might not have been such a favor at all. According to Italian Rules, which I was learning about more every day, when the police department gives up a confidential document, it carries with it the implication that the reporter will put a departmental spin on the story. I was not being hand-fed by DCPI, so I had to do my own reporting. Luckily I'd asked for the phone number at Jeffrey's aunt's place.

Scrambling to get the comment Laura wanted, I called the apartment, and Jeffrey's uncle acted as the family's spokesman. "Even though they have to do their job, the cops were in the wrong," he said. "They have an obligation, in addition to catching robbers, to protect the innocent bystanders, too. They have to be more cautious." I put his quote high up in the story, which ran on page nine under a headline that said: AUTOPSY DOESN'T SHOW WHO SHOT TEEN IN CROSSFIRE. The cops would have preferred definitive blame to have been placed on the fleeing suspect.

As I wrote Jeffrey's story, I could still hear the sound of his mother wailing from behind the bedroom wall. It would last the whole year, gaining and losing pitch, but always lingering.

I was discovering that the line between a law's good intentions and what could actually happen when it was enforced was a lot thinner than I'd ever thought. The morning after I wrote about Jeffrey Vilain, I was supposed to meet a pool of reporters in South Jamaica, Queens, to cover a raid on a row of crack houses. But I overslept, and by the time I got to the meeting point, everybody was gone. I drove to the 103rd Precinct, and the desk sergeant told me to go to Liberty Avenue. When I arrived, the raid was over.

Standing on the street, I felt like the dumbest reporter in the city. Off probation for less than a week, and the bulldog had acted like a poodle. However, as I was doing my catch-up reporting, I realized the story might actually be in the aftermath.

Four families were evicted. On a day so cold the ink froze in my pen, the police had left eight adults and eleven children, ages two to seventeen, many huddling together in their pajamas, out on the street. They looked like tramps, carrying whatever they had been able to stuff in black Hefty garbage bags.

The raid had been the culmination of months of surveillance and arrests by the city's special Tactical Narcotics Team. This elite drug-fighting program had been created in the spring of 1988 after a rookie police officer, Edward Byrne, was assassinated by local drug dealers. TNT units saturated heavy drug areas and were the department's way of telling these thugs that they couldn't fuck with the law because the law would fuck back harder. The TNT cops had staked out the two-family, two-story homes on Liberty Avenue. They had seen crack deals go down, had made undercover buys and had locked up the dealers. But even with all the arrests, the dealers returned like cockroaches. In response, the city brought in the feds to try another strategy: forfeiture.

Under a special federal statute, the police, working with marshals and the U.S. attorney's office, could evict tenants and seize property from the landlord. However, if used indiscriminately, the law could cause tremendous hardship and violate the civil liberties of innocent tenants. The forfeiture statute was one of the most controversial in American criminal justice circles. But in this case the authorities had been so confident that the Liberty Avenue houses were a legitimate target they'd invited the media to witness the raid.

Once I'd briefly looked around, I started talking to a fifty-nine-year-old woman who stood outside, a blue parka over her nightgown and a black scarf wrapped around her ears. Maria Rivera lived on Liberty Avenue with her twenty-seven-year-old daughter, Sally, and five grandchildren. She was not a drug dealer; she was just trying to feed and clothe a daughter and the grandchildren. Now, they were out in the cold, among an estimated sixty thousand homeless.

"Where are we supposed to go?" she asked."I won't take my family to a shelter. They don't want to go to a welfare hotel. I don't understand why we have to leave here. I paid my rent—four hundred dollars —every month. We've gone without eggs, without meat, but we've always made the rent. Why should I have to leave now?"

I was boiling inside. This was New York City, not some Central American banana republic or Southeast Asian dictatorship. What in the hell were the cops doing to these people? If this was drug fighting, I didn't know whose side I was on. The targets were as elusive as the Vietcong, and while the drug barons had disappeared, the Riveras lost their home.

I had to find a telephone. Tom Curran was on the desk at quarter to nine.

"Hi," he said. "I hear you're out in the Arctic this morning."

"Yeah. It's freezing, and you know this crack raid. It didn't turn out to be what it was supposed to be," I said.

"Yeah. What happened?"

"Well, they didn't find any drugs," I said.

"Probably not a story then."

"I don't know. They evicted four families and there were nineteen people, including kids, stranded outside because of it," I said.

"Wow!"

"Think there's something to write about?" I asked.

"You bet," Curran said. "Get back out there."

A copy of the order to seize the property, signed by District Court Judge Reena Raggi, was tacked up on the front of the building, and I copied the information I would need. Under the Controlled Substances Act of Congress, amended in 1984, the U.S. government had granted itself the right to seize real estate used to facilitate the distribution of drugs. I also found Maria Rivera again, and she told me that six months earlier the row of houses had been hell. The people downstairs dealt crack every night, guns went off at all hours and the dealers had threatened to burn down the building and hurt her grandchildren if Rivera reported them to the police. But these people had left a few months ago, and recently things had calmed down. Rivera said she finally thought her grandchildren would have a decent place to grow up.

Then, at seven A.M. that morning, the house began to shake. At first, Rivera thought someone had dropped a bomb. It was like an earthquake. She never suspected the police until they burst in, guns drawn, wearing bulletproof vests, yelling, "Hurry! Hurry! Take what you can carry and get out!"

As I was leaving, Rivera's oldest son, John, who had come to help her after the raid, was lugging a final Hefty bag of belongings from the apartment.

"What's in the bag?" I asked him.

"Drugs," he said with a chuckle. "This is so crazy, you have to find humor someplace."

After a cup of coffee, I returned to the office. For the first time since I'd left the editorial pages, a few numbers in my Rolodex proved helpful. I pulled out a card for the New York Civil Liberties Union and called Norman Siegel, the organization's executive director. When I told him what I'd seen, Siegel was furious and delighted—angered by what had happened but deliriously happy that the authorities had been caught. He called this a sad display of "seizur-itis" by the prosecutors.

While I reported out the story, Hap Hairston and Esposito came by my desk to make sure I knew who to talk to at the Eastern District. I did. I wasn't going to deal with mealymouthed public information people on this one. I wanted to talk to the top guy, U.S. attorney Andrew Maloney.

Still, I had to go through the bureaucratic chain of command to get to him. His spokeswoman put me in touch with an assistant who howled that the press was talking out of both sides of its mouth. "One day, you're yelling at us to do something about drugs. The next, you criticize us for what we do," he said. A few minutes before deadline, while I was panicking over not getting Maloney for the story, he returned my call. Predictably, he defended his office's actions.

This was my first solid scoop, and part of the reason was that I hadn't been able to roll myself out of bed that morning.

Newsday was the only paper to cover this side of the raid, though in the morning, WINS radio picked up on it and the *Times* assigned a reporter to chase the story. Mayor Koch went on a Spanish-language radio station to criticize Maloney. The mayor even suggested that the

U.S. attorney's office let the city refurbish the vacant homes. Best of all, I saw that *Newsday*'s editorial page had a headline that struck the prosecutor right where it hurt most—in the ego.

Andy Looney
The U.S. Attorney meant well
but did he do good?

U.S. Marshals armed with a battering ram to search for suspected drug lords and their possessions barged into four Jamaica, Queens apartment houses last Thursday, but they didn't bag anything.

No drugs. No suspects. No drug-related property. No "victory" in the war of attrition here.

Just four law-abiding families thrown into the ranks of the homeless after the feds summarily evicted them in 12-degree weather. The families were heaved out of their homes under the provision of the federal seizure laws.

U.S. Attorney Andrew Maloney and U.S. Marshal Charles Healey insisted this is how the law is supposed to be applied.

Really? . . .

Maria Rivera's cries were being heard across the city. My reporting had given her a voice, and I thought it might have a real impact. At least it might help her family get a place to live. But the city has a short attention span, and within a few days, Liberty Avenue was a dead issue. The Civil Liberties Union lawyers couldn't find the Riveras and moved on to new cases. The mayor and Andy Maloney had made their political peace in a private phone call. And the editorial pages had found other civil wrongs to rail against. Maybe the story made the prosecutor more cautious in the future, but it hadn't helped any of the nineteen people who'd been evicted that morning.

Shoe Leather

Soon after Liberty Avenue drifted into the city's subconscious, I came across a story that I had to tell for personal as well as professional reasons.

A man had been slashed and nearly killed because he loved a woman who had the *wrong* color skin. I had dated Asian, black and Hispanic women and knew how it felt to be stared at by people who didn't approve of these relationships. It didn't matter if it came from a family member or a stranger, it stung and left an aftertaste that was hard to dismiss. Hate begets hate and these glances set off an uneasiness in my heart. When I saw the slashing on the crime sheets, that discomfort returned.

I remembered a time when a drunken fan at Yankee Stadium taunted a black woman sitting in the row next to mine. I had a date at the game that night, and she was black. Though the taunts were not directed at her, I still wanted to throw the bigot over the railing into the section below. But I didn't have the guts to raise my fists—or my voice.

There was also an evening during college when my girlfriend's brother, a militant Chicano, savaged both me and his sister by saying the only reason a gringo would date her was to engage her Latina rhythms in bed. I told him he had insulted us both and walked away, but couldn't do anything to change the way he thought about whites or our relationship.

I'd never been as courageous as I had hoped when confronted with these situations in the past, but as a reporter, I had a chance to show what had happened to this couple just because they'd fallen in love. First I had to get the desk interested, then I'd have to find the victim. Hap Hairston neither encouraged nor discouraged me from pursuing the story. The paper had run a short on the slashing that morning, and Hap said it covered us.

"Don't worry if you can't find the guy," he said.

"Something's pushing me on this one," I told him.

"Up to you baby. If you can give it wings, let 'er fly."

The sheets had only the barest facts. Juan Iribarren, his wife, Sherry Lewis, and their four-month-old baby, Sophia, were shopping in midtown Manhattan during the evening rush hour. The sidewalks were crowded with commuters and business people, men and women of all sizes, shapes and colors heading home through a crush of grid-locked buses and taxicabs. As Iribarren, Lewis and Sophia waited for a light at the corner of East 46th Street and Madison Avenue, a man asked Lewis if Sophia was her child. Lewis, a black woman, proudly nodded. She was used to receiving compliments about her child and thought nothing of the question.

Then, without warning, the man, later identified as twenty-seven-year-old Kevin Richardson, charged Lewis, screaming, "I oughta slit your throat and kill that half-white baby!"

According to the police, Richardson, also black, drew a ten-inch hunting knife with a six-inch blade and lunged first at Lewis and then at the baby, who was in Iribarren's arms. Iribarren handed Sophia to Lewis, who ran, and Richardson turned on the lighter-skinned Iribarren. Iribarren darted around a taxicab and a hot dog stand. He was leaning against a parked car as the knife sliced through the air and caught him under the chin. Richardson fled west, but Iribarren and a cop took off after him. The cop wrestled Richardson to the ground, and Iribarren, wearing cowboy boots, let go a rib-cracking kick that witnesses said could be heard four blocks away. The kick, at least, was simple justice.

The police wouldn't help me find Iribarren, saying he was "a witness to a crime," so I called every Iribarren in the Brooklyn, Bronx, Queens

and Manhattan phone books. No luck. Having exhausted the old list-
ings, I asked directory assistance for any new Iribarrens. There was
one with no first name on East 96th Street. A woman answered and
said Juan Iribarren did live there, but he was sleeping. I left a message,
and ten minutes later, Iribarren called and agreed to talk.

Hap put the story on the daily budget, and Chris Hatch arranged for
a photographer to meet me at their building. I asked the photographer
to wait in the lobby for fifteen minutes before coming upstairs so that
her cameras and lights wouldn't intimidate Iribarren and Lewis. I didn't
want to take any chances.

Iribarren opened his door wearing a blue, terry-cloth bathrobe. A
six-inch gash that had taken sixty stitches to close ran like railroad
tracks from the base of his chin across his throat. It looked painful. He
said it didn't hurt as much as the stares he and Lewis encountered all
the time.

They'd met in the Copacabana nightclub in the summer of 1984.
Iribarren was thirty-two years old then. He was a real estate broker
from Argentina, but worked as a busboy at the Copa until he learned
to speak better English. Lewis, a twenty-two-year-old aspiring singer
from Trinidad who was working as a Macy's saleswoman, sat at one of
Iribarren's tables. She wore a low-cut dress that night, and Iribarren
wanted to meet her. But when she told him he had a cute smile, he
thought she was asking him for a napkin. By the end of the year, his
English had improved, and they'd moved in together.

They lived in Brooklyn then and took the subway to their jobs in
Manhattan. On those rides, both blacks and whites uttered racist
curses at them. It got so demeaning that Lewis and Iribarren sometimes sat on different sides of the train. When Sophia was born, she
brought joy, tears, lots of laughter and all the other pleasurable pains
babies bring. But she also brought one problem most people don't
associate with the birth of a child: the racism got worse.

"Before, people were never sure we were together. Their stares had
a questioning in them, like they were wondering if we were friends or
partners or something," Lewis said, her eyes focused on my pen as I
copied down her words. "The baby changed all that." They couldn't sit
on opposite sides of the subway anymore.

After Iribarren and Lewis told me about the day of the slashing, I asked them if we could take a photo. They took Sophia from her crib and she sipped formula from a bottle as she sat between them on the couch. Iribarren apologized for his scraggly beard, joking that it was difficult to shave with the slash marks on his chin.

When I got back to the office to write, I was eager to get this story down. I called up the budget, pressing a combination of keys that allowed me to read files in the city queue. Hap had put up a budget note for a story slugged cRACE11 by GELMAN at five hundred words w/ART, and the night desk wanted early copy. The only problem was that I was paralyzed. I kept looking in my notebook for quotes and phrases, but nothing seemed right.

The thoughts racing around my mind could have filled an encyclopedia, but I couldn't find fifty, let along five hundred, words for this story. I tried to shake out all the confusion—from my college girlfriend's brother to the bigot at Yankee Stadium. For Chrissakes, I told myself, this stuff happened a long time ago. What was it doing in the newsroom now? Sure, those memories had driven me to find Iribarren, but I had to get rid of them to write.

I tried the stalking-around thing. That seemed to work for Breslin. I had noticed that when Jimmy Breslin was on deadline, he would stalk around by his desk. Then he would mutter expletives under his breath and march back and forth from his office to the city desk. The faster he marched the louder he muttered. He was this ferocious hulk of man bursting the buttons on his shirt, his tie hanging from his neck like a scarf. He'd gnaw on his cigar until he was ready to write. Then he'd explode on his keyboard. It seemed the cigar smoke he inhaled erupted in his columns, and he wrote with an anger burning somewhere in his gut. I felt that anger, but it wasn't coming out in sentences.

As I was stalking, Barbara Strauch tapped me on my shoulder. "You're very weird, you know," she said.

"Yes, I know," I said.

I was also very on deadline, and being on deadline did weird things to weird people, especially ones with writer's block.

The stalking wasn't helping, so I went for a cup of coffee. As I walked to the kitchen, head down, grumbling to myself, I passed Denis Hamill, one of the paper's columnists and as talented a writer as his older brother, Pete. When I was a copyboy at the *Herald Examiner*, I had opened Hamill's mail. They had called him "the Breslin of South Broadway" in L.A., after the street the *Herald* was on. He'd been born in Brooklyn, and now he was back writing about his hometown. Hamill's writing also seemed like it came right from his gut.

"How you doing?" he asked.

"Lousy."

"Yeah. Me, too," he said. "What are you workin' on?"

"A story that says this city is as bad as Johannesburg," I said.

"Huh?"

"This guy and his wife are walking down the street in midtown. He's white and she's black and they have their baby. So, some guy who doesn't like this interracial romance decides to try to cut the guy's head off," I said.

"Nice story."

"Sucks," I said.

"Race is the biggest issue in the city. It's ripping it apart," he said. "Look at the crime, homelessness and the politics and it's all divided on race."

"Right. But how do you write something like this?" I asked.

"Just write it. Let it tell itself," he said.

I went back to my desk and Hap sauntered over, noting that deadline was approaching fast. I had only a few scattered paragraphs on my screen. I kept starting and deleting my lead. I'd type a few sentences, pull a quote from my notebook, then backspace and delete the whole thing. Hap gave me a quick shoulder massage and offered a few words of encouragement: "Bang it out, baby," he said. "The best don't even think when they are writing. They just bang it out and it comes out pretty good that way."

After five more minutes of typing and deleting, the story started to take shape. It wasn't a work of art, but all the facts were there. Joe Gambardello, on the night desk, read it and called me over. He had been a wire-service reporter for ten years and was a master at tailoring a story. Gambardello picked out a salient detail, a quote, and in a few swift strokes fashioned a top that tied the beginning, middle and end together.

"Why don't we try this," he said, rewriting my lead.

> Juan Iribarren showed the six-inch slash on his face that required 60 stitches to close.
> The cut runs from his left ear, down his chin toward his throat.
> For Iribarren, the wound is just the latest he's had to suffer apparently because of racism.
> "Sometimes it feels like the whole city is looking at us," Iribarren said. "On the subways, in the street. But my wife reminds me we're not the only black-white couple in New York."

That was it. Clean. Neat. And poignant. Like Hamill said, the rest of the story told itself. It appeared in the next morning's paper beside a picture of the interracial family on their couch, touching and in love. The story was a personal adventure for me, the kind I had hoped to do when I came to *Newsday*. I still needed editors to turn my drafts into publishable prose, and I was learning how a reporter finds his way around the city. But as long as I could take the initiative on stories like that one, I was happy.

On Saturday, January 14, my education continued when I got to learn from a legend. After admiring him for as long as I could read or follow a dinner-table conversation, I got to work a story with Breslin.

An eighteen-year-old woman had been killed by a stray bullet while eating with friends at a McDonald's. She was the second innocent bystander killed in ten days. The police had made an arrest and had scheduled a press conference at the 70th Precinct in Flatbush. Breslin was writing his column on the victim and called the Cop Shop to find out when the "presser" began. I offered him a ride, and we agreed to meet at Police Headquarters. As soon as I hung up, I started getting butterflies.

I'd read all his collections, most of his novels, knew his characters Marvin the Torch, Klein the Lawyer, Fat Thomas and Un Ochio, the boss of all crime in America. A longtime columnist for the *Daily News*, Breslin was known as the voice of working-class New York. Anyone could cover big events. Breslin had always been able to pique the city's conscience by writing about people who were usually ignored: Harlem mothers who couldn't make their grocery bills; junkies who needed drug treatment; the New York Mets when they were in last place. His Pulitzer Prize wasn't for breaking news out of the White House; it was for uncovering police brutality and climbing tenement staircases in Queens.

Listening to him type was like hearing Sinatra warm up before a concert or watching Ted Williams take batting practice. He was not a touch typist. Breslin used two fingers and attacked the keyboard in bursts that sounded like someone was popping popcorn in his office. Every few minutes, he would pause to smile or sneer. If he liked what he'd written, he would lick his lips and admire the poetry created by a guy nearly all knuckles.

Newsday dropped its biggest bomb in the War of the Tabloids when Breslin's contract with the *News* ran out in 1988 and he signed with *Newsday*. To make sure everyone in the city knew where Breslin worked, the paper ran an advertising campaign for months that said BRESLIN SWITCHED, and on his column days his picture was across the top of page one.

Breslin had always written a column for the Sunday paper, which meant he worked on Saturday like any other day. Saturdays were usually quiet. Most of the Sunday paper—the business section, editorial pages, book review, longer features and entertainment news—had already been written. This was a day when young reporters worked with new editors to fill in the rest of the space. But Breslin was in early. He'd deposit a bag of muffins on the city desk, retreat to his office, read the wires and work the phones.

He'd never had the finest phone manner. When he called to speak to my father when Dad was editing his magazine stories, my sister, Jan, thought he was the rudest man in the world. "Steve dere?" he'd demand in a tough-guy accent. And Jan would run across the apartment, yelling, "The Steve-dere man's on the phone. It's the Steve-dere man for Daddy."

I didn't think he was rude at all. I figured Jimmy Breslin was a busy man who had the ear of mayors, ball players, governors and senators, and he knew whom he wanted to speak to. As far as I could tell, he was just being direct. After all, he always got Steve when he called. Now he was calling me, and it didn't even really matter that all he wanted was a lift to a press conference.

While I waited for him, I combed my hair, tightened the knot on my tie, and the butterflies fluttered faster. I felt like this was a first date. And I was terrified I'd get lost on the way to the precinct.

"Am I late?" he said, walking in.

"No, I'm early. Car's out on the triangle," I said.

"What time's this thing?"

"Supposed to start at four. We should be okay," I said, knowing we were really cutting it close.

"I want to see how many people come out, compared with last week," he said.

The one last week was a press conference after the killing of a thirty-year-old white doctor at Bellevue Hospital. The doctor, Kathryn Hinnant, from a small town in South Carolina, was five months pregnant. Her husband and a hospital security guard found her body in her laboratory after she didn't show up at an art gallery opening. Her red dress had been pulled up above her waist, and she had been raped and bludgeoned to death. The police set up a command post right at the hospital. Chief Aaron Rosenthal, the head of Manhattan detectives, who was known as the Supreme Allied Commander among his minions, assigned fifty investigators to the case and supervised it himself. The mayor called Hinnant's killing "the number one murder in the city." The police commissioner came to the hospital and both Hamill brothers and Breslin wrote columns on it. A week later, Breslin wanted to see how the death of an eighteen-year-old black college freshman would be treated by the press corps and public officials.

The way we were covering Tondelayo Alfred's death showed me it wasn't getting the same attention Hinnant's slaying had received. For that one, the desk had beeped Esposito and called in a handful of reporters who had the day off. For Alfred, we were going with just our regular Saturday crew, which meant I was the only reporter handling it.

Driving across the Brooklyn Bridge, Breslin asked me to turn the radio up. The bridge's cables screwed with the reception, and he wanted to stay up on the news. To make conversation, I asked him how he liked living on the Upper West Side, where he'd moved to be with his second wife after living in Queens for most of his life. "Fuck it," he said. "I don't know where I am half the time. No fucking idea."

By then I was clearly getting us lost, so I hoped we were in one of the halves he knew. "You know how to get to the precinct?" I asked. He shrugged. I glanced at a map I had unfolded on the dashboard and as I was driving toward Flatbush, my beeper went off. I pulled over and ran to a pay phone. The desk wanted me to pick up a photograph of Tondelayo on my way back. They said this as if getting a picture of a dead person was like picking up a carton of milk.

"I'm going to be tight on deadline as it is. Can't photo send somebody?" I asked.

"They don't have anybody to send. Do what you can."

I hated being told "Do what you can." Did they think I wouldn't do what I could if they didn't tell me to? Sometimes editors had been inside too long. Breslin told me I didn't have much of a chance getting a photograph. The family hadn't even talked to him when he went out to their house in the morning.

As we drove along Prospect Park West, I felt I was wasting an opportunity. Here I was sitting next to one of the great journalists of all time and I wasn't picking up any lasting wisdom. Our conversation was sounding more like an interview.

"What do you make of the way it's getting out here with all the killing?" I asked.

"Never been so bad," he said.

"It's got to get better."

"Does it?"

As we spun around a circle at the end of the park, Breslin popped up in his seat. "Are we near Farrell's?" he said. "Fuck it. I'm going to Farrell's. Yeah. Pull over. You know the place?"

"I've heard of it, but . . ."

"Best fucking Irish bar in the city. I don't care what anybody says. Wait here. I gotta use the bathroom."

Here I am, a fool waiting for him to tell me something brilliant, and he's thinking, Where's a bathroom? A few minutes later, we turned from Ocean Parkway onto Lawrence Avenue, and amazingly, the precinct was right in front of us. While I looked for a parking space, Breslin stared up at a footbridge across the street.

"Most difficult zoning variance in the city. Can't get fire trucks under it. The fire department fights those things like hell," he said.

I thought he was just talking trivia before I realized this guy could smell a fixed contract from a footbridge. They don't teach that kind of reporting in journalism school.

Outside the Seven-oh, cars with NYP plates and television trucks were parked horizontally and diagonally up and down the street. I drove around the corner to find a space. The station house was one of the oldest in the city. Its original bronze plaque from 1909 had rusted green with the years and remained embedded in the precinct's stone façade. Inside, a huge American flag was draped across the back wall and a desk sergeant paced behind a classic fifteen-foot oak desk.

"Fourth estate's in the basement," he said.

"Has it started yet?" I asked.

"Nope. Not until the chief comes downstairs," he said abruptly.

The press conference was delayed, and I still didn't have much on Tondelayo Alfred other than her name and where she went to school. To make matters worse, Rose Arce, Elaine's curly-headed friend from the *News*, had a full notebook. She told me that Tondelayo had been a cheerleader at Midwood High School and said they already had a photo of her in her cheerleading outfit. I looked around and saw Breslin, who didn't seem at all concerned that our deadline was creeping up. He was stretching, yawning, reading signs and memos posted on bulletin boards and watching a black cat scurry around the podium. Then he sat down with his head bowed over his notebook. I bought a pack of peanuts from the candy machine and chewed nervously until a row of investigators marched into the basement at four-twenty P.M., following their boss, Deputy Chief Ronald Fenrich, head of Brooklyn detectives.

Breslin raised his head in synch with the first sound from Fenrich's mouth. His concentration locked onto every word and he took rapid-fire notes. The chief gave a straightforward synopsis of events. Tondelayo and two friends had gone to McDonald's after a homecoming basketball game at Midwood High School. A man with a 9-mm. automatic handgun was shooting at another man who ran into the fast-food restaurant. One of the bullets struck Tondelayo. Based on information from "an individual in the community," the detectives located and arrested the gunman.

When the press conference ended, Fenrich and Breslin said hello to each other. Having been through the motions so often in the past, they did their version of the DCPI dance, communicating mostly in body language.

"Nice work," Breslin said with a quick nod.

"Thank you," Fenrich nodded.

"Is there anything else?" Breslin indicated by shrugging his shoulders.

"Like what?" Fenrich responded with raised eyebrows.

"Names of the girls with her in the McDonald's?" Breslin asked.

Fenrich shook his head.

Breslin nodded.

On our way out, I reminded Breslin that I had to swing by Tondelayo's house to get a picture.

"Okay, drop me. I'll get a cab. Naw. Fuck it. There's the El," he said, pointing to the elevated train tracks that ran past the precinct. "I'll take the subway. What time is this thing due?"

"Deadline's in less than an hour."

"Easy. That's easy. I'll write the fucking thing on the El," he said.

He grabbed his overcoat from my car and I took off for Tondelayo's street. Breslin was right about her family; they still didn't want to talk, but luckily I found a group of kids who knew her, one of whom had one of her cheerleading photographs. I tossed the picture in my notebook, and nearly knocked the carriage off the bottom of my car when I hit an inverted pothole as I raced to the office.

By the time I was settling in my seat, Breslin had finished typing the column he'd written on the train. He dropped a printout in front of me and told me to make sure the facts matched what I was writing. Of course, I hadn't written anything yet, and even if I had, I'd have been more inclined to make my copy match his than the other way around.

Breslin had changed the subject of his column slightly. The mayor hadn't shown up, but there had been enough press coverage that he couldn't really say the city had ignored the death of a young black woman. Instead, he wrote that we were losing our best and brightest:

> Tondelayo Alfred was a freshman at Brooklyn College....
>
> Her father is a sergeant in the police department of the City of New York. Somebody said that her mother had been going to college, too. I don't know that. I do know that her city needed Tondelayo Alfred as much as it needs the sunrise.
>
> She was on her way to something, and she was going to take all of us with her, and here comes some degenerate walking in from the street with a gun. She loses her life and we lose her.
>
> One week ago, a doctor named Kathryn Hinnant was murdered in Manhattan. Now, an eighteen-year-old woman in college in Brooklyn is gone. Through much of last year we counted the bodies of people whose resumes were not impressive. We begin a new year by murdering the best in sight....

It was a great column, but he implied Tondelayo would have stayed and contributed to the city. That didn't jibe with what I had heard. The kids in her neighborhood said she wanted to do well her first two years in college and then transfer out of state. I mentioned this to Breslin.

"Does that mess me up?" Breslin said.

"Not really," I said, realizing this was a matter of conjecture, not fact, and that all the times, places and names in his story were solid. It was too late to change much anyway. "Your point is that we lost her one way or another, right?"

"That's it," he said and headed out the door.

I still had to write my story. I wrote as fast as I could, trying to keep my sentences conjunction-free. On my way home, I replayed the afternoon, looking for some technique I could pick up from the master. But nothing Breslin had done or said seemed particularly remarkable.

Then, it struck me. After forty-three years as a reporter, after winning the Pulitzer Prize, after seeing his novels on the bestseller list and his articles in national magazines, he still went out on the streets like any other working stiff. He got up early and stayed out late. He listened to the radio and went to the far end of Brooklyn hunting for an angle that wasn't even there. He had pressed the detective for information and had pushed the deadline to the wall. And from home that night, he'd call the desk three times before midnight to see if anything else had happened. Sure, Breslin had a great ear for dialogue. He could write like a poet and had more opinions than a parliament. But a lot of people could listen, write and boast. He worked. I stopped looking for a magic formula. The secret was in the shoe leather.

The next day, I drove to the house my father owned in upstate New York, where he and his girlfriend were spending the weekend. I'd been concentrating so hard on reporting that I'd almost forgotten there were trees and lakes in other parts of the earth. Just being away for twenty-four hours was refreshing. There was snow on the ground, and my father and I skied that afternoon. For the first time in months, I was someplace where cops, killers and deadlines couldn't find me.

When I got back to the Shack, the mornings were quiet. Joe Cotter hadn't been feeling well and had taken a few days off. I'd gotten into the habit of talking to Joe when I arrived, running down the overnight crimes and chatting about the way the papers had played stories from the day before. Mornings dragged without Joe's daily greeting, but nobody thought his illness was serious.

When I came back from lunch on Tuesday, January 17, I saw Ginny

Byrne from the Associated Press and Anne Murray of the *Post* sitting on either side of Joe's desk. They were eating cookies out of a box of assorted Pepperidge Farm classics and were looking at each other in shock.

"What happened?" I said.

"It's Joe," Anne said.

"What?"

"Joe's in a coma," Anne said.

"He went into the hospital over the weekend for a nosebleed, and I saw him and was talking to him on Sunday," Ginny said. "He looked fine. Then, it just happened."

"What do the doctors say?" I asked.

"They have no idea," Ginny said.

"It's too soon to tell. But Joe's a tough old Irishman and they don't go down easy," Anne said.

"Worst thing is he's in intensive care and they're only letting family visit," Ginny said.

Ginny and Anne considered Joe family. He was like a father to them. Whenever Anne was depressed, Joe knew it immediately from the number of cigarettes she chain-smoked or how long it took her to go through the box of cookies. And Ginny would sit with Joe for half an hour every morning, sipping tea and chatting about life, love and the news until a story broke.

With Joe out, I missed a good word in the morning. Anne and Ginny missed a friend, a colleague and a surrogate father. But like Anne said, Joe was a fighter. They weren't giving up yet.

In the first few days, everybody—from the highest ranking chiefs in the department to the morning custodian—came by to ask about Joe. Anne even put a note on the door that said, "Joe Cotter is in a coma. Cards and flowers are appreciated." I bought a card for Joe, and Esposito sent flowers from our bureau. Anne promised to update Joe's condition on the note as soon as it changed, but the note remained the same for weeks.

Joe was the link between the old and the new at the Cop Shop. In the old days, reporters and police officers were part of the same clique; they drank together and kept each other's secrets. Along with district attorneys and judges, they were part of the same criminal justice family. However, as the number of papers declined and jobs became less stable, cop reporting was no longer seen as a lifetime calling, but rather as the low rung on the journalistic ladder. The police bureau was the place where kids served time before moving on to more prestigious assignments. To climb that next rung, reporters were more apt to criticize the department than ever before. Our role had changed from insider to outside observer. Joe was the last of the real old-time cop reporters in the Shack. He maintained special relationships with chiefs he'd known since they were patrolmen, yet he accepted the stringent ethics of new reporters.

The *Post* replaced Joe with a former police officer who had left the department after he was injured in an on-duty scooter accident. Mike Koleniak came from a cop family and landed his job after sending a letter to the editor, which the paper ran as an Op-Ed piece. He sat in Joe's chair, but nobody could fill it. Koleniak knew about police work, but he was a novice journalist compared to the other reporters assigned to Headquarters.

The reporters at the Shack were extensions of the styles and personalities of their papers. The four *News* reporters had the biggest office, at the end of the hallway, and didn't spend much time talking to other reporters. Larry Celona's father ran a fish market in Bay Ridge, Patrice O'Shaughnessy was a young mother, and David Krajiek had come to the paper from Nebraska, lived in Brooklyn and was the bureau chief. James Duddy, the night reporter, had been in the Shack almost as long as Cotter. The first time I met him, he told me that if his door was closed, it meant one of two things. "I'm either breaking an exclusive and you'll read about it in the morning, or I'm taking a nap and you'll never know," he said. Then he tipped his hat and ambled off behind a closed door. Duddy was a classic, but he didn't have Joe's charm or wit. Like their readers, the *News* reporters were connected to the city's white, working-class neighborhoods.

At the other extreme were David Pitt and Don Terry of the *Times*, a paper that saw the police bureau as one step up from copyboy. Most *Times* reporters wanted a national or foreign assignment. Pitt, a laid-back man with a beard who'd worked in the Berkshires before coming to the *Times*, and Terry, an aggressive young black reporter from Chicago who was skeptical of anybody in power, were very serious about covering police, but they were less inclined to remain on the beat as long as the rest of the group.

Although the Shack has its rivalries and jealousies, there is also a sense of togetherness among cop reporters. They may not all be friends on a day-to-day basis, but they join in crises, either to fight with DCPI or to offer support when someone is warring with an editor. Police reporters share something special—how many other people had to leave dates and family functions for crime stories? —and know that if they can't keep other relationships going because of their jobs, they can rely on each other. I saw all of this, but at the beginning of the year, while most of the reporters would shoot the breeze or cultivate sources between breaking stories, I always seemed to be working on a feature, answering phones, watching the sheets or cranking out another two-hundred-word short for the next day's crime briefs. I was writing an average of two to three stories a day.

Around this time, I was getting carried away with the competition between the three tabloids. It was fun being in the middle of an old-fashioned newspaper war, but I learned my lesson about taking this too far when Hap told me to find and kidnap a Bronx bodega owner who had shot and killed two robbers.

"Bring him to the office. Take him to a hotel. This guy is the Dominican Bernie Goetz. I don't care how you do it. Just don't let the *Post* or *News* near this guy," Hap said.

The banner of the paper waving from my antenna, I flew up the FDR Drive, over the Willis Avenue Bridge and into the Bronx. I was on a mission from Hap.

The bodega owner's name was Ramon Guzman. He ran the Rainbow Mini Mart across the Harlem River from where the old Polo Grounds used to be. This was a place where my white skin, sport coat and tie made me stand out like a blond-tasseled corn stalk in a wheat field. Guzman's store was shuttered closed, but after talking to a few people, I found someone who knew where he lived. The guy said his name was Pedro, and he promised to keep the address our secret.

As I was leaving, I saw two other white people walking up Anderson

Avenue. One was Peter Moses, a reporter from the *Post,* and the other
was Bob Gearty from the *News.* I tried to sneak away, but Moses saw
me and came over.

"Let's go see the landlord," Moses said.

"You guys go. I gotta call my desk," I said.

"Gelman! What are you holding back?" Moses said.

"Guzman is not there. He doesn't live here. I checked that already,"
I said.

"You know where he is. Level, Gelman," Moses said.

Gearty didn't say a word.

"You guys go. I'll catch up with you later," I said.

As I walked off, Moses said, "You're lying, Gelman. Give it up. We
share out on the street. Because if we don't, next time we're the one
who gets burned."

Hell, Hap's instructions were simple: No *News.* No *Post.* I found
Guzman and was talking to him for five minutes when there was a loud
knock on his door. In walked Moses and Gearty.

"And look who's here. Surprise! Surprise!" Moses said.

Already sunk down as far as I could, I wanted to crawl under the
couch.

For the next twenty minutes, as Gearty questioned Guzman, Moses
peppered me with threats. He was going to put me on his blacklist if I
ever lied to him again. I guess I should've known Moses and Gearty
would find Guzman on their own. And I was a moron for thinking
Pedro would keep a secret.

Esposito and Hap were in the newsroom when I returned. Hap had
led me into enough trouble for one day, so I told Esposito what had
happened. I explained how pissed off Moses was, but Esposito didn't
think it was such a big deal. He said Moses was a good reporter and
not to worry about it.

"Yeah. I know that," I said. "But what's the right thing to do when
you have information and you're trying to hold on to it?"

"When I was on the street," he said, "I always had enough to share."

The stuff between me and Moses would pass. My biggest challenge
was developing relationships with cops, particularly the ones in DCPI.
Every morning I talked to my friend Alex, but when you're covering a

department of 27,000 officers, a friendship with one headquarters security guard does not make a well-sourced reporter. I wasn't going to find a solution in a textbook or learn it from an editor. I'd have to adjust my personality to fit the environment I was working in.

But how?

Living Dead

I was upstairs in the public information office at eight forty-three A.M., just two hours before George Bush would promise a kinder and gentler nation during his inaugural address, when a report crackled in over the scanner.

A cop was frantically calling a "Ten-thirteen" into his radio, and every head in the room turned. A dispatcher picked up the call and broadcast flashes from the scene over the citywide frequency. *"Shots fired ... Confirmed officer down ... Perp on roof ... Eighty-two Hancock Street ... Brooklyn ... All units respond. ..."* Chris Hatch and Tom Curran were monitoring their scanner, and Curran sent a reporter from the Brooklyn bureau to Hancock Street and told me to go to Kings County Hospital, where they were taking the cop.

When I got to the redbrick hospital, one of the paper's photographers was leaning against a pillar in the lobby. He told me an unmarked silver car outside the emergency room was the one the cops used to bring the stricken officer. The car's backseat was soaked with blood, and streaks had dried along the rear side door. Suddenly, the magnitude of this story started becoming clear. The emergency room entrance, a cement ramp, was a few yards in front of the car. By nine-forty A.M., a dozen cops huddled in small clusters nearby.

The scene reminded me of the 72nd Precinct the night Joe Galapo was killed. Only much bigger. And again I felt like an intruder crashing an extremely private gathering. This was a tribal ritual and I did not belong. As a member of the press, I just reminded the officers that something tragic had happened.

Whenever they spotted someone they knew, their eyebrows lifted and they reached out for each other, leaning on each other's shoulders and cradling each other's heads. They hugged and cried and I heard them saying, "Is he okay?" "I heard it was Billy." "Yeah." "Jeez." "I just saw him last week. He was doing great." "What happened?" "Did he get off any shots?" A few went inside to give blood. Others brought steaming cups of coffee. Yet there was still a tension among the cops. As they talked, their jaws tightened. Even as they held one another, they seemed to be trying to push away the fear they all shared, the knowledge that the one on the operating table could have been them.

Back at *Newsday*'s main office, editors were putting together a package of stories—what we called a "pak"—on the shooting. They'd want to know the cop's name, what he'd been doing at Hancock Street, if he had a wife or kids and how long he'd been on the job. Esposito was writing the main story in the Cop Shot Pak. A few minutes past ten, he beeped.

"What do you have?" he asked.

"All I know is they brought the cop here in a silver car."

"Get more," Esposito said.

He was in his Ferrari speed, up on two wheels, racing around that corner. He spoke so fast that his sentences sounded like multi-syllabic chatter. "Get-me-quotes-from-the-mayor, the-police-commissioner, mood-at-the-hospital, bio-on-the-cop, his-wife, children, the-caliber-of-the-gun, color-of-the-cop's-hair, his-condition, what-the-doctors-are-saying. I-want-every-lick-and-splatter," he said.

"I'll try," I said.

My problem was that the officers didn't want to talk to the press and the department hadn't released the cop's identity. The hospital was also being tight-lipped about his condition because they didn't want his family to find out what had happened from the news. I found one officer in a thick blue parka who didn't mind talking, as long as I agreed not to use his name.

While I was pressing him for background on the cop's family life and hobbies, a helicopter landed on a football field across the street. Two police supervisors and a priest hustled a young woman wearing a white silk blouse into the hospital.

"His wife?" I asked the officer in the parka.

He nodded.

By noon, television cameramen, reporters and radio people were gathering for a press conference on the hospital's second floor. Microphones were lined up like toy soldiers on a table. This, too, was its own peculiar ritual—a media mob scene. Seats and camera angles were on a first-come, first-served basis. Cameramen and still photographers jockeyed for position, pushing and shoving and yelling back and forth. "Hey, what do you think this is, a TV show?" "Gimme a break, man. Just gimme a little room here." One television reporter checked her hair in a hand-held mirror and asked her technician how she looked. "Fine, honey. Just darling," said the tech, a thickset balding man in his union windbreaker. Reporters who hadn't seen each other since the last big story caught up on the latest newsworld gossip.

Intoxicated with anticipation, I watched intensely as Mayor Edward Koch, his lips pursed and his glasses on top of his head, walked in. Police Commissioner Ben Ward was with the mayor, along with two surgeons in hospital gowns and a coterie of police brass, including Alice McGillion.

Koch massaged his temples as Ward opened the press conference with a brief statement. He said two officers had been shot during an attempted arrest of a murder suspect. One of the officers, twenty-eight-year-old William T. Gunn, had been seriously wounded. Koch and the doctors spoke briefly and then took questions. At press conferences, I usually waited for another reporter to ask what I wanted to know, but this time nobody was asking Ward about a key element of the story.

Gunn had come to the aid of a detective who'd been left standing alone outside the suspect's apartment. Why had this detective been by himself? Esposito and the editors—who were always looking for ways to find fault and assign blame—would want to know if this was standard procedure. I understood that the police commissioner wouldn't want to condemn anyone in the aftermath of a tragedy like this, but it was a question I had to ask. Ward said he didn't know yet and told me to check with McGillion later.

When the press conference ended, the radio reporters dashed for the phones and cameramen packed their gear. I waited until the room had cleared and walked up to McGillion. The usually soft-spoken deputy commissioner was not so soft this time.

"Can't you see we just had a cop shot?" she said sharply.

"Yes. I'm just trying to find out what happened. I'm sorry about the officer...."

"Are you? We're still finding out what happened," she said.

"When should I call about the question?"

She glowered at me and walked away.

In a few days, I learned that there was a perfectly reasonable, even heroic explanation for the detective being alone in the hallway. But because McGillion had so indignantly dismissed my question, I spent the morning trying to find out what she was covering up. That preoccupation temporarily took me away from the more important matter of Billy Gunn's story.

Gunn was on the trail of his first killer when his squad got a tip that the suspect was holed up with a girlfriend in Bedford Stuyvesant. Gunn was going to spend his day off with his wife, but he canceled their plans to look for a twenty-year-old felon named Ralph Richardson. This was important to Gunn because, as old detectives say, even if they catch hundreds of killers, they never forget bringing in their first homicide. It's a milestone in any cop's career.

Gunn woke early on January 20, put on a new suit, a dark blue trench coat and an Inspector Clouseau hat he'd bought after his recent promotion to the detective bureau. He drove from his Long Island home to meet four other detectives at the 67th Precinct. They took two cars to the Hancock Street brownstone. When the landlord confirmed that a man fitting Richardson's description was staying in one of the apartments, the cops took positions. One detective went around back to guard the fire escape. Gunn and Detective Louis Rango set up outside the apartment's door. The team's supervisor and the fifth detective walked down the street to call the department's legal division to be certain they had the right warrants to arrest Richardson at his girlfriend's place. Just then, Richardson heard the commotion in the hallway and started throwing clothes off the fire escape. The cop in back radioed for help, and Gunn headed toward the yard, leaving Rango isolated. The fifty-one-year-old Rango, a first-grade detective with twenty-eight years on the job, tried to stall Richardson until Gunn could get around back.

"Police, Ralphie! Come out, Ralphie, come out," he said.

"I'm coming out," Richardson responded.

And he did—firing! A .25-caliber automatic in each hand, he spun toward Rango, who was crouched five feet away. The first shot struck the detective in the shoulder. Rango squeezed off a bullet that hit Richardson in the leg, but didn't stop him. Rango fell back and Richardson stood spread-eagled over him. Richardson put a gun to Rango's head and tossed one of his .25's aside. Richardson didn't kill Rango, but took the detective's .38-caliber service revolver.

Gunn heard the shots and was churning back up the stairs when Richardson leaned over the bannister with Rango's gun. Two shots echoed in the hallway. One blasted off half of Gunn's head, the other hit him in the stomach. Gunn and his Inspector Clouseau hat tumbled down the staircase. Richardson escaped in his pajamas, climbing through a hatch to the roof.

By two forty-five P.M., Gunn had lost fifty pints of blood. Doctors said his condition was "extremely critical." The police department went a step further, and prepared a memo announcing his funeral.

Newsday's editors were looking for as many angles to the story as possible. They kept one reporter at the brownstone, had Esposito check with DCPI for any developments in the case, and told me to find out what I could about Richardson's trail of death. I went from the hospital to the Flatbush neighborhood where police said Richardson had killed a young electrician five days earlier. The electrician had tried to break up a fight between his cousin and Richardson.

It was dusk by this point, and shadows were cast across the empty streets near the electrician's home. With my press pass clearly visible, I approached a group of young men wearing orange armbands cut from the crime scene tape the detectives had used to cordon off the sidewalk after the murder. The young men were friends of the electrician's cousin. They said that Richardson was a freelance enforcer for crack dealers and that his street name was "Caprice"—slang for cocaine. They also said he'd had the letter "C" engraved on gold caps over his two front teeth.

"He just a nigger who thought he was the new *Big Man* around 'cause of the Titan he got on his hip," one said.

For some reason—and I didn't want to be there long enough to find out—the guys with the armbands seemed nervous. I left the street before it turned dark and drove toward Manhattan to find a phone to call in my notes.

That night, the cops did all they could to continue the job that Officer William Gunn, who was still fighting to stay alive, had started. They put out a $25,000 reward for Richardson and broadcast his description— five feet eight inches, 150 pounds, medium complexion, short brown hair—citywide every thirty minutes.

At nine A.M. the next day, Hancock Street was frozen in silence. Barriers sealed off the traffic and bitter gusts of wind swept over the hoods of two unmarked police cars. The cops had combed the street with helicopters, detectives and bloodhounds, and they were still guarding 82 Hancock as if it were an active crime scene. But the only sign of Richardson was his mug shot, which lay flat on the dashboard of both detectives' cars.

In the photo, Richardson stared directly at the camera, his eyes cold as petrified wood. He wore a red long-sleeve T-shirt. His thick lower lip curved slightly toward the bottom of his rectangular face. The police wouldn't let me get anywhere near the brownstone, so I went back to the Cop Shop, where DCPI had a folder that included Richardson's six-page rap sheet. He'd been arrested half-a-dozen times since he was fourteen years old and had been convicted of armed robbery, harassing a state police officer, jumping a turnstile and possessing weapons. He'd served time in a juvenile detention center, city jails and state prisons, and had jumped bail while awaiting trial for trying to kill a police officer in November 1987. Since then, he'd allegedly murdered a man in Philadelphia in a fight over a woman.

His life hadn't always been marked by crime, though. His mother, Hazel Richardson, was eighteen years old when she got pregnant and twenty when she learned that her husband wasn't coming home from Vietnam. Friends said that his death devastated Hazel but that she pledged to them that Ralph would not be deprived of anything because he didn't have a father.

While other young mothers in the neighborhood were buying clothes at discount stores, Hazel treated Ralph with three-piece suits from Saks Fifth Avenue and bought him a gold ring before he was old enough to go to kindergarten. And she wouldn't scold him. Not at an office Christmas party in 1972, when four-year-old Ralph stuck his hands onto the buffet and pulled a baked ham off the table, nor a year later, when he stomped to bits a toy airplane Santa had given another boy. Ralph's mother was convinced he was just going through a stage.

By the time he was sixteen years old, he'd served ten months in the Harlem Juvenile Detention Center. Although he briefly attended Thomas Jefferson High School after he was released, Richardson dropped out during his sophomore year. His mother kept a bed for him at her apartment in the Fairfield Towers, a housing complex in East New York, but he rarely stayed at home and never slept there while he was on the lam. Still, the cops staked out his mother's apartment, along with his street haunts.

Richardson was making a mockery of the entire NYPD. If they couldn't catch a cop-shooter, who could they catch? Richardson became a symbol of the violence that was sweeping the city. Word went out from Headquarters: He had to be apprehended—dead or alive.

While the police hunted for Richardson, I took a few days off. The early morning beeps and late-breaking stories had made me overly tired, and my nerves were frayed. I hadn't been able to run or go to the gym in weeks. Esposito told me to take some comp time. Richardson seemed to have drifted off the face of the city, and I didn't think the story would unfold as quickly as it did. But while I was reading and relaxing at my dad's house, I was missing a lot of action back home.

On Tuesday night, January 24, Richardson walked with a limp into the Request-A-Movie video rental store in East Flatbush. He was holding a .38-caliber revolver in one hand and a .25-caliber automatic in the other. He didn't know that the counter clerk, Janet Caban, lived a double life, working during the day as a cop in the 77th Precinct. And Caban had no idea that the man robbing her store was the most wanted criminal in the city. Richardson, who had a stolen car with its motor running outside, ordered Caban to give him the money in the register.

"That's not enough, bitch!" Richardson said when Caban handed him two hundred dollars. "Where's the stash?"

"Look, sweetheart, that's all there is," Caban replied.

Richardson started toward the counter, saying, "If I find any money when I come around here, I'm gonna kill you."

In four years as a police officer, Caban had never fired a shot on or off duty. Now, she had no choice. She grabbed her gun from a shelf beneath the cash register. The pair were just a few feet from each other during the gunfight. Bullets went everywhere except where they were aimed. Nine shots were fired. One shattered the glass of the front door, another went through a window. Half a dozen shots went into walls and into the ceiling; one hit Richardson in the groin. As he dragged himself to the car, Richardson had a parting word.

"I'll be back to kill you, bitch!" he said.

It was around ten P.M., and a light rain and clouds blocked the moon. Wounded, Richardson drove his stolen silver Oldsmobile along Avenue D toward East New York. At the 79th Precinct, manhunt headquarters, detectives didn't know their quarry had been shot.

Richardson steered the car through a desolate land of auto body graveyards and burned-out factories, where the only life after sundown was a few drunken night watchmen and junkyard dogs guarding gutter, sewer and water-main warehouses. He turned into a rutted alley that ended in a heap of rubble, and parked beside a tin fence among splintered two-by-fours, crushed crack vials and tires stripped to their steel belts.

At three-eighteen A.M., two police officers, partners named Jeffrey Rosen and Martin Kennedy, responding to a factory alarm, came upon the stolen car. According to police reports, they pointed their flashlights inside and saw Richardson's body. The car door was slightly ajar. The left front window was rolled down four or five inches, and the officers said Richardson was lying across the front seat with a bullet wound to his left temple. Rango's .38-caliber revolver lay between his legs, and a gnarled bullet was on the seat next to his knit hat. The police said that Richardson had masturbated and then shot himself through the brain.

When I crossed the city line early Thursday morning, I saw *Newsday*'s front page on the newsstand. There was a picture of four cops looking into the stolen Olds. The headline said: DEAD END. I dropped a quarter on the counter and yanked a copy off the top of the stack. Then I slammed my fist on the roof of my car, upset that I'd missed the story.

When I saw Esposito later, I apologized for not being around to help with the coverage.

"Yeah, remind me to never let you take a four-day weekend again," he said. "I had to get up at six A.M. on this one, and I'm getting too old for that."

Richardson was dead, but in people's minds the circumstances surrounding his death hadn't been put to rest. In the Cop Shop, in the halls of Headquarters, around the newsroom, in precincts and at a party I went to at the end of the week, everybody asked: Do you think he really killed himself? Nobody completely accepted the police department's version; at the same time, nobody seemed overly concerned. Only one reporter at the Shack was visibly angry. He believed the cops had been so happy when they found Richardson, they shot him and then celebrated by jerking him off. The general attitude among the rest of us was that it couldn't have happened to a nicer guy than Richardson. If we found out a cop had killed him—and it was unlikely we would find out—we'd have reported the hell out of the story. But even if it had happened that way, it would have only further satisfied the primal urge for vengeance in a lot of souls.

Not even Hazel Richardson, whom I called while reporting a follow-up story on her son's death, wanted to protest. A close friend later said she was relieved that at least her son would not kill again.

Breslin was the only journalist who explicitly questioned the police version of the story in his column the following day.

> The police say that an alarm did go off on that block last night and that officers in a patrol car then found Richardson dead in the stolen car.
>
> But yesterday, as you looked around the place, a phrase came to mind naturally: "taken for a ride." I don't know anybody who believes the police story. At the same time, most people don't care. Which is fine at first drink. Great! Gone. As vicious as we've ever had.

I read Breslin's column, heard what everybody else was saying, and found that my own emotions were mixed. I had always believed the death penalty was revenge and not justice, and that vigilante killing was the same as murder. But this seemed different, mostly because I knew more now. The city's court system, which cops didn't trust and criminals didn't respect, was backed up in an interminable logjam. Police officers cursed turnstile justice, and thugs laughed when they walked out of jail with slaps on the wrists for serious crimes. Frustrated cops combined with arrogant crooks made the streets a place where rules were ignored and survival often meant kill or be killed.

Since coming to the Shack, I had been exposed to an environment where things didn't fit into neatly balanced arguments about right and wrong. And it shook the roots of much of my thinking to realize that, in a lot of ways, the law didn't apply to Ralph Richardson's world. And though I was disturbed by the idea that the police might have taken Richardson's life, I also felt he deserved to die just as brutally as he had lived.

Virtually no more information about Richardson's death was coming from the police department, certainly not from any of the officers in DCPI. One reason they had such a bunker mentality was Commissioner Ben Ward—an equal opportunity offender. He would insult anyone, male or female, black, white, brown or beige, regardless of race, creed or color.

In the past, the commissioner had offended Sweden's female police officers by making sly comments about the slits in their uniform skirts; he had angered black ministers by warning them about black burglars, robbers and killers in their parishes; and he had recently upset Hispanic leaders during the announcement of a new car-seizure program by asking them to "tell your relatives to be careful where they buy their drugs, because we don't want to confiscate their cars." Whenever Ward spoke—at a corporate luncheon or at a department promotion ceremony—McGillion could be seen holding her breath, always ready to begin damage control.

On February 1, he met with Hispanic community representatives to smooth relations after his "be careful where they buy their drugs" comment, but instead made things worse. When the leaders asked Ward about his minority promotion policy, he answered with a saying popular among white South Africans.

"They say, 'You can't give the Zulu white bread; you have to give them black bread. Because if you give them white bread, then they'll be back asking you for butter,' " he said.

When Walter Alicea, president of the department's Hispanic Society, came down to the Shack to tell us about Ward's latest insult, Elaine Rivera's eyes almost burst from her head.

"He what? He said what?" she asked.

"Not for nothing, from his mouth to God's ears, and you can ask anyone else who was there, that's what he said. There was five seconds of silence. We were dumbstruck," Alicea said.

"How could he be so stupid? You know what? I think he is a self-loathing black man. That's his problem," Elaine said.

"Well, are you going to write something?" Alicea said.

Not only did Elaine write something, but she made sure David Pitt at the *Times* and Anne Murray at the *Post* and everyone else within earshot wrote something, too. A Puerto Rican born in Cleveland, Ohio, Elaine was always sensitive to bigotry, but even more so when it involved Hispanics.

Elaine was pretty frank about this with cops, too. They would visit her all the time, and she always seemed happy to see them. They would sit down and she'd tell them straight out that they were racist or sexist and that they knew it. As they sheepishly smiled and tried to defend themselves, she would tell them they were going to die in La Revolución. Guilt-ridden and totally disarmed by her honesty, they'd leave and return in a few days for the same conversation.

Elaine, who treated me like a little brother, joked with me one day that being a woman gave her an advantage in developing sources. Or as she put it: "Na-na-na-na-na, I've got something they want that you don't have." But if that were the case, why couldn't I cultivate female cops as sources? No, it was more than what she was referring to. She had an unwavering integrity that even the most deceitful police officers wanted to be infected with. She charmed them with the truth.

No matter what peace-keeping efforts I tried, my fights with most of the officers at DCPI only got worse. We just had too much mutual distrust. They suspected that I was always looking for dirt, even if it meant sneaking glances at reports on their desks, and I was convinced that they conspired to cover up stories they didn't want written. Working together was complicated even further by the police department's numbing bureaucracy.

On February 3, I received their official denial of the FOIL request for access to the homicide list. I had thirty days to appeal to the office of the deputy commissioner for legal matters. Forst and Curran hadn't asked me about the list in awhile and I didn't want to cause any more problems with DCPI, so I tossed the denial in my top desk drawer, telling myself I'd worry about it later.

I did get along with two cops on the thirteenth floor. Sergeants Mo Howard and Norris Hollomon worked the Saturday morning and afternoon shifts. Mo and I'd bullshit for fifteen minutes or so as I checked the sheets when I came in. He was about to retire and enjoyed going on about the wretched state of the city and what he thought should be done about it. Norris, soft-spoken and a splendid dresser, was one of the most polite human beings I'd ever met. He would often help me out by calling if any stories broke close to our early Saturday deadlines.

Besides Mo and Norris and a couple of others, I found the crowd at

DCPI too deeply entrenched in the NYPD establishment to communicate with anyone who didn't see things the way they did. These guys couldn't exactly be called flexible thinkers. They were primarily concerned with not rocking the boat, keeping their desk jobs and getting promoted. Loyalty to a never-erring, blue-is-thicker-than-blood NYPD came before anything else. And no one served that vision with more undying dedication than Sergeant John Clifford.

Clifford and I came from different backgrounds. He was a Catholic raised on faith in the Lord's word and obedience to anyone of higher rank. I was a Jew told always to question and to speak my mind if I did not agree with a policy or the person making it. I wanted to be a muckraker; he was a good soldier. In a way, Clifford and I made each other possible. We also made each other miserable. Ginny Byrne once told me that even if I didn't learn anything else, after a year covering cops, I'd know how to think like an Irish Catholic. I still had a way to go. But in addition to a clash of cultures, Clifford and I had a clash of personalities.

We had our worst blowup over a story I wrote about a woman whose car had been seized. The cops had taken the car under a state version of the forfeiture action that led to the Liberty Avenue evictions, and wanted the woman to pay a twelve-hundred-dollar fine to get it back. When I found out the money would go to a police department pension fund, I asked Clifford about the case and the law and if this involved a conflict of interest. Three days later, he still didn't have any answers. Before he went home for the weekend, after I'd threatened to put a line in the story saying, "The police department refused to comment," he called to say the fine had been waived. I added that last-minute reprieve to the story, but noted that it came only after the media expressed interest in the woman's situation.

On February 7, the day after the story ran, Clifford was fuming.

"You distort things. You just write what you want. That's why nobody will talk to you," he said.

I should have simply smiled and walked away, but I didn't.

"Well, I thought the story was fair," I said.

"Oh! You did? You did? Anybody reading that would think what we did was illegal. That's the way you slanted it."

"Show me where it says it was illegal!" I said.

"Any layman reading that story would . . ."

"Do you have a copy? Let's see," I said.

As the other cops looked on, astonished that we were yelling at each other across the office, Clifford told Norris Hollomon to find the story from Sunday's paper.

"An-an-an-and that stuff about a reporter's inquiry getting the car back free. Pure bullshit! That was a routine review of the case," he said.

"Yeah, right! Routine, as if I didn't have the request on your desk for three days before you got back with an answer at five-thirty Friday night."

"There you go. See, you're a liar! I wasn't even here at five-thirty. I called you at two-thirty! Two-thirrrrrty! With Norris as my witness, you're a liar," he said.

Eight people called that day, all complaining that the cops had impounded their cars and wondering if we'd do a story on them. Still, that shouting match made me feel even more isolated from these cops I had to work with. But the only thing to do was try to put it aside and move on.

The top department brass were unveiling a plaque for Monsignor John Kowsky, a police chaplain who'd recently passed away. The ceremony wouldn't make a story, but it was good politics to show respect for police traditions. And it turned out to be important for other reasons. Unexpectedly, Lori Gunn attended, making her first public appearance since her husband was shot. I remembered a story that Mike McAlary, a former *Newsday* reporter who had left to take a column at the *Daily News*, once did about a widow of a slain police officer, and I wanted to write about Lori Gunn, whose husband was in a coma. After the ceremony, I asked her if she'd sit for an interview, and she agreed. That night, I drove to her home in Massapequa Park, Long Island.

During the interview, Lori Gunn stretched out on a couch wearing a dark gray sweat suit. Her twenty-month-old daughter, Jennifer, climbed across her lap.

Psychologists say people react to tragedy in five stages: shock, rage, grief, resignation and acceptance. Lori's suffering was still fresh that night. Love and depression mingled in the stories she told about how she and Billy met and what they had planned for their lives. She seemed to be emerging from shock and holding back the rage that seethed beneath her soft brown eyes and gentle features.

A miniature replica of her husband's police shield—No. 1054—dangled from a thin gold chain around her neck, and like all cop wives, Lori said she'd been scared something might happen to Billy. But things had been going so well with them she hadn't really thought that anything could disrupt their lives so totally.

Billy's career was on a roll, and things at home were good. He was squirreling away money in his suit coat pockets for a family trip to Disney World. He and Lori also wanted to get away to St. Martin for a second honeymoon, and they had everything a young couple could want: a house, healthy parents and dreams of one day sending Jennifer to a good college.

Sitting on the mauve modular couch in her living room, Lori remembered the first time she saw Billy. She was twenty-four years old and working as a secretary at the Lake Success, Long Island, branch of Chase Manhattan bank. He was twenty-two years old and already a police officer. She was running some errands on a lunch break with her friend Annette from the bank. Annette lived on Billy's street in the Bellerose section of Queens, a block of Archie Bunker houses crowded with big, Catholic families, far from the Jewish enclave in South Merrick, Long Island, where Lori grew up.

While Annette ran into the cleaners, Lori stayed in the car and saw a tall, dark man with a mustache walking a Doberman pinscher. When Annette came back, Lori pointed to him.

"My God! Look at that guy," she said.

"Oh, yeah, that's Billy Gunn," Annette said.

"You know him! Do something," Lori said.

"Oh, no. He's married."

"Damn."

The next day, Annette told Lori that Billy was getting divorced. "Well," Lori said. "Do something."

Annette got word out through Billy's mother that a gorgeous young woman wanted to meet him. After a little prodding, Billy called Lori. When he came to pick her up on July 26, 1983, it was kind of like a blind date. She knew what he looked like, but he had never seen her and they hadn't talked for more than a few minutes on the phone. The son of a Bellerose forklift operator and the daughter of a South Merrick plumber made the best of it.

Lori's father sensed that Billy was special. After they left on that first date, he turned to his wife and said, "He's trouble."

They went to a bar where they sipped drinks and watched airplanes take off, then to dinner and to an amusement park, staying out until four A.M. He told her how he and his six-foot, seven-inch partner, Richie Orzack, were known as the Twin Towers at the 107th Precinct. She told him about her two sisters, her family and her job. He had a great time and she passionately kissed him good night.

"It was wonderful," Lori remembered.

When Billy asked Lori to marry him, she said yes, on one condition. In October, Billy met her demand and gave away Max, his Doberman.

They were married by a rabbi on November 18, 1984, and took out a $104,000 mortgage on a custom Cape house on a quiet, residential street. Less than three years later, Lori set a home pregnancy test on the dining room table beneath the chandelier. She went upstairs to read the instructions on the box; blue meant the rabbit was dead. When she peeked around the wall at the bottom of the stairs, she saw the color of a cloudless sky and ran back upstairs to wake Billy. He immediately started calling relatives. Eight months later, when Jennifer was born, it was the happiest day of their lives together. Billy bought pink cigars for all the guys in the Brooklyn South Crack Unit.

For Jennifer's first birthday, he decorated the entire house with characters from the *Alf* television show. Billy and Jennifer watched the show every week, and he wanted her to have the television extraterrestrial for her first birthday.

Each day, it seemed, the Gunns grew closer.

My tape recorder sat on the arm of Lori's couch. She was lively, even animated, as she spoke, but she paused when I asked about the day of the shooting.

"Do you want me to turn the tape off."

"No, that's okay. Just let me collect myself," she said.

"Did he ever talk to you about Ralph Richardson?"

"When he got the case, he did. He called him 'an animal' and said he wanted to catch him before he hurt someone else."

Lori took a deep breath and closed her eyes before continuing. "Billy was out jogging the night before when his sergeant called to say they knew where Richardson was hiding. I didn't want to give him the message, because we hadn't been spending much time together and were supposed to go to the city on his day off. I put up a snit when he said we had to cancel, but I knew how much the case meant to him."

At five forty-three A.M., the clock radio buzzed and Billy climbed quietly out of bed. He kissed Lori gently on the forehead and she felt the caress of his mustache and the warm touch of his lips. She watched through sleep-clouded eyes as he walked toward Jennifer's room, stopped to admire her, and tiptoed downstairs.

Around ten A.M., Lori had her wallet in hand and was on the way to buy some clothes for Billy. He had the Inspector Clouseau hat and the dark blue trench coat and was still trying to expand his detective wardrobe. He needed a few more suits, ties and dress shirts, and had told Lori about a post-Christmas sale at a Tall and Big Men's shop. Before she could get out of the door, the white push-button phone on the kitchen wall rang.

Lori answered in a cheery voice. It was Richie Orzack, Billy's former partner. Richie, a few years younger than Billy, did not know what to do. He assumed Lori already knew what had happened and was calling to tell her to sit tight, that he was on his way to pick her up. When he realized she didn't know, he didn't say a word. Lori heard only silence on the other end of the phone.

"What's the matter, Richie?" she asked.

No response.

"What's the matter?"

"You don't know?" he answered in what she described as a really scary voice.

"Where's Billy? Richie, where's Billy?" she said.

"Let me call you back. He's okay. He had a little accident. Let me call you back," Orzack responded.

Lori first called her mother, then dialed the 67th Precinct. Every time she identified herself to the cops at the Six-seven, they told her, "Hold on," and she had to wait. Nobody was authorized to tell her anything.

Things started moving as if somebody had put them on fast-forward. Lori remembers a neighbor coming over to stay with her. The neighbor told her not to turn on the television or the radio. Her mother came, as did a Nassau County police car. Then, a priest.

"As soon as I saw a monsignor standing on my lawn, I knew it was not a hangnail," she recalled.

A helicopter took them to the football field across from the hospital. Lori was whisked up the emergency room loading dock into the long, sallow hospital corridor. The hallway was lined on both sides with police officers. Lori saw a tunnel of blue and recognized a friend of Billy's.

"Are you going to tell me what happened to my husband?" she asked the friend.

His head fell. His mouth didn't open.

Lori remembers waiting in a room with Detective Rango's wife. Periodically, Billy's doctor walked in dripping with blood. He tried to give her a medical explanation of Billy's wounds, but all she wanted to know was, "How bad is it?" He told her, but the answer wasn't what she'd hoped to hear. Lori tried to act calm, telling her mother, father and sisters, who'd arrived at her side, "It's going to be all right."

She would later wonder if Billy, who was tall and sometimes awkward, had been shot because he'd been clumsy. She would question his decision to run to Rango's aid instead of going in the other direction. But in the hospital that afternoon, all she wanted to do was see him. Her father suggested he take a look at Billy first. When Mel Gonchor came back to the family waiting room, he said to Lori as softly as he could, "Don't see him. Please, remember him the way he was." Twice in the next few days, Lori made funeral arrangements, but Billy refused to die.

As she talked, it was clear that, deep inside, Lori still hoped Billy would make a miraculous recovery. She showed me a photograph of him finishing a marathon as evidence that he had always been a survivor.

After the ceremony at Police Headquarters, Lori had gone to see Billy in the hospital. His head remained bandaged and swollen, and an intravenous tube extended from his arm. Propped up in a recliner, sheets covering his chest, he wore a white hospital gown and pale blue slippers. When she told him she loved him, Lori swore she saw a tear drop from the corner of his left eye. "I think he heard me," she said. Billy's doctors were not as certain.

It was late when the interview ended. Yet Lori remained more than hopeful. She was buoyant, bright, awake. Even inspiring.

On my way back to Manhattan, I listened to the tape on my car stereo, picking out the quotes and anecdotes I wanted to use. Impressed by her courage and inner strength, I was thinking how small any problems I might have had seemed compared to what she faced. I was going home to write a newspaper story. Then I'd be on to a new one. For her, the story would never end. Lori Gunn was about to enter a year of the living dead.

Little Italy

I was beginning to believe I'd never fit in with the cops.

My liberal politics and Berkeley education just didn't jibe with the backgrounds of most patrolmen and investigators. I couldn't charm them like Elaine, banter with them like Richie or belly-up to the bar with them like some other cop reporters. I dressed too much like an executive, talked too much like a lawyer and still looked too much like Joe College for them to trust me.

A colleague said I should have told cops I went to Fordham, because they all had cousins who went there. But it was too late. I had to look elsewhere, outside the department, for sources who could help me break stories on my own.

One Saturday afternoon in the middle of February, I was covering a truly horrible crime when, completely by chance, I met a remarkable man. Dr. Kildare Clarke was the associate director of the emergency room at Kings County Hospital. I met him tracking down the condition of one of his patients.

Norris Hollomon had called on the hotline with a late-breaking story. A sixteen-year-old Catholic school student had been arrested for trying to kill her newborn infant. It was a sensitive case, a latter-day *Agnes of God*, so the police department only released the bare details: the name, age and address of the teenager. A spokeswoman for the Brooklyn district attorney's office had a bit more. But it was a routine call to the hospital to check the infant's condition that opened up the story. The switchboard operator mistakenly patched me through to the emergency room, instead of to the administrator, and Dr. Clarke picked up the phone.

I knew Clarke's name from a series the *Post* had done on the problems of inner-city hospitals and health care in which he'd spoken out on the ills of the underfunded and overburdened municipal hospital system. Some of the things Clarke said had made Mayor Koch angry. I told him how much I had admired his honesty, and he talked openly about the teenager and the infant.

The teenager was a student at Brooklyn's St. Saviour High School in Park Slope, a nice section of the borough. She'd been voted the smartest girl in her class. Everyone said she had a bright future ahead of her. She also had a secret she didn't want to share with anybody— not her mother, with whom she lived, or the nuns, who were her teachers.

On February 10, she tried to keep her secret forever. She told her mother she was constipated and went into the bathroom. Moments later, an infant boy plunged from her womb into the toilet. She cut the umbilical cord with a kitchen knife and flushed, but the baby wouldn't go down. She later told doctors and detectives she tried to kill the baby, but her mother and sister, who were in the next room, heard the crying and ran into the bathroom. As she washed the knife and placed it on a shopping cart in the back of their apartment building, her sister wrapped the bleeding baby in a blanket. Her mother called an ambulance.

When they got to the hospital, Clarke said, the baby had puncture wounds in his chest and abdomen and had been slashed on his arms and legs in his genital region. But he was alive. Back at the apartment, detectives found the knife. While she lay in a hospital bed, the student with the bright future was read her rights and arrested for attempted murder.

I offered to quote Clarke anonymously on background, but he said he didn't mind if we used his name. I was shocked. When I asked him why he didn't want anonymity, he asked why he should. "There's a lot wrong in this society," he said in the lilting tones of his native Jamaica.

"There's teenage pregnancy, AIDS, so much senseless violence and crack and crack violence all over the place. You cannot make these things go away by pretending they do not exist." Clarke's voice pierced the armor of bureaucracy that prevented official New York from hearing the cries of its people. Clarke was as aware of the streets as any beat cop. And he and I clicked right from that first phone conversation. After hanging up, I filed a few hundred words on the attempted infanticide, and hoped that he and I would connect again.

We did, talking frequently through the year. Speaking with Clarke was refreshing. And KCH was a great place to have a friend. It seemed whenever a big crime occurred in Brooklyn, the victims—cops, kids and everyone else—ended up in Dr. Clarke's emergency room. He was concerned about many of the city's social ills. But none bothered him more deeply than what drugs—especially crack—were doing to the inner city. Crack was everywhere. Four out of ten murders were crack-related, according to police, and thousands of other people lived helplessly as slaves to the Devil's candy. An entire generation was sucking its soul through glass pipes, losing its mind in vapid, vaporous puffs of smoke. Crack attacked the city with greater fury than anything I could remember. Even the cops couldn't stop it; and sometimes the ones who tried became crack's victims, as well.

Moments after midnight on March 3, Robert Machate, Jr., a twenty-five-year-old police officer, was struck by a slug that went beneath his bulletproof vest, through his midsection, and lodged in his heart. Doctors pronounced him dead at Kings County Hospital at one-forty A.M. I got a call from editor Laura Durkin a few minutes before seven A.M. telling me what had happened, and I headed straight to East 23rd Street and Newkirk Avenue in Brooklyn. All that was left of the crime scene was a yellow chalk circle beneath a NO PARKING sign, where Machate's body had fallen. Smaller circles marked the places where the police had found shell casings or other bits of evidence. The bloodhounds and helicopters were gone, but a few undercover and uniformed cops were still hunting for witnesses.

On the street corner, a group of hooded thugs with gold chains banging off their chests joked about the cop's death. When a television reporter pointed a microphone at one of them, he slapped her. A police officer standing nearby seemed as scared of the hoodlum as the reporter was, but he grudgingly chased the thug away. This all seemed like some futuristic urban nightmare, but it was for real. Outgunned and outnumbered, the cops were more scared of the punks than the other way around.

I picked up a few quotes from people on the street about the state of the neighborhood. Then I got a cup of coffee. Rose Arce from the *News* was the only other print person there.

"You're late," she said.

"Plenty of time to catch up," I said.

"Everybody on the block who saw anything's gone to work," she said.

"So, fill me in."

She didn't have much more than was on the sheets. Or if she did, she wasn't sharing. As we talked, a television reporter did a take, walking somberly toward his cameraman, recounting what he knew of the shooting. He commented that Machate was the second law enforcer killed in three days: two days earlier, an undercover DEA agent had been killed while investigating a Staten Island cocaine case.

"These things are becoming routine," Arce said.

"Yeah, I can't believe what's going on," I said.

"Soon, dead cops will be shorts, like kids who bring guns to school. Hey, why study when you can rob stuff?" she said.

"I know. We hardly even write about guns in school now. You have to be in fifth grade or under to get a mention," I said.

"Next month, it'll be preschool."

From there, I drove to the headquarters of Machate's unit, the Brooklyn South Task Force, a converted park house off of Prospect Park. Machate's colleagues were slouching on desktops, drinking coffee and talking softly in a back office or playing chess and watching television in the muster room. Machate's commanding officer, Lieutenant Raymond Powers, agreed to talk to me, and I called DCPI so that they would know I wasn't trying to get him behind their backs. Sergeant Clifford cleared the interview.

As I waited for Powers, I met Joe Dwyer, a representative from the Patrolmen's Benevolent Association who'd spoken with Machate's partner. He could talk to the press without official sanction because he was an officer in a powerful union. Dwyer said that Machate and his partner, Gus Checcini, were working a six P.M. to two A.M. plainclothes anticrime detail when they saw a suspicious-looking group on Newkirk Avenue near 23rd Street.

"One of the guys in the group had a bulge in his waistband, so Bobby and Gus went after 'em. Bobby got out and Gus followed him in their unmarked car," Dwyer said. "The perp with the gun ran around the corner to an Oldsmobile and tossed the gun under it. Bobby tried to grab the driver, but there was a scuffle. When Gus got there, Bobby yelled, 'I've been shot. He's got my gun!' Gus and the perp exchanged several rounds and that's about it."

"Is Gus okay?" I asked.

"Yeah, he's doing okay," Dwyer said. "He's probably on his way home now."

Talking to Dwyer was liberating. I'd still have to call Inspector Mayronne to confirm Machate's last words, but it was a relief not to be a total slave to DCPI.

When Powers came out, I asked him what kind of a police officer Machate had been. Powers was tired, but he impressed me as a sensitive and experienced police supervisor who knew the world didn't stop at the end of his billy club. He described Machate as "an active young cop, one of the best in the unit." Powers said Machate and Checcini took more guns off the street—Nines, Mac-10s, Uzis and small-caliber revolvers and pistols—than any other team on the task force.

A week earlier, a sergeant had talked to Machate about his productivity. "The sergeant told him he was too active and to slow it down, for his own sake," Powers said. "But you couldn't hold the kid back. He told his sergeant, 'No way, I can make a difference out there.' What can you say to that?"

I called Elaine Rivera at the Cop Shop with my notes and headed toward Machate's house. Powers and Joe Dwyer had said that Machate's father wouldn't mind talking to reporters.

As I was leaving the task force building, a bitter wind blistered off the park, and I saw four officers pull a cardboard box from the back of a station wagon. They unfurled two strips of purple and black bunting and draped them over the parkhouse entrance. Stretching that cloth was a practiced and somber ritual for the cops, one that was occurring too often.

Machate had lived with his wife, Grace Ann, in Sheepshead Bay, on the west side of Ocean Avenue, the Mason-Dixon line of South Brooklyn. Sheepshead Bay was an Irish-Italian enclave that was a ten-minute drive but a cultural millennium away from the Caribbean-black, Afro-American and Hispanic neighborhood where Machate had been killed.

Machate came from a cop family. Policing was in their blood, passed down from generation to generation like a priceless inheritance. Machate's father was a retired lieutenant with the city's Human Resources Administration police force; his grandfather had been a cop; his uncle was a retired mounted police officer; his stepbrother a correction officer; and his brother, Thomas, was a cop in the 84th Precinct. Machate and Grace Ann, who was seven months pregnant with their first child, had recently bought their house on Banner Avenue, and hoped to keep the tradition going.

Cop cars were parked around the light green wood-frame house, and visitors came and went, bringing food and tears to share with the family. I watched from the end of the block, where an officer assigned to provide for the family had set up a barricade. I told the officer that Powers and Dwyer had said Machate's father wanted to see the press, but the cop told me that had changed. A television reporter had done what television reporters often do. Showing a complete lack of sensitivity, he had thrust a microphone in front of Machate's grieving mother, making her cry uncontrollably. The reporter had been sent from the house—along with orders to keep the rest of the media out, too. Television types fucked up a lot of interviews for print journalists. I often wanted to have a big bonfire and melt down their cameras. And that afternoon, I wanted to throw at least one television reporter on the sacrificial pyre.

I had to try another tactic to get to the family, so I walked to the far side of Banner Avenue, where there wasn't a barricade. On the way, I picked up a cake to camouflage the intrusion I was hoping to make. I didn't want to be a hypocrite, but I wanted to talk to Machate's parents and his wife. The cake was my way of saying I was sorry for what happened, and it was also part of the con job a reporter sometimes has to do to get a story. I had learned the cake trick from my late Uncle Abe. He never had much to say to anybody when he showed up for Thanksgiving with my mother's side of the family, but he always brought a pie. His motto was the same as a million New Yorkers': "Bring a small pumpkin pie and the hell with 'em," he used to say.

I snuck behind Machate's house with a store-bought cake, my face filled with as much sorrow as possible. I walked around to the front and offered the cake as a bribe to a young cop guarding the door. His shield said his last name was Tallarine. He accepted the cake but turned me away.

When I got back behind the barricade, I ran into David Firestone, another reporter *Newsday* had sent to write a front-page profile of Machate. As I gave him my notes on Machate's police career, I remembered the first time I met him, at a *Newsday* party a few years earlier. He and Esposito had introduced themselves using each other's names. Like a dummy, I spent the whole night calling Richie David, and David Richie. It struck me as funny that now I was working on a big story with them.

When I returned to the Shack, Jimmy Breslin called to ask what had happened, and Elaine took down the quotes and details I'd gotten throughout the day. We sent the story to the desk. DCPI called down to say detectives had picked up two suspects, and I drove to the 70th Precinct, where they were being questioned. When it became apparent they wouldn't be formally arrested until past our deadline, I went back to Newkirk Avenue.

I peered through a steel mesh security grate into a rancid tenement lobby near where Machate had been shot and saw two detectives and Mike McAlary, of the *Daily News*, inside. McAlary was smoking a cigarette, and the detectives were pacing back and forth, canvassing for witnesses. An old man followed me into the lobby. He walked up to McAlary, told him he knew all about what happened and asked for a cigarette. McAlary gave him one and they walked to a corner. A few seconds later, he came back shaking his head.

"That guy doesn't even know who he is," McAlary said.

"Same guy tried to get me to buy him breakfast this morning," I said.

"He got his smoke. He's happy," McAlary said.

The detectives had been sent to find anyone who could identify the suspects in a lineup. They distributed COP–SHOT fliers that offered a ten-thousand-dollar reward for information concerning the killing.

As we waited, addicts shuffled out and residents hustled in from the cold. The lobby had art deco designs, high ceilings and marble floor tiles that had been layed down in figure eights stretching around the perimeter in a pattern of infinity. It must have been majestic once, but now a film of soot had caked onto the marble, and dirt had crusted over the fluorescent light bulbs that hummed from the ceiling and cast shadows on paint-chipped walls.

One of the detectives, a fat man wearing an olive fedora, chomped a cigar. His thin partner wore a cheap tweed sport coat. I was still trying to bridge my communication gap with cops, so I listened and watched while McAlary bantered with the detectives. He seemed to have an innate understanding of these guys.

McAlary even looked like a cop, with his rough Irish features, brown hair, mustache and deep eyes. He spoke in short bursts with a barroom roll that sounded like he was telling an inside joke every time he finished a phrase. He chatted up the fedora and the sport coat, dropped names of commanding officers and made them see he wanted to be friends. The detectives were bored and enjoyed anything that broke the monotony, especially having a columnist follow them around. It made them feel important, which they needed because they hadn't had much luck finding witnesses. So far, all they'd done was rack up six hours overtime.

A woman walked down three marble stairs from an apartment in the building's east wing. She was wearing tight, faded jeans and a denim jacket, and gave a sexy shake as she passed by the detective in the sport coat. He reached out with a COP–SHOT flier, but she smiled, showing a quarter-inch gap between her front teeth.

"You guys gave me one on my way in. Remember?" she said.

The detective in the fedora remembered. "Could I forget? Preach me some more of that Bible," he said.

The woman took a pocket-size Bible with a dark green cover out of her jacket.

"Read us da plagues," the fedora said.

The woman turned to Exodus, thrust her free hand on her left hip and started rattling them off. She punched out the scriptures in the spasmodic cadences of a Baptist preacher: the plague of the blood. The plague of the frogs. The plague of the gnats. Of the flies. Of the livestock. Of the boils. Of the hail.

"Then the Lord said to Moses, 'Go to Pharaoh, for I have hardened his heart and the hearts of his officials so that I may perform these miraculous signs of mine among them . . .'

"And the Lord said to Moses, 'Stretch out your hand over Egypt so that locusts will swarm over the land and devour everything growing in the fields,' " she read. Then she continued in her own words: "So, Moses stretched out his hands and locusts smote the earth."

"Hey," I said. "How could you smite the earth?"

"Ooooooh!" she said, tossing back her head and twisting her hips. "By being sooooo despiteful."

Despiteful. It was her own use of this word, and we all knew how she meant it. It was doing something despicable and delightful. It was everything crack and crackheads and crack dealers were doing to the city. It was the gospel of the crack world, a way to get back at everything white, rich and in authority. Being despiteful meant beaming up to Scotty with a sweet drag on a glass pipe. It meant wearing hooded sweatshirts, swallowing vials when cops came, and dancing and slapping high-fives on the street corner the morning after a cop was killed. Cops were bad for business. Despiteful meant that young, hard, inner-city blacks, Colombian and Dominican immigrants and anyone else who wanted a piece of the action could score their chunk of the crack trade and smite the city.

The gap-toothed preacher pushed her Bible back in her pocket, smiled devilishly and darted into the dark, cool East Flatbush night.

After leaving Flatbush, I stopped off at the office to read the final draft of our Machate story. Bob Drury, a reporter who used to be in the Shack but now worked out of the midtown office, had rewritten the version Elaine and I had filed, twisting our straight narrative into a better read. Our original story had a regular cop-news top:

> A 25-year-old police officer was killed early Friday during a struggle with a suspect who fired a shot from the officer's own gun that went underneath his bullet-proof vest, striking him in the heart, authorities said.
>
> Robert Machate, who was assigned to the Brooklyn South Task Force as an anti-crime officer, was rushed to Kings County Hospital, where he died at 1:40 A.M. after he had been shot once by one of two assailants he and his partner were chasing in the East Flatbush section of Brooklyn.
>
> Machate, whose wife, Grace Ann, is seven months pregnant with their first child, is the first New York City police officer slain in the line of duty this year. His death comes two days after a federal Drug Enforcement Administration agent was assassinated in Staten Island.
>
> "I've been shot, he has my gun!" Machate apparently yelled after he was struck by the bullet. . . .

Drury pulled the quote from the fourth graph to the top and, using the same facts, created more drama:

> Police Officer Robert Machate managed to shout a warning to his partner before he fell mortally wounded—apparently by a bullet fired from his own service revolver —on a Brooklyn street yesterday.
>
> "I've been shot, he has my gun," the highly decorated 25-year-old officer said.
>
> Machate, an officer assigned to the Brooklyn South Task Force's anti-crime unit, was shot once by one of two suspects he and his partner were struggling with in the East Flatbush neighborhood. He was rushed to Kings County Hospital, where he died at 1:40 A.M.
>
> Machate, whose widow, Grace Ann, is

seven months pregnant with their first
child, is the first New York City police officer to be slain this year. The officer was
wearing a bullet-proof vest, but he was hit
below the protective gear.

His death occurred two days after a U.S.
Drug Enforcement Administration agent
was assassinated on Staten Island...."

Elaine thought I should have been pissed off that the editors brought Drury—and Firestone, for that matter—in on a big story instead of letting the bureau handle it. I'd been disappointed, but figured I had a lot to learn and would have a chance to grab some of the glory the stars at the paper received in the future.

It was late, but I still had time to catch the last act of the Inner Circle rehearsal dinner, a song-and-dance variety show put on by the City Hall press corps, who spoofed the commissioners and politicians they covered. In 1987, when I was a researcher, Tom Plate had given me a ticket to the show. I remember being shocked that the reporters on-stage were not the objective stewards of the people's interest I'd imagined they were. Two years later, this cozy little scene didn't seem so foreign. I sat down feeling somewhat uneasy but more confident than I'd been before. I kept reminding myself that I'd done legwork that day for the paper's front-page feature and main news stories and was earning the right to be among the city's real reporters.

The cops from DCPI were hanging out at a table with the reporters they liked. Other reporters and sources chatted behind pillars in the hotel ballroom. The atmosphere had the same trappings as a high school lunchroom. It seemed fun, though, and I wished I was in one of the cliques. Elaine Rivera and Rose Arce were with a group in the last row of chairs stage right. Arce was wearing the same casual black outfit she had had on that morning. "Your tie has spots," she said, flicking my tie, yellow silk with small blue dots. She called it a company tie and said it wasn't good for the image of a police reporter. "Wear more loose-fitting clothing and don't shave as much," she said. "You'll look like you spend more time in the trenches."

I was trying to be more relaxed with colleagues. I was still tense, but

I was beginning to get a sense of familiarity I hadn't felt before. I was also discovering that I thought Rose Marie Arce, of the New York *Daily News*, was very sexy.

The next morning, *Newsday* went on the stands with a photograph of Machate on a raspberry-red page one, a color that underscored the emotion of the story. The headline, HE WENT LOOKING FOR TROUBLE, was from a Powers quote, and Firestone's profile also began on the cover. There was a misty rain in the air and the ink streaked across the words like bloody teardrops.

> It was the highest compliment that Lt. Ray Powers, or for that matter any cop, could pay.
> "He went looking for trouble," said Ray Powers, commander of the Brooklyn South Task Force. "That's the kind of officer he was."
> Officer Robert Machate, 25, spent night after night on the streets of Brooklyn looking for trouble, and frequently found it. He made so many arrests, garnering so much contraband and so many commendations, that his superiors begged him, for his health's sake, to slow down a bit.
> Early Friday, at a dark intersection in East Flatbush, Machate again found trouble....

At a morning press conference at Police Headquarters, Richard Condon, the department's first deputy commissioner, accompanied by Chief of Detectives Robert Colangelo, announced that two men had been arrested. The alleged gunman, twenty-three-year-old Renaldo Rayside, was charged with murder, and twenty-two-year-old Kurt Haneiph received reduced charges for ratting out his alleged accomplice.

Rayside was from Panama, Haneiph from Trinidad. They met in their late teens when both were serving time in state prison. According to police, when they were released in 1988 their friendship turned into a partnership. Drug dealing was the new American Way to get rich quick. Rayside had five hundred dollars on him when he was arrested, and the cops found Haneiph's gun—the bulge in the waistband—under the Oldsmobile.

Rayside's parents lived in the Fairfield Towers, the same apartment complex where Ralph Richardson's mother lived, but no one was home when I went there Saturday morning. Haneiph's family lived in an apartment building on Ocean Avenue. When I told Haneiph's mother who I was, she slammed the door in my face.

A security guard in Haneiph's building had a copy of *Newsday* on his desk. He was young, no more than three years out of high school, and had written something in blue ink next to the headline. Beneath where it said HE WENT LOOKING FOR TROUBLE, he had written, "Why?"

My friend Alex, the security guard at headquarters, was on duty that morning. Machate's killing bothered him, too, because it made him question his own worth to the department and to the city. He was feeling guilty that he wasn't out on the streets. He wanted to be a role model in the ghetto or a cop trying to help a community fight crime and whatever caused it. Realistically, he didn't want to risk his life in a losing battle, but his sense of duty made him want to leave the cushy Headquarters security detail and transfer to one of the higher-crime precincts.

I felt a similar conflict. One of the key reasons a lot of reporters like myself chose the profession was that we hoped we could solve problems by writing about them. But the more crime I covered, the more I began to feel that nothing I wrote could really help. After awhile, it seemed I was just going through the motions, reporting one vile act after another, with no reason to believe things would get any better.

Up at DCPI, the sheet from the Machate killing remained on the top of the clipboard. A dozen other crimes had occurred overnight, but Martians could have landed at LaGuardia Airport and it would have been buried under the police officer's death. Mo Howard went through the sheets of the crimes he'd taken down in the last twelve hours. "Let's see, we had a car accident with one dead, a manhole explosion in Manhattan, a man shot in Brooklyn, a fire with two dead, a demonstration at an abortion clinic, three arrested, an attempted suicide by a teenager, a booby-trapped UPS package in the Bronx, and a rapper, LL

Cool J, shot and wounded in what may have been an attempted chain snatch at a local club," he read, stacking the sheets on his desk.

Some of these were worth looking into, but Mo wasn't in the mood to get more details and I didn't feel like asking him to do something he wasn't up for doing. "Just another night in the city," I said. He promised another one the next day, and the day after, and the day after that.

"It's the same things again and again. Only the names and ages change," Mo said.

Police reporters who worked the beat for too long found a way to detach themselves from stories they covered. It was almost a defense mechanism, but it also seemed dangerous to me. There were some reporters who saw crime as good for business, which meant they had lost their humanity and had become cynical. The ones who let themselves be pressured by the police brass became tools of deception, and others who accepted the suffering as inevitable in a city of thieves and killers became victims themselves. Virtually all veteran crime reporters, whether they were cynics, defeatists or police department pawns, ended up indifferent to the stories they covered. I didn't want that to happen to me, yet I didn't know another way to stay sane in the job.

Maybe with spring coming, I'd be able to lighten up. A few people were already tossing baseballs and Darryl Strawberry had walked out of spring training. But the crime on the streets had such a constant grip on my brain that diversions like plays, books and movies were difficult to focus on. One place I did go to let it all hang out was Madison Square Garden for New York Knicks basketball games.

I shared a mini-season-ticket package with Joey Queen, another *Newsday* reporter. We were in the green seats three-quarters up, off the corner of the court, and during games we would cheer, jeer and talk about everything from newspaper politics to our meandering love lives. On the night after the Machate killing, the Knicks, with guard Rod Strickland filling in for an injured Mark Jackson, beat Michael Jordan and the Chicago Bulls. It was a great game and a good diversion.

The next evening, I went to a Chinese restaurant with a friend, and during dinner let loose with a chaotic ramble about how the entire city was crumbling. My ranting hit on shattered family values and how the school system had been destroyed and religious institutions defiled by greed. The only sustenance people looked for was money and the only way a lot of people could get money was drugs, I said, drumming my chopsticks on the table. So, who did the president name to lead the nation's war on drugs? You guessed it. The Veep. Dan the Man Quayle. George Bush had just announced that Dan Quayle would represent the U.S. at a hemispheric drug conference to convene in New York City the next week. Holy shit! I mean, this guy knew as much about East Flatbush as he knew about Da Nang, and he had fought that war from the farmland.

Politely, my friend let me go on. Eventually I shut up and we moved on to discuss more hopeful things, like her acting career. She was preparing to audition for a part in a revival of the play *Does a Tiger Wear a Necktie?* I thought we had shifted topics, but not really. The original production, in which Al Pacino launched his career, was set in the sixties in a halfway house where the residents were strung out on heroin. The new version would reflect modern times and my friend was reading for a role as a crack addict. Oh, well, at least that was something I could help her prepare for. I even knew a place in Washington Heights where we could use the change from dinner to buy a couple of trey vials, or if she wanted to drive to East New York or Tremont, we could get a good deal on ten-dollar Jumbos. In work, in art, in friendly conversation, crack was everywhere.

I dropped my friend at her apartment and kept going, up through East Harlem, by the dealers, past the sirens, off the island of Manhattan, into the Bronx and beyond. I'd had no plans to leave, but just kept driving north. Two hours later, I was at my father's house upstate for a few moments among the trees.

The next afternoon, back in the city, I parked for twenty minutes in the middle of a snowstorm in Greenwich Village and somebody smashed my rear window and took off with my cassette player. The thief left a U2 tape I'd had in the player on my dashboard. I didn't know whether to be grateful that he didn't take the tape or insulted that he didn't like my music.

At the Sixth Precinct, another man was also reporting a stolen car stereo. A veteran of such thefts, he told me to go to Lamston's, a five-and-dime store, and buy a plastic covering to tape over the broken window. Taping windows had become another skill to pass along to fellow New Yorkers. It reminded me of the guy who stuck a sign in his car that said NO RADIO; his window was broken anyway and the vandal left a note: THEN GET ONE.

By the time I got home, it was late. Esposito had left a message on my answering machine, telling me to cover the Machate funeral in the morning. I set out a black suit, black wing tips, a white dress shirt and a dark blue tie, and went to bed.

Snow flurries fell on Grace Ann Machate's heavy gray coat when she left the Banner Avenue house. She leaned on Gus Checcini's right arm as he led her to a black limousine. The young cop who had been guarding the door the other day, Joe Tallarine, stood behind Grace Ann. His eyes darted from side to side, as if he were trying to occupy himself so he wouldn't cry. Machate's father, Robert Sr., and mother, Vivian, marched quickly into the limousine for the ride to the Torregrossa Funeral Home, where the twenty-five-year-old cop's body lay in a metallic-blue casket.

Instead of following them to the funeral home, which seemed more like voyeuristic espionage than legitimate reporting, I drove to St. Mark's Roman Catholic Church. I arrived early and staked out a spot on a balcony above the sanctuary before the press—which would be admitted after family, friends and fellow officers—was allowed in. Inspector Mayronne saw me and didn't say a word, just pointed down the stairs, and I went back outside.

The mayor, police commissioner, city council and borough presidents and prosecutors were there. And with the mayoral election just starting, David Dinkins and Rudy Giuliani, the men who wanted to unseat Koch, were also there. Dinkins, the Manhattan borough president, was running against Koch in the Democratic primary, and Giuliani, a law-and-order U.S. attorney, was running as a Republican. They stood with the others in the cold, flanked by five thousand officers wearing white gloves and dress-blue uniforms. The officers stretched fifteen deep and three hundred yards long. And the department's Emerald Society bagpipers played a solemn dirge. As the Machates' motorcade approached, a drummer tapped out a soft, steady roll on his snare.

St. Mark's, a half mile from Machate's house, was part of his family's history. His parents were married there, he was baptized there, and he and Grace Ann wed amid the church's marble pillars on October 5, 1986. Now St. Mark's wouldn't hold everyone who came for his funeral.

Once the officers from the Brooklyn South Task Force had entered, Mayronne escorted the press to the balcony.

The service began with the seating of Machate's family in the front pews. The Reverend Gerald J. Arella pleaded for survivors to temper their emotions: "We are angry and justifiably so, but we must not let that anger turn to hatred." Mayor Ed Koch also spoke, and he didn't hide his frustration with the drugs and death that plagued the city: "We have got to bring back the rule of law," he said.

After the mass, Grace Ann Machate followed her husband's flag-draped casket down the church steps. She gripped a wooden cross in her right hand and dabbed her eyes with a handkerchief. Machate's mother and father, heads bowed, walked behind his wife. The wall of blue once again lined the avenue. A man handed out fliers accusing Governor Mario Cuomo of being an accomplice in the cop-killing because of his opposition to the death penalty. A woman's howl mingled with the rustle of air from three helicopters that flew overhead to honor the city's latest hero.

Machate's family and friends attended a short service at the Green-Wood Cemetery in Sunset Park. Once the service ended, I approached Gus Checcini, who graciously paused to offer a touching comment about his friend. "This guy was more than a partner to me," Checcini said. "My son always called him Uncle Bobby and you can write that his kid will always have an Uncle Gus." With that quote, I had enough to file, but I knew that the best story would say something about Machate's unborn child. I still wanted to talk to Machate's parents or widow.

The family was hosting a reception at a local Knights of Columbus Hall along the water in Sheepshead Bay, and I decided to crash. When

I got to the hall, Joe Tallarine was standing at the door to the banquet room.

"You again!" he said.

"I was wondering if Lieutenant Machate or Grace Ann had anything they want me to say about Bobby in the paper. That's all," I said. He left and came back.

"Okay, fella," Tallarine said. "But give them twenty minutes until they finish eating."

The buffet was loaded with pasta shells, meatballs and lasagna. An oak-paneled bar was crowded with boisterous cops drowning their fears in beer. I waited until Tallarine summoned me to a table in the rear of the hall.

Morning snow clouds lifted over the bay, and the sun turned the water a crisp, clear blue. Lieutenant Machate said he had not had time in the past few days to really reflect on his son's death. The countless hands to shake, calls to return and condolences to accept had not given him a chance to mourn.

"All weekend, I stood by my son's coffin and people came by and said they were sorry. There were Bobby's friends and cops he worked with, people from the community, people we didn't even know—thousands of them. All I could say was thank you," he said, his eyes pressed into his head with grief.

"I'm sorry," I said. "But I'm sure you have a lot of good memories of Bobby."

"The best."

"Can you tell me some of them?" I asked.

And he did. Lieutenant Machate told a few stories of playing baseball with his son, taking him boating and watching him grow into a police officer. Then he recalled the pride that had welled up in Bobby's throat when he told his old man he would be a grandfather. They already had plans for the baby.

"The other night on the couch, we were talking and Grace Ann says, 'If it's a boy in my belly, he'll be a cop,' " Lieutenant Machate said.

I scribbled that into my notebook as he went to bring Grace Ann over to the table. She was still gripping the wooden cross, and I expressed my sympathies and tried to ask gentle questions. She said she wasn't angry, that she didn't have enough energy for anger. She preferred to remember the good things about her husband, his understanding and his humor. She mentioned the note he left her with flowers when she went to the doctor to get her pregnancy test confirmed: "Congratulations if it is, but don't worry if it's not. We'll have a lot of fun trying again. Love, Bobby." She smiled remembering that. And with her husband now dead, she said, "I still feel him. I still have some of Bobby inside me." I asked her about the baby and what she wanted it to be if it was a boy. She said she wouldn't mind if he wanted to be a cop, but didn't put it as dogmatically as Lieutenant Machate said she had the other night. Still, it was too good not to use.

I called Laura Durkin and read her the quote as if Grace Ann had said it to me. She put it on the budget. "Okay, Snookie, that's good. Now, you've got to hurry back to write the story, though. It's getting late." I raced back to the Shack, typed away and moved the story to the desk. Joe Gambardello called to say the editors wanted Grace Ann's quote up high because they were going to pull it for the cover. We worked out a lead that let us use it in the second paragraph.

> Grace Ann Machate, seven months pregnant and suddenly widowed at 26, made a prediction yesterday after attending the funeral of her slain police officer husband.
> "I don't know what tomorrow is going to be like," she said. "The only thing I have now is Bobby's child. If it's a boy in my belly, he'll be a cop. That's what Bobby would want."

I made a printout of the story and took it home, terrified I had violated some sacred trust by attributing the quote directly to Grace Ann. I had trouble falling asleep and called a friend in California to confess my crime. After a few fitful hours of rest, I forced myself to run. I'd have to keep my head about me, and I always felt sharper after I exercised.

My emotions were mixed when I saw the paper on the newsstands. There it was, IF IT'S A BOY IN MY BELLY, HE'LL BE A COP, in two-inch type running vertically down the front page next to a photograph of Grace Ann following the casket from the church. I was excited the story made the cover, but felt I had somehow perpetrated a fraud on the city. I also wondered what kind of pressure this story might add to the child if he didn't want to be a cop; this would extend the dark shadow he would have to grow up under. And worst, I wondered what Grace Ann would think. If someone from her family called one of my editors to deny the quote, I'd be relegated to whatever the computer age newspaper equivalent of changing typewriter ribbons was for the rest of my career.

A friend called to say he liked this story, but I couldn't appreciate his compliment. And a female colleague called with the line of the day: "If it's a girl in her belly, will she be a nurse?" I tried to force a laugh, but I had to deal with my own anxiety until I was able to summon the guts to call the Machates later that morning.

"Are you the guy from *Newsday*?" Lieutenant Machate asked when he came to the phone.

"That's right. I talked to you and Grace Ann at the banquet hall yesterday," I said.

"Listen, guy, Grace is reading that story right now. Your paper did some job," he said. I couldn't tell whether that meant they did or did not like it. Then he said, "We can't thank you enough. Tell you what, guy. Give me your phone number. In two months, when this baby is born, you're going to get a call."

Phwew!

I let out a sigh of relief that lasted all day. Still, I felt that something wasn't quite right about the way I had reported that story. That night, I went to a hockey game with a group of *Newsday* reporters and editors. Between periods, one of them patted me on the back.

"Nice one on the funeral," he said.

"Thanks," I said, hoping he'd drop the subject.

"Nobody else had the widow," he said.

"The *News* talked to her, too."

"But you got the great quote."

"I didn't *get* it. I just wrote it down," I said.

"That's what I meant," he said with a smile.

By the next day, everybody had forgotten the story existed, such was the attention span of newspaper people.

On March 15, I went uptown to pick up my mail. Usually it was nothing more than outdated press releases, an occasional letter from a psychotic reader, interoffice memos on management policies and self-congratulatory reports from nonprofit groups. But that afternoon, there was an official-looking envelope from the New York City Police Department. I'd forgotten that two weeks earlier, just before the deadline, I had appealed the Freedom of Information Law request for the homicide log. I'd decided the best way to fight DCPI was with persistence. The envelope contained the department's response:

Dear Mr. Gelman,

Please be advised, in connection with your request for 1988 homicide data, that the Chief of Detectives has granted you access to the 'Homicide Log Book' maintained by the Detective Bureau.

I trust this will satisfy your needs.

I flipped the letter in the air and spun in my swivel chair. It was a small victory, but the Mets couldn't have been more elated when they won the '69 World Series.

A few days later, I returned to Banner Avenue to do a profile on three of Machate's closest Police Academy friends. In a corner of the living room were six shopping bags overflowing with mass cards. Machate's silver shield, embossed on a slick, black plaque, hung on the wall above the bags. *The Morton Downey Jr. Show* had done a tribute to the slain officer and a video cassette of the show played on the television.

Grace Ann and Vivian Machate were in the kitchen, drinking coffee and eating Italian pastries. Robert Sr., his white hair combed into a fifties-style quiff, offered me a Budweiser, which I nursed while watching Machate's buddies on the Downey special.

"Yo, Tommy," the ever-present Joe Tallarine said to Bobby's brother. "They let you on TV?"

"Morton Downey knows star quality," Thomas Machate said.

"You look lousy. Look lousy," Tallarine said.

"And you're a regular Marlon Brando," Thomas said, getting a wink from Tallarine.

"You guys ready to get started?" Robert Sr. asked. "Let's move it to the basement."

Walking downstairs, Robert Sr. told me that Bobby had turned the basement into a playroom for his expectant family. He spoke with love and hate in his voice, love for his son's memory and hate for the man who killed him. The state legislature needed one more vote to override the governor's veto of the death penalty and the lieutenant was using Grace Ann and her unborn child as symbols in a campaign for vengeance. His son had lost his life and Robert Machate, Sr., it was so sadly clear, had lost his smile. I tried to steer our conversation from politics to the story I'd come to write.

Robert Sr. wasn't going to participate, but he sat behind me and monitored the interview. For me, this interview was a personal test. There was no purer cop family than the Machates, and no cops were more regular than Bobby's pals.

Bobby's friends were Anthony Brognano, Chris Potenza and, of course, Tallarine. Their Academy teachers called these four cadets "Little Italy." They were bound by the vowels at the end of their names, and had remained close after they graduated onto the force in 1986. They would call each other in the middle of the night to brag about big arrests, and they did stuff together on weekends. In the end, it took a bullet to tear Little Italy apart.

Sixteen days after Bobby died, I asked them what had made him special. At first, they talked slowly and cautiously. Then they warmed up and told their favorite Bobby stories: The time he mooned the guys on the other boat while fishing. When he put gum on the seats of female cadets at the Academy. The way he impersonated sergeants. He was a prankster and a mimic. But only two weeks after his death, it was Bobby's appetite that had become legendary.

"He ate like a brontosaurus," Potenza said.

"How about the night he had all those sundaes and got sick?" Brognano recalled.

"The fat fuck," commented Tallarine. "One time, he runs up to me and says, 'Let's go get a burglar,' and I thought he said, 'Let's go get a burger.' He was always getting burgers."

For a few minutes, I could feel Bobby's presence in the room. I liked Bobby Machate, missed him and wanted to write about him as best I could. I started to see Machate's cop friends, guys from the west side of Ocean Avenue, as people, not uniforms.

When I asked how March third had changed their lives, the humor quickly lapsed into bitterness. After closing the lid on their friend's casket, seeing him dressed up all pretty at the Torregrossa Funeral Home, they could never make an arrest the same way again. They said they would always be aware of the danger. Bobby's death wouldn't paralyze them—"No, Bobby wouldn't want it that way. Somebody's got to police South Brooklyn," Brognano said. But it would make them more cautious. The worst part, they said, was there'd be no justice.

"You know what's going to happen to his killer?" Tallarine asked. "While Bobby is laying there dead on a cold slab of board, this animal is sitting in a nice, warm jail cell, playing cards, doing push-ups and getting three square meals a day."

"They treat cop killers like celebrity inmates on Rikers," said Potenza.

I nodded understandingly as they said this, and I thought about Lori Gunn. At least she didn't have to deal with this added unfairness. She was lucky in a way, not having to go to sleep worrying about whether Ralph Richardson had enjoyed a better day than she, whether he'd won or lost a pack of cigarettes at the card table. Nor would she have to live through the agony of a trial. For her, the verdict on Billy's shooting came fast and final.

After I turned off the tape recorder and was packing my notes and capping my pen, Tallarine came up to me. This time, he was preventing me from leaving.

"By the way," he said. "Are you the one who brought the cake?"

"Yeah. I know it didn't work. But was it any good?"

"We took it out back," he smirked. "It was a pineapple upside-down cake. We turned it right side up and dumped it out. Then we played Frisbee with the box."

We both laughed, which paved over the tension from before. There would always be a natural distrust between cops and reporters, but that night I realized we were of the same species. Although he carried a gun and I carried a pen, Tallarine and I were linked by our mutual infatuation with the city. That evening in Bobby Machate's renovated basement, I broke through the thick blue line I feared I'd never be able to cross.

Actually, Tallarine had gotten one thing wrong. I had brought a coffee cake that afternoon. A *New York Post* reporter, who'd seen my cake, had brought one of his own. I don't like pineapple and never would have picked that kind of dessert.

Still, Tallarine's credo held: Beware reporters bearing cakes.

Keeping Faith

The first day of spring was my birthday. A few friends from the editorial pages asked me to come to the main office for cake and champagne. It was a nice surprise. Esposito sent me a computer message: "Happy birthday, you hump!" Then he came across the newsroom to ask how old I was.

"Twenty-seven," I said. "I'm getting too old to keep up this cub reporter image. Soon you won't be able to tell the cops at DCPI I keep fucking up because I'm a kid."

He wasn't concerned. "That's all right. We'll come up with another excuse for your existence," he said.

Hap stopped by my desk and asked how I was going to celebrate. He did a double take when I told him I was meeting two cops at a high school basketball all-star game. He didn't think of me as someone who'd hang out with cops on my birthday. To him, I was still the kid from the editorial pages he owned 65 percent of.

That night, the city's public high school all-stars were playing the best of the Catholic high schools at the Felt Forum, the small arena in the back of Madison Square Garden. I met Iron Mike and a buddy of his at the game. I had done a profile on Mike and his colleagues in a Bronx narcotics unit a few months earlier, and we'd stayed in touch. He got his nickname because of the tireless work he'd done before his promotion to the Narcotics Division. He was a fan of high school sports, and we'd made plans to see the next big game that came around. By offering scholarships and smaller classes, the Catholic schools were usually able to recruit the best of the city's young players. But their superstar that season, senior Kenny Anderson, had chosen to play in a national all-star game that week, and the public school all-stars won a close contest.

After the game, we went to Beefsteak Charlie's for a few beers. Despite the bonding I'd had with Bobby Machate's Academy pals, I still felt out of place around police officers, especially Iron Mike and his partner, who were on the streets every day, fighting America's war on drugs. Iron Mike, an Irishman as short as a fire hydrant and as wide as a Volkswagen bug, and his partner worked in the middle of crack hell. They gathered intelligence, made undercover buys and arrests, took down crack rings and busted the profits out of street-corner drug sellers. I was just a spectator, up in the press box, zooming down whenever there was a pause in the action. It never occurred to me that night, as we drank and tried to find some common ground of conversation, that they were as nervous around me as I was around them.

I tried to act tough, using cop jargon I'd picked up—like TNT, collars, raids and cases—and referring to suspects as mutts and skels—short for skeletons. But when I said I'd heard they were making progress, Mike smirked at me like I was nuts.

"Get real!" he said. "You been up to the Bronx lately? It's like nothing's been done up there."

I admitted that it had been awhile, and he said he'd rekindle my memory with a few recent war stories. His favorite was the time he spent an entire day hidden under a porcelain bathtub turned upside down so he could surprise a team of dealers operating in a vacant apartment next door. The dealers had chained the roof and side entrances shut and had lookouts in front of the building all night. The only way Mike and his team could get in was to infiltrate the building after the lookouts went home. They made a good bust, but the dealers were back within a few weeks, this time with a twenty-four-hour watch. In another case, he and his sergeant were making undercover buys one afternoon when they witnessed an assassination on a Bronx street. They chased the two gunmen and collared them three blocks later. Though Mike had almost been killed that afternoon—a minor point he left out of the story—he was more concerned that he'd lost his lucky trombone case in the chase.

"Your what?" I asked.

"My lucky trombone case." He had found it in the garbage and had used it to disguise himself as a musician when he made undercover buys. "It was special to me, kinda like Capone's violin case with the machine gun. The dealers, they never knew if I was a music student or a gangster."

After booking the two gunmen, Mike checked every gutter and trash can for the case, but never found it. Now he'd have to come up with another prop.

We drank more beers and the conversation shifted from crime to women. Mike and his buddy both said that single women in bars were hotter on them since they got married. They suggested I invest in a simple gold band to improve on the recent drought in my love life.

"They like married guys," Mike's buddy said. "No ties. No calls. No questions."

"Sure, like the movie *Fatal Attraction,*" I said.

"My wife took me to see that," Mike said. "Then she got the video!"

Basketball and beer were good ingredients for male bonding, and the drunker we got, the more comfortable we felt. Mike said he had something for me, taking out a credit-card-size piece of plastic. It was a PBA card, issued by the Patrolmen's Benevolent Association, the police officer's union. It was green and white and had a police officer's shield underneath the PBA logo. Cops kept them in their wallets and gave them to wives, brothers, sisters and friends. They were passports that admitted the bearer across the border of the secret cop community. There was a silent cop code that said one cop should pay courtesy to someone who was tight with a fellow police officer, and the PBA card was that proof.

"This is so, ya know, if you ever get jammed up or something," Mike said sheepishly.

Mike was showing me his trust, but a shiver of discomfort came over me, as if I were about to do something I knew was wrong. The feeling was more immediate than I'd had with the quote from Grace Ann

Machate. Here there was no deadline-induced adrenaline, only the warmth of cold beer. But this was Mike's way of saying we were friends, a gesture I had wanted.

I reached out tentatively and looked at the card, wondering if taking it would in some way obligate me to keep the cops' secrets, be on their side. My father had drilled me on the ethics of the business but he had also once told me it was better to accept gifts it would be more awkward to refuse. I wasn't sure Mike would understand if I didn't take the card. Most police officers believed that you were either procop or anticop, no inbetween. I wanted Mike to see me as what he called "a stand-up guy." I accepted the card and said thanks, telling myself I'd bury it in a desk drawer at home.

On my way home, though, I could almost feel the sides of the card in my pocket. It was like having a good luck charm. It gave me an angle on the city that would put me above the law—if I used it. I worried about succumbing to that temptation, and whether if someone like Sergeant John Clifford found out, I'd become his hostage. But when I got home, I slipped the PBA card into the part of my wallet that flipped open with my driver's license.

Around this time, journalistic ethics were a hot topic in the newsroom as the result of a two-part series in *The New Yorker* by a writer named Janet Malcolm. In her articles, "The Journalist and the Murderer," Malcolm charged Joe McGinniss, author of *Fatal Vision*, with lying to his subject, Jeffrey MacDonald, a Green Beret doctor accused of killing his wife and two children, in order to keep pumping him for information. Sometime during the trial, at which MacDonald was found guilty, McGinniss came to believe MacDonald was a killer, though he didn't tell MacDonald what he really thought. Malcolm also painted an entire profession with a broad and nasty stroke, saying that all journalists were, by nature and necessity, sly and deceitful. She began with this shocking indictment: "Every journalist who is not too stupid or too full of himself to notice what is going on knows that what he does is morally indefensible."

Almost every reporter I knew was punctured by this. The newsroom became a constant debate between McGinniss-backers and Malcolmites. One reporter said he read the articles to pick up some tips for modeling himself on McGinniss, whose books were national best-sellers and made-for-television movies. Others found his techniques abominable and felt he'd used MacDonald for his own ends. A few reporters in the middle said both McGinniss and Malcolm were partially correct, that he did what he had to do but she had caught him and was justified in criticizing him for it.

The debate raised questions in my mind. McGinniss was a friend of my father's, and I'd known him for a long time and came readily to his defense. But whether I realized it or not, I was changing around the end of March. I was starting to see gray areas where I'd never noticed them before. No matter how much I wanted to shoot down Malcolm, my own experiences had shown me that there were seeds of truth in her generalizations.

It was important to keep a distance from the people I wrote about, but sourcing was part of covering a beat. After taking the PBA card from Iron Mike, I worried that I was getting too close to someone who might be the subject of one of my stories. I feared I'd crossed a line that implied that I, as "a stand-up guy," shared Iron Mike and his buddy's views. I wondered if I'd ever be in a position to betray my new friend.

My skin was thickening to the daily sparring at DCPI and I was starting to get a more consistent flow of information and better access. One reason was because I was picking my fights more carefully. Instead of being the bulldog bent on every scrap of meat, I told myself it would be better to write as much truth about the department over the course of a year than it would be to cut myself off by trying to tell it all in a day or a week. This required some restraint, but it was more sensible. This way, I'd neither get iced by the cops nor become part of their long-term public relations apparatus.

The homicide log book, however, remained a problem. Although we had won access, the department still controlled how and when we could see it. They wouldn't let us photocopy the book, so *Newsday* assigned an intern to cull through the pages of the leather-bound ledger. The intern brought a portable Tandy computer to the chief of detectives' office, where he would copy what we needed. Day one passed without incident, but on his second afternoon, the cops took away the book.

Inspector Mayronne said it contained material that could damage pending cases against suspects. He was right. There was a line of comments next to each homicide, but everything in the book could also be found in the detectives' case folders. What the cops were really afraid of was the computer, which they knew we could use to figure out the breakdowns of victims by age, race or the types of weapons used. This was exactly the kind of information they didn't want in a newspaper. If the story showed how many young men, particularly blacks, were murdering people with semiautomatic pistols every day, the department feared it would convince readers the cops had lost control of the city. As they continued to stall, I became livid, but the department possessed the book and had the upper hand. We were still playing by Italian Rules and they didn't owe me any favors. Getting another Freedom of Information Law request approved could take months. At this rate, we'd get the 1988 list around the year 2000. Finally, Esposito stepped in and worked out an agreement in which the cops would tape a piece of paper over the line of comments they were afraid of getting out. In exchange for that concession, they'd let the intern back at the book.

This kind of paranoia was common among cops, and nobody was as consistent with it as Chief of Detectives Robert Colangelo. Around the time of the Battle for the Log Book, I attended a ceremony at headquarters. Before it started, the top brass were gathered around a table of coffee, juice and Danish pastries. These occasions were a good time to meet the chiefs and make small talk. As I was standing behind Colangelo, trying to listen in as he bantered with a group of four bosses, the Chief of D's pivoted toward me. He pulled my press pass from behind my tie.

"So, who do we have here?" he asked.

Colangelo was a short man, but an imposing figure to a young reporter. Nicknamed the Dapper Detective, he wore fancy suits and hand-painted ties, had artificially tanned skin that made him look as if he were mummified, and wore his hair in a pompadour that lounge singer Vic Damone would have been proud of.

"So, you're the new guy," he said.

"I've been here a few months, but I'm still getting to know the department," I said.

"Good to know you," he said.

Colangelo patted me on the back and spun back to finish his conversation. He seemed like a nice man to me, and he left me feeling good. Later that morning, Mayronne called down on the hotline. "Get up here," he said. He was angry and I had no idea what I'd done this time. "The Chief of D's is pissed off at you. He said you were eavesdropping on him at the ceremony."

"I thought we had a good chat this morning," I said.

"Another good chat like that and nobody'll ever talk to you again. If you keep getting in trouble, I won't be able to send you over to see the chiefs when you need them," he said, escalating from a reprimand up to a threat.

Then the consummate ball-buster decided to have a little fun by telling me that he didn't know if he was going to have to mention this episode to Esposito. This time, I recognized a pattern in the old DCPI dance and told Mayronne that I'd tell Esposito myself. Esposito reacted exactly as I thought he would.

"Did you pick up anything?" he asked.

"No."

"Don't waste your time with that guy. Colangelo hasn't known anything worth hearing for years," he said.

Italian Rules also meant that some things weren't worth getting caught for. Colangelo was one of them. My forced introduction to the Chief of D's, however, taught me a lot about how detectives think. To be good, they have to create a myth of their power. They are gamesmen, psychologists and hustlers, lying, scheming chameleons who believe anything is fair in the pursuit of a perp. They spend so many hours trying to understand the criminal mind that they develop similar traits. They are skeptical of everyone and everything. Whether they are charming, slick, hot or cold, they always have an angle. The best detectives, the ones that television cops like Kojak and Columbo are modeled on, take their rap to the streets where they actually solve cases. The worst ones coast on their gold shields and wait around to retire. But all of them can be dangerous.

One detective I knew explained how they worked.

"Mitch, let me share something with you," he said, using a phrase I suppose he thought would win my confidence. "These guys jerk you off with one hand and drag you away by the ear with the other."

The best illustration of this is the detective in the 75th Precinct who told a murder suspect that the human eye takes a picture of the last thing it sees. In this case, the detective told the suspect that the incriminating photo showed him pulling the trigger. The guy was so convinced he'd been caught that he quickly made a full confession.

I was catching on to the way the job worked, and already there were some mornings when I dreaded going to Headquarters. But love it or hate it, the Shack had become my center of gravity. My routine was to pick up the papers and a muffin on my way in, read the sheets, get a cup of Community Affairs coffee, call the desk with the overnights and wait to go out on my story of the day. Occasionally, if I had gotten an early start, I'd pick up a few steamed pork buns in Chinatown and some hot Chinese tea for myself, Alex the security guard and Mike Koleniak, who was still sitting in Joe Cotter's chair. Cotter remained in the hospital without any significant change in his condition. We tried to put his absence out of our minds, but we missed his company in the Shack. One of the good things about being downtown was our independence from the main desk. Editors were constantly calling, but they were four miles north. We could also stay isolated from the politics of the newsroom—a galaxy of rising and falling stars and a playground of sandbox bickering.

I had loosened up a lot since my first months on the beat and was getting along better with Elaine and the other Cop Shop reporters. Anne Murray got pissed off with me now and then because I was constantly bumming cookies from her to satisfy deadline jitters and rarely replacing them. But it was good-natured fooling around. If I was having problems with my love life, I could talk to Koleniak in the morning or share stories about romances lost and hoped for with

Ginny Byrne on the days she asked me to tie a knot "like men do, you know, with the regular tie-knot" in the ribbon around the collar of her red blouse. The *Daily News* guys spent most of their time in their own spacious office. The *Times* reporters were in limbo, David Pitt hoping to be pulled off the beat to go down to Central or South America, his area of expertise, and Don Terry waiting to be transferred to City Hall, the next step for a *Times*man. Some days, we'd sit around and bullshit, but never for long. Stories were always breaking.

Covering death was debilitating as well as intoxicating and caused my mood to change as frequently as the weather. On sunny days, I'd take walks in the park to escape the killing, or throw a softball around with one of the other reporters or photographers at the paper. On gray days, there was no way out. The East River reminded me of industrial strips along the Rhine, and the glittering and glamorous city looked like someone had painted it with a damp cloth dipped in sludge.

Coming back from a story in Brooklyn on one of those days, I turned right against a red light onto the Brooklyn Bridge. There wasn't any traffic, but a police car was staked out on the side of the bridge, waiting to catch drivers who made that illegal turn.

The cops waved me over and one came to my window. I took my registration out of the glove compartment and opened my wallet. The PBA card Iron Mike had given me was next to my driver's license. The cop asked me where I'd gotten it. I told him a buddy on the force had set me up with it. The officer went through the motions of preparing a ticket and came back to my car.

"Now, you be careful out there," he said, wagging his finger at me. "Don't do any more naughty things." He handed back my identification but no summons.

I steered my car across the bridge toward Manhattan. Not only was this job affecting my thoughts, but it was also controlling my actions. My arrogance easily superseded my humility. My heart beat fast. I wasn't thinking about whether I owed the department anything or dwelling on any favors I might have to return to Iron Mike. I just felt like I was wired to some supernatural power.

*   *   *

Tricked by this sense of invincibility, I vowed to start running around the reservoir in Central Park before work. I figured that with a little willpower I'd get out there early. This lasted about two days, and then I got even worse about getting up in the morning than before. Maybe it was spring fever or the rigors of homicide coverage that made me start looking for shortcuts, but I began rolling out of bed at quarter past eight, fifteen minutes before I had to call the desk. Instead of reading the sheets myself, I'd lie in bed, listening to the headlines on the radio, and would call DCPI to ask if anything was going on.

That was dangerous, because the cops were not paid to have news judgment. To them, one murder was nearly the same as another. Also, the charming Janice Swinney—who yelled, "Hush, Mitch is coming. Watch what you say," whenever I walked into the office—didn't like hearing me on the phone any more than seeing me in the office. It was a great inconvenience for her to go through the sheets. For a while, I tried to be courteous, but with Janice courtesy was wasted breath.

"Good morning Janice, how are you?" I'd ask.

"Don't give me that crap. What do you want?" she'd say.

"Well, I was wondering if you could give me a rundown of the overnights," I'd say.

"Honey, I ain't got time for that. Hold on," she'd say.

My phone would go blank. As I waited, sometimes as long as five or ten minutes, I'd get angry at myself for not getting down to read the sheets. Then Janice would pick up again and say, "Forgot you were on there." She'd giggle and continue: "Now, what was it you wanted?" By then, I wanted to strangle her.

The worst was when my beeper would go off while I was on hold with Janice. It was usually Esposito or the desk, so I couldn't return the beep until I knew what was on the sheets and I couldn't know that until Janice picked up the phone. It was like being caught between the Devil and DCPI. On mornings like that, I hated the job.

Fortunately, my work developing sources was starting to pay off. A man I'd tried to cultivate earlier in the year was in a position to leak a report about a high-profile investigation that had been going on for nearly a year. He was a member of the Civilian Complaint Review Board, a twelve-member panel that consisted of six police department officials and six civilians. The board was charged with reviewing complaints made against police regarding alleged acts of brutality, corruption, bigotry or any other misconduct. Its civilian members were, for the most part, open-minded, but the board's department members spoke and voted with a single voice. And its investigators were virtually all cops who'd been assigned to the CCRB by the department.

The board's biggest task of the year was the investigation of a police melee that had occurred the summer before in Tompkins Square Park. Four hundred officers in riot gear had converged on the East Village park shortly before midnight on August 6, 1988, to confront a few hundred homeless people and residents who were protesting a one A.M. park curfew. The minor demonstration quickly turned violent, with cops flailing nightsticks at protesters, who pelted them with rocks and bottles. The cops, perhaps tired and frustrated by the demonstrators' verbal taunts, covered their shield numbers with black mourning bands and went on a rampage. They clubbed spectators, knocked photographers to the pavement and smashed video cameras that were filming the chaos.

In the morning, the investigation into what went wrong fell to the CCRB. It would be months before the board would have anything to report, and during that time, I got to know one of its members. One night, we met for dinner at the Oyster Bar, a restaurant in Grand Central Station. During dinner, we talked about how little time reporters had to write about the larger issues surrounding crime. He understood the priority of breaking news, but stressed the importance of putting it in context.

I used my *Newsday* corporate American Express card to pick up the check. The board member offered to pay, but I said journalistic ethics wouldn't allow that. Besides, I'd been waiting weeks to use my AMEX card, a plastic sign that I was becoming a real reporter. Still, the check startled me—$76.00 for two salads, soups, entrées and bubbly water—and I hoped my editors would approve the expense when I handed it in. It seemed a large investment, and I had no idea if it would pay off.

At the time, the board member impressed me. He was smooth and intelligent, but I thought he would be like so many of the charming power brokers I had run into during my time on the editorial pages. I had discovered that very few had the courage to back up their ideals with controversial action. But he turned out to be different.

I called him occasionally for updates as the Tompkins Square Park investigation proceeded. It turned out that the board was having difficulty getting anywhere. Of the four hundred officers, including the forty sergeants, lieutenants and other supervisors who'd been at the scene, not one would cooperate with investigators. The Patrolmen's Benevolent Association encouraged the cops to maintain this blue wall of silence. At one press conference, PBA president Phil Caruso waved a manila folder and told the media that hundreds of "good New Yorkers" had seen the demonstrators provoke the police. Caruso said he had their names right in the folder, but when I asked to see them, he refused to reveal a single one. His antics were pure McCarthyism, but his goal of stifling the investigation seemed to be working.

Although the board was able to substantiate about two thirds of 121 complaints filed against the cops, it was having trouble identifying any of the officers. During the first week of April, the board was almost ready to forward its report to Ben Ward. The department did not intend to release it to the press until they had a chance to review its language. I knew an advance copy would be a great exclusive. When I phoned the board member that week, he said the board had met the day before and that the final draft was in the last stage of preparation.

"What happened at the meeting?" I asked.

"We agreed to sign off on the majority report," he said.

"No dissenters?"

"No. The truth is there in the last draft. We'll see how the department reacts. Telling the truth is always a bit of a shock to the police department," he said.

"Getting there is never an easy process, either," I said.

"Not at all. We went through a lot of lively debate to get from the self-congratulatory tone some members proposed in the early drafts to this one. This draft states three things. One, the events of the night comprised a 'police riot.' Two, the department, which could have granted supervisors immunity in exchange for their help, preferred to see, hear and speak no evil. And three, the board needs more independent investigators to do an effective job," he said.

"Do you think I can get a look at the report?" I asked.

"Let me think about it," he said.

He called back half an hour later and invited me to his office, where he handed me an envelope with three drafts of the report enclosed. The contrast between the self-congratulatory early drafts and the final one was dynamic: it was the difference between a whitewash and a reckoning. Rather than give the department a chance to change the language, the board member decided to leak the report to the press. I couldn't believe he was giving the report to me rather than to someone at the *Times*, and my natural skepticism kept me trying to figure out why he was leaking it at all. I wondered if he was in cahoots with the mayor or the police commissioner or if he had his own political ambitions. But nothing tracked. He didn't want any publicity for himself and was going around the police commissioner and mayor's backs, releasing the report before even they had seen it.

I had to accept the board member's word for why he leaked it. He really wanted to preserve the integrity of the report so people would consider the CCRB a legitimate, if limited, check on police power. This way, the police brass couldn't try to put their spin on the board's findings. He knew it was important for the CCRB to show that it was not simply a rubber stamp for department decisions. Many thought the police commissioner, who seemed to interpret his job as a mandate to run an agency in the short term, didn't understand this. But the board member kept the long view. By going around Ward's back, he had acted as a surrogate commissioner, which in the world of Italian Rules made him a "Shadow Caesar." Woodward and Bernstein may have had Deep Throat, but I had the Shadow Caesar.

I walked out of his office thrilled I had the report before Koch, Ward or McGillion. I promised the board member the paper would hold it until the day it went to Ward, but Koch and McGillion would read the results of the CCRB investigation for the first time in *Newsday*. I found Esposito at a function he was attending and showed him what I'd uncovered. He was pleased and agreed we'd hold the report until a copy landed on Ward's desk. Then we'd blow it out in the paper before the rest of the press received their copies.

After nine months as a reporter, I was starting to take on a degree of cynicism when a story that seemed to push me further in that direction came along. Surprisingly, the story showed that it was more difficult to become cynical than I had thought.

On April 11, Chris Hatch, the photo editor, who sometimes went out on stories, was driving to work before dawn when he heard about a shooting on the radio. The announcer said a boy, Shawn Motayne, was in Kings County Hospital with a bullet lodged in the base of his skull. He was likely to die. Instead of going to the office, Hatch followed his instincts and drove straight to the boy's neighborhood in Flatbush.

As a newsman, Hatch covered all the bases by getting up early, listening to the radio, knowing the scanner frequencies and the neighborhoods around town. Yet there was something intangible, uncanny even, about his ability to identify stories. A tall man, Hatch had a nagging knee injury and walked with a limp. He was often in pain, but he never let his personal hardships detract from his work. He had tremendous pride, and his handicap seemed to contribute to the empathy he felt for victims and their survivors.

Hatch rang the Motaynes' apartment and a woman who had not slept all night came to the door. She did not want to talk to any press, but Hatch just nodded. His foot in the door, which was open only a crack, Hatch could sense Gail Motayne's suffering and made her see that he understood her agony. He told her about the son he nearly lost at birth from spinal meningitis; he knew the pain of having a child almost die. At that, Gail Motayne let him in. Hatch remembers an almost religious bonding with her that morning. He was a Connecticut Yankee and she was an immigrant from Guyana, but they were both parents who loved their sons. She gave Hatch an eight-by-ten color photograph of Shawn sitting with a book open on his lap, an American flag behind him and a chipmunklike smile on his face. A few minutes later, Denis Hamill arrived on Hatch's coattails, and Gail Motayne, in a melodic Guyanese accent, shared her story with him.

Hamill was writing a column on Shawn and the paper wanted me to do a news story to go with it. I called in the sheets and Hap sent me to Flatbush. By then, another story about a kid shot in the head seemed almost formulaic. Shawn Motayne was Jeffrey Vilain and all the other kids who had been killed in recent weeks. The name, the age, the quote, the tears were typed into a story about the city's youngest being mowed down for no reason.

The lobby of the redbrick building smelled of detergent, steam heat and home cooking. I climbed the stairs to Gail Motayne's apartment and apologized for asking her to tell her story again, but she was kind. Wearing a babushka wrapped around her head and a GIRLS AND CURLS sweatshirt, she sat in the living room and remembered sending Shawn to meet his sister at the Wash Land Laundromat at six-thirty P.M. It was still light out.

The family was moving to New Jersey to get away from the violence in the neighborhood, and was washing their clothes before packing them. Shawn and his sister took turns watching the clothes, and Shawn brought back a bagful at a time. An avid soccer player, he was wearing white sneakers, red shorts and his yellow Canarsie Amity Soccer team jacket on his last trip to the Laundromat. As he walked down Hawthorne Street to Nostrand Avenue, 120 child's paces from his front door, bullets started flying and Shawn went down. A neighbor ran to Gail's apartment and told her Shawn had been shot.

"Is he dead?" she asked.

"No. Come fast," the neighbor told her.

Her nightgown whisked back and her hair suspended in flight, Gail Motayne ran to her son. He was conscious, rocking back and forth, and looked up and smiled at her.

"Don't worry, Mommy. I love you. Don't worry, Mommy," he said.

A car rushed him five blocks to the trauma unit at Kings County Hospital. Gail Motayne called Shawn's father, who coached his son's soccer team but didn't live with the family. She cried, and then she prayed.

When I left Gail Motayne with her family and her prayers, a team of detectives was taking photographs and measuring the distance from the back of the Barrett-Saunders Funeral Home on the corner of Hawthorne and Nostrand to the point where Shawn had been shot. The night before, while Shawn was heading to Wash Land, there had been a wake for a slain drug dealer at the funeral home. One of the guests yelled at a neighborhood homeboy who had double-parked, making it difficult for the guest to get by in his gray two-door sedan. The yelling turned into posturing and both men's manhood came into question. They had been "dissed," shown disrespect in public, which was a slight worth dying for. The man from the sedan went into the funeral home and emerged with a team of comrades sporting full-length black leather coats. They drew handguns and sprayed more than twenty bullets at the homeboy and his friends. One shot grazed an old lady from Shawn's building, and another hit Shawn in the head. The next morning, the detectives drew a diagram of the crime scene, but had no suspects. They knew the gunmen had attended the wake, but had no idea who or how many had fired the shots.

Hamill was writing about Shawn, so I had to find another angle for the news story. I wanted to know more about the murdered drug dealer whose death had brought the gunmen into Shawn's path. I got his name, Johnny Harpe, Jr., from the funeral home marquee, and from a pay phone across from the funeral home, I called the detective squad that had handled Harpe's killing. I'd met the squad commander through Elaine, and he remembered me when I called and got the case file. *Newsday* had recently given AT&T charge cards to reporters, so instead of feeding quarters, I just waited for the bong and punched in my numbers. Still, I had to scrunch the receiver between my neck and shoulder and balance my notebook on top of the phone while the detective filled me in.

Johnny Harpe, Jr., was a celebrity in southeast Queens and East New York. Only twenty-four years old, he'd amassed hundreds of thousands of dollars and controlled a stable of crack and cocaine distributors. His street name was "Unique," and the cops called him the Donald Trump of the drug world because he'd invested in a series of boutiques, hair-styling salons, fast-food restaurants and other small businesses along the Brooklyn-Queens border and had named them after himself. The Brooklyn district attorney's office had been investigating his holdings when he was killed. Harpe had survived for a day after being shot three times in the chest, just long enough to tell police that four men wearing masks had done him in. Harpe had so many rivals who were happy he was dead that it was doubtful the cops would find the masked men.

What a sick character. Even when he was dead and nearly buried, Johnny Harpe still wreaked misery. Bullets followed him to his grave. I called Hap with the update, and then I wandered around Shawn's neighborhood, looking for anyone who had seen what happened the night before.

The streets were lined with small businesses, apartment buildings and single-family homes. Novelty stores sold silkscreens of idyllic scenes of palm trees and lakes, the fond memories of the islands that local residents had left behind. The aromas of West Indian and Caribbean spices wafted from restaurants and bodegas. Amid all of this were the hard young men in bomber jackets, bleached denim jeans, baseball caps with the brims turned up. They lugged thick gold chains around their necks, and the women by their sides wore gold hoop earrings. Even during the day, these streets seemed harsh. At night, the shops shuttered their windows, and reggae and calypso music, salsa and rap would beat against the sky, their sweet sounds punctuated by honking horns and gunshots. Crime had stolen the streets from the people of Flatbush.

At one time, they had been able to sit on stoops, chat and act like a neighborhood. That was no longer. They'd been forced into their apartments. But even there they were not safe; crime had entered the area's homes as well. The week before, Shawn's apartment had been robbed of a television, a VCR and some jewelry. "We called the police when we came home, but the cops never came," said Shawn's great-aunt, who lived with the family. "It takes a beautiful little boy to get shot, almost snatched of life, before you get a cop to come around here." Gail Motayne had had enough and was planning to move, but her family's exodus would come too late.

When I got back to the office, Hap was nervous. Driven by the eight-by-ten Hatch had picked up, Hamill's column and the stuff about Johnny Harpe, Jr., the Shawn Motayne story was strong enough to lead the paper. While Forst was sketching a headline—A VICTIM OF THE CITY

—Hap was worried I didn't have the right drug dealer. Bob Drury had called a source to double-check my information, and Drury's source hadn't heard of Harpe. That made Hap concerned I had mixed him up with someone else.

"I'm putting my ass out there for you. So, are you sure?" Hap asked.

I was going on what I'd seen on the funeral home marquee and been told by the detective squad commander, but I didn't have enough confidence in my reporting to be beyond doubt. Then the district attorney's office confirmed they'd been looking into Harpe through his businesses. I told Hap not to worry.

"The guy's the guy," I said, using a phrase obviously influenced by cop-speak.

That night, I called the Kings County Hospital administrator to get an update on Shawn's condition before our final deadline. He was in critical condition, and as with most neurologically damaged patients, it would take seventy-two hours before a preliminary prognosis could be developed. The neurologists had put him into a barbiturate-induced coma, and he was breathing on a respirator. "It's wait and see," the administrator said.

I also called Kildare Clarke, who had something more on his mind. He was furious at the continued violence caused by drugs, and he used me to vent his anger.

"You see what is happening here, man?" he said.

"What do you mean?"

"It's the drugs," he said. "They're destroying this community. You see the signs of it here every day."

"It's all over the place," I said.

"And it's only getting worse. The police can't stop the violence and the politicians are just talking nonsense when they say they are trying to do something about the problem," he said.

The thirty-six-year-old doctor from Jamaica spoke with a strong sense of purpose, but these days not even the upbeat melody of his native dialect could hide the anguish in his voice. He had worked at Kings County for the better part of fifteen years, and his rage at the establishment had been building longer than that. He was the seventh of eleven children born on a farm without electricity or running water in a place called Fat Hog Quarter, in Hanover Parish, Jamaica. Clarke went to college in London and came to New York for medical school when he was seventeen years old. He attended school at Downstate Medical Center in Brooklyn, which is across the street from Kings County Hospital, and was elected president of the student body. Never one to be afraid of taking on authority, Clarke organized a boycott of the final exam in one class to protest the way the school taught about tuberculosis. It included TB in a course on statistics instead of letting students work in community health centers that treated the epidemic. The boycott resulted in a change in the curriculum, and it also marked Clarke's first confrontation with medical school and hospital leaders.

As a student, Clarke did a rotation through various departments at Kings County, and although he was trained as a psychiatrist, he found a home in the hospital's emergency room. In the mid-1970s, while doing his residency in psychiatry, Clarke worked nights in the E.R. The head of the emergency room hired Clarke as associate director in 1979. During the next ten years, Clarke kept that job, graduated from law school and earned a master's degree in labor relations. He also continued to be an outspoken critic of the city's multitiered health care system. He seethed when he saw how privileged patients had private doctors and access to good hospitals while the mostly black, Hispanic, poor and uninsured ended up in badly managed municipal facilities. Clarke, who had three children, continued to work long hours in the hospital, and identified with the patients. His heart was often troubled by the lack of compassion he saw in fellow doctors and administrators. Nothing, however, bothered him more than what drugs were doing on the streets. Clarke could work through the doctors union or the media to change hospital policies or challenge insensitive government bureaucrats, but he was frustrated when it came to fighting drugs.

Shawn Motayne was not the only victim of a drug dealer's bullet in Kings County Hospital. Upstairs in the adult neurological intensive care unit, Billy Gunn was still in a coma. Almost three months had gone by since Ralph Richardson shot Billy Gunn on the stairwell of the Hancock Street brownstone. His condition remained unchanged. Although he, like Shawn, was now under the neurologists' care, Clarke took the time to keep up with any patient who had come through his trauma unit. He also offered an ear to Lori Gunn and Billy's mother, Mary, who visited the hospital every day. To them, he was just another doctor, a white gown with a hospital identification card like the dozens of doctors they saw and listened to each time they came to the hospital. But Clarke paid attention to their mood swings and noticed that while Lori seemed to accept the doctors' views when they said Billy would never recover, Mary Gunn maintained an unflinching belief that he would someday come out of his silent, mostly motionless existence.

Clarke's many hours in the trauma unit made him look at doctoring differently than a general practitioner does. He had seen enough violent head injuries like Shawn's to know that they could end a life rapidly. He also knew that the line between the world of the living and the world of the dead was very slim. He shared the conventional wisdom that the first seventy-two hours—three days—after a head wound determined which side of that line a patient would land on. The human body, like a car battery or computer chip, had a task to perform; some bodies lasted longer than others, but all came to a time when they were through.

Clarke sought a balance that would allow him to work feverishly to save a human life but also know when it was time to step away and let that life slip along its natural course. He treated medicine as a combination of art, philosophy and science. But unlike an artist's pursuit of infinite beauty, a philosopher's unending quest for truth or an astronomer's search through space, he believed that medicine had a finality: death.

As Shawn began the second day of his fight to survive, the morning paper came out with his picture on page one. Hatch had gotten the only photograph of Shawn, so none of the other papers had reported the story. It was ours alone. The editors put me on the budget for a follow-up story on his condition. I thought I knew what the story would say and already dreaded reporting it. I figured that the doctors would tell me the kid was brain-dead and, in more gentle terms, had become a ten-year-old vegetable.

Prepared for the worst, I called the hospital's public relations person and asked to speak with Shawn's neurologist. The spokesman explained that I'd be talking to a neurosurgeon, not just a neurologist, and cautioned me about the doctor's ego.

"Be careful the way you talk to him. Really, I know this sounds funny to you, but you have to understand, neurosurgeons think they're gods," the spokesman said. The neurosurgeon was helpful if not humble. He went into some detail about Shawn's injuries. The bullet had severed a portion of his cerebellum—the part of the brain that controls motion and balance—and had lodged against the base of his skull. After removing the damaged brain matter, doctors had used drugs to slow Shawn's metabolism to the rate of a person in a coma. The bullet was still set against the bone, but it couldn't do any more harm. As expected, the neurosurgeon played down Shawn's chances of recovery.

Later in the morning, I talked to Gail Motayne, who wanted no part of the doctor's prognosis. A devout member of the Assemblies of God church in Guyana, she did not believe that the neurosurgeons had any healing powers. What they had was science, not religion. She was adamant about this. "The hands of God will guide the hands of the doctors," she said. "I know God and Shawnie knows God and God will give him back to us." She asked that all the readers pray for Shawn. She made this sound more important than the medical treatment, and I treated her prayers with similar significance in the second day's story.

Late that night, I called my friend Karin Muraszko, who was a pediatric neurosurgeon at the National Institutes of Health in Washington. During a recent weekend I'd spent at her house, I had seen a book on head injuries and had scanned a chapter on bullet wounds. Before going to NIH, she was the head resident at Columbia Presbyterian Hospital in Washington Heights, where she saw her share of gunshot victims. I often thought about the pressure she was under every time she went to work. With newspaper reporting, we could run a correction if we made a mistake.

Karin was very interested in Shawn's case. I explained his injuries, and we talked for half an hour about what happens when someone under age twelve loses part of his cerebellum. "Kids are amazing," she said. "They are frankly downright awesome sometimes. Their ability to recover is such that they can be back on their feet ten days after leaving the hospital sometimes. But when they go bad, they go quickly." The key to Shawn's chances, she said, was how much swelling had occurred before the doctors got to the wound. If a large hematoma had developed, putting pressure on the brain stem, which carries messages from the brain to everywhere else, he might never regain his faculties to think, speak or breathe. But if the damage was only to the cerebellum and his brain stem reflexes came back as doctors weaned him off the drugs, he could make it. He might never dance like Baryshnikov or play soccer like Pelé, but since he was brought to the hospital so quickly, Karin said he might be lucky.

In the morning, I answered the phone in the Shack and an angry Gail Motayne was on the line. She was upset with the headline on the story, which said SHAWN'S MOTHER HOPES, PRAYS FOR A MIRACLE.

"I'm not praying for a miracle," she said. "I *know* there will be a miracle."

I tried to be sympathetic. "Okay. Okay," I said to try to calm her down. "We'll try to fix it in today's story."

I thought she was a mother who didn't want to face the truth that her son would never recover. I was thinking, *C'mon lady, get real. Your son's got a bullet in his head. He ain't going nowhere.* Yet she had such a dispassionate fervor to her tone. She was not ranting irrationally, but complaining as if I'd spelled her name wrong or reported an incorrect address. I realized that to her, miracles were absolute facts, and she wanted to set the record straight. I had never encountered anyone who was as filled with spirit as she.

She'd been raised in the sanctified church in Guyana with a strict, moral upbringing that demanded a clean life without tobacco or alcohol. She attended church three or four times a week, always tithing and paying attention to the Lord's word, and had brought Shawn up in the same kind of traditionally religious household. He went to Sunday school, prayer meetings and regular services. Since the day he was baptized, she had made sure he was in good with God. And now it was time for the Lord to give something back. She was certain He would not let them down.

For my third-day story, I wrote that doctors were cutting back on the drugs and waiting for Shawn to emerge from the coma. I also reported that his mother said, "I know Shawnie will be fine." After filing, I got a call from my friend Alex. He'd joined Cops For Christ and the group was holding a youth crusade at the New Gethsemane Baptist Church in Crown Heights to pray for Shawn that night. I told him that I wasn't sure if I could make it, but Hap thought I should go because I would need an angle for my next story about Shawn.

The church was a plain brick building on a pot-holed street of boarded-up tenements with rusted fire escapes in a section of Brooklyn known for corrupt cops and crack. A dreary rain had made the roads wet. Yet as soon as I walked into the church, I was overcome by the vital and infectious spirit of the congregation, which pulsed with the joy of life and faith in God. Whenever I entered a Christian church or a Moslem mosque, I always muttered the Sh'ma, the one thing I remembered from Hebrew school: *"Sh'ma yisraeil: adonai eloheinu, adonai echad."* It offers praise for Israel and pledges the Lord is one, separating Judaism from religions that worship a trinity or any other God. I'd always thought the stuff about being the chosen people was pure arrogance, but just in case it was true, this would cover me.

A female detective was preaching about the various forms of love. The highest love, she said, was the love of Jesus. And as she went on, the church swayed to the steady beat of a bass drum that pounded in rhythm with the sermon. When she finished, the Reverend Ellis Washington stepped to the pulpit and urged everyone "to reach out and hug someone, not just the person sitting next to you, but someone who shares with you the love the sister shared with us." Next thing I knew, my arms were wrapped around an old black lady with a beard as thick as steel wool. After a litany of praise-the-Lords, Washington offered one more remark.

"Not far from where we rejoice this evening, a young boy is fighting for his life," he said. "Please join me in a moment of silence to pray for Shawn's recovery."

After the service, I walked down a hallway and saw an altar for Shawn in a prayer room. On top of a lace-covered table was an open prayer book, two brass vases with red and white carnations and a copy of the issue of *Newsday* that had Shawn's photograph on page one. Behind the altar was a print of Leonardo da Vinci's *Last Supper*. The prayer book was open to Psalm 49: "But God will ransom my life; He will snatch me from the grasp of death." I knelt on a pillow in front of the altar and remembered something I hadn't felt since I'd bowed before the Wailing Wall during a trip to Jerusalem with my grandparents seven years earlier. I swore that if Shawn recovered, I'd never doubt the Lord's existence ever again. The service had touched the religion that had been latent in me, though perhaps closer to the surface since Shawn's shooting. Maybe Gail Motayne was right. On the way out Alex and I exchanged smiles and a handshake.

Seventy-two hours after the shooting, Shawn's condition was still "critical but stable." The doctors said he was emerging from the drug-induced coma, and his mother maintained her fervent belief that he would recover. The next day, we ran a picture of the special altar at the New Gethsemane Baptist Church.

I was leaving to visit a friend in Las Vegas that afternoon, but I had one more story to write. This time the lead was straight from the doctors. The story was so easy and so simple that I read it over and over on the terminal to make sure it said what I thought it did.

> Shawn Motayne woke up yesterday.
> He flashed bright, brown eyes at his father. He answered doctors' commands to move his arms and legs. And, the boy's mother said, he continued to respond to her prayers.
> The 10-year-old, who was shot in the head by a stray bullet fired in a traffic dispute outside his home Monday night, was listening to music through headphones attached to a cassette player yesterday afternoon.
> "He's doing better," one hospital neurosurgeon said. "There is no question that he will live."
> ...The boy's mother says she's certain the young soccer player will be back in uniform.
> "I've known all along Shawnie will be all right," she said confidently yesterday. "We just want to thank everyone who has been praying for him. When you talk to him, he opens his eyes and looks at you."

A few weeks later, when *Newsday* posted the monthly awards that the editors gave to reporters, I got a fifty-dollar pat on the back for the stories on Shawn. I put half of it in an envelope in Chris Hatch's mailbox, but he wouldn't take it. "This is yours," he said the next time he saw me. But I knew Hatch had made that story happen. In addition to getting the photo from Gail Motayne the first morning, his kindness in returning it to her by hand the following day was a large part of why she continued to speak with the paper. I learned something important from him that week. When dealing with real people rather than institutions or politicians, empathy is more important than intimidation or subterfuge. If a reporter could win a person's trust, the person would give up almost anything you asked for, often a lot more than you ever expected.

During the same time that I was writing about Shawn's saga, I was also working with Esposito to get the story on the CCRB's Tompkins Square Park report in the paper before I left for a week's vacation. I'd already given Tom Plate a copy of the report so he could time an editorial for the day we broke the exclusive. On the day I was going to Las Vegas, Esposito was in the newsroom putting the final touches on our story. He had a headline running around in his mind—IT'S A RIOT—and needed to ask the board member a final question. But the Shadow Caesar wouldn't return his calls. Esposito beeped me at the airport and asked if I'd give the board member a call.

I looked at my little red address book, which was nothing like Esposito's. I had only one phone number worth mentioning, but that evening those seven digits I dialed seemed like they could break any secret code in existence. Our story was strong, and I wondered as I flew across the country how Ward and McGillion would react in the morning.

Two days later, in Las Vegas, I bought a copy of the national edition of *The New York Times*. They had a story chasing ours. We'd scooped them cold. I used my company AMEX to send a telegram thanking the Shadow Caesar. I had no doubt that I'd get the charge approved.

When Ginny Byrne saw our story on the report, she thought Esposito had gotten it from one of his sources. That was okay by me. This was a case where I was better served by anonymity than recognition. Although it had been a while since I'd asked Esposito how he got the memo on the police-fire feud, I hadn't forgotten that secrecy was part of his method. The riot report story allowed me to help undermine the department's tendency to lie and deceive, and I'd played by Italian Rules in the best way possible—with an almost imperceptible hand.

This was also the last story Esposito and I would be working on together for a while. He was beginning a leave of absence to write a book about the international drug war. Before I left for Las Vegas, he gave me a key to his desk uptown so I could get to any files I needed, and I gave him the names of a few friends in Hong Kong, where he was going on the first leg of his book research. It was nice to be able to do something for him after all he had done for me. But after relying on him for a lot, I wanted to find out if I was any good at this when I didn't have someone to reach out to every day.

"See what you can do," he said before going. "You're going to learn things nobody could teach you. Try to carry the paper a little when you can."

I was scared and up for the challenge. But first, I was ready for a rest.

The Wild Thing

My mind was mush when I got to Las Vegas. My synapses had stopped synapsing and my neurotransmitters had stopped transmitting. It was classic crime-beat burnout. I spent my days toasting in the desert sun, jogging among the cacti and lying in an air-conditioned apartment. My friend Eric and I occasionally wandered around the strip, where we dropped a few bucks at the five-dollar crap tables.

When I wasn't comatose by the pool, I was listening to Edie Brickell and New Bohemians, whose lyrics were just the antidote I needed. "I'm not aware of too many things; I know what I know if you know what I mean," she sang, and went on to compare philosophy to a walk on the slippery rocks and religion to a smile on a dog. Even if I had been looking for an intellectual challenge, Brickell, singing, "Drown me in the shallow waters before I get too deep," made sure I wouldn't find it. Amen. I just wanted to wade around for a while.

Vegas was perfect for five days. Then I picked up a copy of the *Times* and saw that hell was breaking loose back home. Once again, I was out of the city when a big story broke. A twenty-eight-year-old, white female investment banker was attacked by a group of teenage blacks as she jogged through Central Park. The woman had come to the city from suburban Pennsylvania, via Yale and Wellesley, to take a job at Salomon Brothers, an investment banking firm.

On April 19, her path collided with ten to twenty youths out looking for excitement. Many of the suspects lived in a middle-income, government-subsidized housing project on 110th Street at Fifth Avenue named for the famous curator of black history, Arthur Schomburg. The youths tackled the woman and dragged her down a ravine into a puddle. They gagged her with her white sweatshirt, tied her hands in front of her face, tore off her black leotards and removed her panties. They bashed her head with a brick and spread her legs, taking turns on top of her. Satisfied, they left the jogger to struggle a few feet up the ravine before she collapsed across the roots of a budding maple tree. Gurgling and bleeding, barely breathing, she stopped on a bed of moist leaves, broken twigs and mud.

This was the same kind of angry violence that was tearing the city apart, but this case was different. This crime happened in a place many considered the city's front yard and made people, especially white New Yorkers, realize that crime wasn't going to stay in the black and Hispanic parts of town.

When I returned from Las Vegas, I could sense that New York's level of fear had heightened. I hadn't covered the story, so I could see it from a distance and get a broader view of people's reaction to it. Everyone had pretty much become numbed by crime in East New Yorks and East Flatbush, but this dehumanizing attack on the Upper West Side was met with outrage. There and in other affluent parts of the city, residents used their money and clout. Now that crime was on their front stoops, they wanted something done. They were afraid and their fears were reported, analyzed, catered to every day in the press.

The story made *Newsday*'s cover for four straight days. In addition to news, profiles and sidebars, columnists and experts took on the psychology of race-based rape and the failure of social policies to close the income gap, make life better for single mothers and improve schools. The papers and magazines were full of fury, explanations and solutions. They called for more cops, jails and judges, tougher penalties for youth crimes, and stiffer sentences for mob violence. Almost all of the commentary said that young men and women had become alienated from their environment. They sensed the city hated them, and the poverty so many of them lived with left them with a feeling of lesser importance. And this led to the city's intense volatility. The commentators all seemed to agree that this was a cycle that would breed upon itself. As Pete Hamill wrote in the *Post*:

> Atrocities like this will go on and on and on. The details will change. But there will be more broken bodies, more scarred psyches, more temporary outrage, more numbed retreats from the horror. . . . It is no consolation to say we've seen this coming from the mid-60s and nobody did anything serious to stop it. Now, the fierce and terrible future is here. You reap what you sow.

A few days later, I went to the Golden Gloves finals. Between the red ropes of the boxing ring, young, half-naked boxers fought for the same things the pack in the park had wanted: manhood, domination, conquest. Many were from similar backgrounds, had the same scores to settle and frustrations to express, but they were led by Marquess of Queensbury rules, not the lawlessness of the jungle. These young men knew the boredom of an inner-city night, the sense of being second-class citizens, the desire for wealth, for love, for adventure. That night, with the Golden Gloves titles on the line, the fighters battled each other on the turquoise canvas. Taped up and rubbed down, they transformed frustration into punches. Their muscles, which released explosive bursts of violence, were finely toned expressions of the only power available to have-nots in a land of haves. The fighters let out their aggression in the ring, and a boxing referee would be their judge; the teens from the park attack would hear their verdicts in a courtroom.

The assault on the jogger terrified the city, and rape became the tabloid crime of the month. Twenty-eight other rapes had occurred the same week the jogger was attacked, but none of them had received any significant media coverage. With this in mind, Hap told the police bureau to keep tabs on rapes. Although he never said it explicitly, the implication was that we needed to look for a comparably heinous violation of a black woman in order to balance the scales of our coverage.

In late April, as the Central Park rape suspects were being indicted by a grand jury, detectives at the Brooklyn Sex Crimes Unit had collared a man dubbed "the Bicycle Rapist." For months, he had ridden a bicycle alongside cars driven by lone women and faked accidents. He'd tell the women that he was all right but his bike was damaged. He would ask them for rides home, and a few blocks later, pull out a silver gun. He would force the women to drive to a desolate area of warehouses and housing projects near the East River, rape and sodomize them, and steal their cars to get away. Seven instances like this had been reported.

I'd already written about the attacks, so I was the one who hustled to the 81st Precinct for a press conference. Lieutenant Donald Kelly, commanding officer of the Brooklyn Sex Crimes Unit, which had hunted the Bicycle Rapist since his crime spree began, said that as soon as twenty-five-year-old Willie Gonzalez was put into the holding cell, he went to sleep, a sure-as-hell sign that the suspect's mind was at rest and he was guilty. After the press conference, the cops walked Gonzalez from the precinct to a car waiting to take him to Central Booking. This gave photographers time to take his picture and reporters a chance to try to get a comment from him.

Gonzalez was not a normal-looking kid like the jogger suspects. He *looked* like a rapist. His eyes were sunken and insane. He walked with the slinky steps of a man who knew his act was over. His cheeks were covered with a fuzzy sheen of black beard, and he wore a leather jacket, a white T-shirt stained with oil and grease, faded gray jeans and black work boots. Willie Gonzalez's face expressed no remorse and invoked no pity.

As he passed, a television reporter called out, "Willie, why'd you do it?" No answer; he kept walking to the car.

I went back to the Shack and wrote my story, checking a few more details with Lieutenant Kelly as I typed. Jim Dwyer, whose column "In the Subways" ran three times a week in the paper, had been writing about a man who attacked young women on the trains. Dwyer had even dubbed him "the Subway Stalker." The Stalker's description—short, Hispanic, feathery mustache—fit the Bicycle Rapist, and they had both used a small-caliber silver-handled gun. In addition, the bicycle rapes started just after the subway attacks subsided. Dwyer suspected the crimes were by the same man. He called me to ask who he should talk to about the bicycle case and I gave him Kelly's phone number. Dwyer asked Kelly why the city and transit police departments had not shared the descriptions they had of the Stalker and the Bicycle Rapist earlier so that this possible connection could have been explored. Kelly admitted the two agencies could have cooperated better.

I covered the possible link in the news stories by writing, "Transit police detectives are investigating whether Gonzalez is responsible for any of seven attacks on women that occurred in the subway system last year and early this year, said Al O'Leary, a transit police spokesman. Two subway victims, however, viewed Gonzalez in lineups and said he was not the person who attacked them, O'Leary said."

Dwyer's column was not so charitable. He was able to express opinions, which aren't allowed in an objective news story. He liked to say that American journalism was about "tweaking the noses of people in power." And with this one, he really tweaked the cops' noses.

> At times, the police departments of New York City are a marvel. At times, they are a comedy.
> And when three different departments—don't forget the housing police—are chasing what may be the same criminals, they flirt with tragedy. . . .
> "I don't have all their [transit police] information," said Lt. Donald Kelly of the Brooklyn Sex Crimes Unit of the city police. "I won't interview their people [witnesses and victims]. They have established contacts with victims and I don't want to break in on that.
> "They brought two of the [subway] victims in and one said it absolutely was not him. The other said it looked like him but wasn't."
> Maybe there are two different short, His-

> panic guys with feathery mustaches and sil-
> ver-handled guns raping women. But it
> doesn't do much to make people feel safer
> to assume that because one incident occurs
> in the subways and one happens in the
> street that two different police depart-
> ments are needed to investigate.

In the morning, Ronald Fenrich, head of Brooklyn detectives, didn't wait long to phone Kelly.

"Chief, I know this isn't a social call at nine thirty A.M. What's up?" Kelly said.

"You see the paper yet?" Fenrich asked.

"I'll take a look and get right back to you," Kelly said.

Kelly called me later that morning and said that his face had dropped when he saw Dwyer's column. He was able to deflect some of the heat from Fenrich by referring him to my news story. Kelly said he was calling to thank me and to tell me it helped him out of hot water. I didn't know what to say. That wasn't my intention, but I was glad the story worked out for him. I put Kelly's phone number in my book. When it came time to play by Italian Rules, you had to remember all your allies. A friend in Brooklyn Sex Crimes, particularly that month, was good to have.

Commanding a sex crimes unit was not like anything Donald Kelly had ever done before. During his twenty-five years as a cop, he'd been a patrol officer in Harlem and a squad commander in Brooklyn. He thought he'd seen just about all there was to see until the first day of his new assignment in 1986, when he was welcomed by a room full of life-size male and female dummies propped up at typewriters. Kelly knew that running that group would be a new challenge. The squad consisted of a mixed bunch of twenty detectives, each one saddled with between 120 and 125 cases, for a total of over 2,000 rape and sex abuse cases a year. The detectives split the cases into five unofficial categories, based on the types of victims. There were crack addicts, whom the cops called skels; prostitutes, whom they considered rob-bery victims as much as sex crime victims; women attacked by ex-boyfriends, which was akin to domestic violence; and sex crimes against women the cops called "decent" or "upstanding" citizens, who were usually attacked on their way home from work or some social outing. The fifth category was reserved for children, who always got special attention. By sorting the cases this way, the squad maintained a credible 50 percent clearance rate.

Sex crimes detectives have to try not to let their jobs affect them personally, but investigating a rape charge involves a living, breathing, shattered victim, and even the most grizzled of the bunch occasionally let go of his façade. In talking to Kelly and a few of his detectives, I came to understand some of the day-to-day pressures they faced. Not only were the victims more vulnerable than most, but rapists were more ruthless than average criminals. They were sicker, colder, more deranged, impulsive and arrogant than many murderers.

Psychologists have a lot of long, involved analyses that say rapists hate their mothers or had bad sexual experiences at critical developmental stages. The sex crimes detectives had studied all the theories, but were less meditative. They had caught and cuffed enough of these scumbags to know why the majority of them acted: unlike killers, who usually wanted revenge or money, rapists have a sick, addictive desire to feel dominant and invincible. That was all the psychology Kelly's detectives needed to do their jobs.

On Tuesday, May 2, I went into the midtown office after my Sunday-Monday weekend and Julie Shpiesel, the clerk on the desk, told me Lori Gunn had called. When I returned the call, Lori said that the doctors were moving Billy, whose condition was unchanged, by helicopter from Kings County to a nursing home in Connecticut the next day. She asked if I could cover it. Cops and courts editor Laura Durkin had no problem with that and said I could start the day at the hospital.

As I was arriving at Kings County the next morning, my beeper went off. I could see the helicopter landing on the football field, but I had to return the beep. It was Hap, and immediately I could tell he was agitated.

"Where the hell are you?" he asked.

"At Kings County Hospital," I said.

"What for?"

"They're moving Billy Gunn and I'm going to do something on how his wife and their daughter are doing. I cleared it with Laura yesterday."

"You did! ... I don't give a shit about some fucking brain-dead cop and his publicity-seeking wife. There was a woman raped and thrown off a roof last night," he said.

This was the rape that the paper had been waiting for since April 19 —a black victim who had been as brutalized as the jogger. I got the address from Brooklyn Sex Crimes and drove to Lincoln Place in East Flatbush, where it had happened. I started talking to residents and detectives and jotting down what everybody said. At around 11 P.M. the night before, a thirty-eight-year-old woman asked a young man for a cigarette. He grabbed her and dragged her into a building, where they were met by a second man. The men took her to the roof of the four-story building, where a third man was waiting with a knife. (A few people speculated that the woman went to the roof to turn a five-dollar trick, but I didn't have enough solid information to put that in the paper.) When she got there, the men pressed her down on the gray and white tarpaper, raped and sodomized her, and then carried her, now clad only in a blue blouse, to a parapet. They threw her like a piece of garbage down a fifty-foot air shaft.

A building resident heard the woman scream "Oh God!" as she fell, followed by a loud *whoomph,* like a piece of wood hitting the concrete.

I stood on the roof and looked down the air shaft. There was no way the three men could have expected her to live, but she had. She had landed on her right side, broken both ankles and a leg and suffered a fractured pelvis and internal injuries. About half an hour later, the resident found her whimpering like a wounded puppy but still conscious. She was taken by ambulance to Kings County Hospital, where Dr. Clarke described her wounds as "extremely volatile" because her pelvic region, a very vascular area that serves as the body's center of gravity and axis of motion, had shattered when she hit the ground.

Only one other print reporter and a camera team from the local CBS television news were at Lincoln Place when I arrived. I was disappointed to see how few reporters had showed up. The police department had done a better job than the press of treating this case with the same importance as the rape of the jogger. By early morning, the cops had flooded the street with Emergency Service Unit spotlights, and Lieutenant Kelly's sex crimes guys, who kept expecting the woman to die and homicide to take the case, were at the building almost before the woman got to the hospital. When I arrived, they'd already interviewed more than one hundred people in the neighborhood.

I needed a quote from someone, and this was a high-profile case, so I knew I'd better go to the borough commander, Fenrich, instead of Kelly. I didn't want anybody's ego out of place. I tried to get Fenrich to say something venomous about the crime, but he was not one for the tabloid quote. He was informative, precise and thorough: "It was a crime of opportunity, a forcible rape and sodomy followed by the men throwing the woman over the side of the building," he said. "This is an unusual crime, but it has happened before. It might have been because they were afraid if she lived she would identify them. We have some suspects."

I filed this story and still managed to write something about Billy Gunn's transfer to the nursing home, even if it only made page thirty. By this time, Lori's cycle of mourning had passed through shock and rage; she was progressing from grief toward recovery but was a long way from acceptance. Although I didn't see the helicopter take off from the football field, Lori's honesty and expressiveness in our phone conversation gave me plenty to write about.

Wife Fights Despair As Cop Slips Away

For Lori Gunn, the wife of a critically wounded police officer, these are the toughest of times.

Her husband, Officer William T. Gunn, was shot in the head while trying to arrest a murder suspect Jan. 20 in a Brooklyn apartment building. He remains in a coma from which doctors say he may never awake.

"He is getting skinnier and skinnier, just dwindling away," she said from her Long Island home. "When I look at him, I still see the old Billy. Otherwise, I lose all hope."

After six operations and more than three

months in the intensive care unit at Kings County Hospital, doctors say there is no more they can do for Gunn. Yesterday morning, he was taken by helicopter from Kings County to the New Medico Coma Rehabilitation Center in Waterbury, Conn.

Gunn, 28, will remain there, medical experts say, until he either recovers or a decision is made to take him off life support systems.

The former marathon runner now breathes through a respirator and is fed through a tube in his stomach. He wears jogging suits and size 14 high top sneakers [to support his swollen ankles].

In public, Lori Gunn, 30, smiles and talks easily about her tragedy. At home, she plays with her two-year-old daughter, Jennifer, and tries to make Jennifer's life as normal as possible.

It is when she is alone, she says, that she falls apart....

Three weeks ago, Lori Gunn opened a letter that came for her husband. It was from the police department.

Inside was a card that notified Gunn that he had done well on his sergeant's exam and should expect to be promoted.

The next morning, Billy Gunn's mother called me. She was furious. "Who are these doctors?" Mary Gunn said. "He is in there fighting to beat this thing and you write about taking him off life support. Never. Over my dead body. I'll go to court to fight it if it ever comes to that." As hard as I might try to understand how she was feeling, I would never be able to. Every day, she saw someone she had given life to teetering on the brink of death. Unlike Lori, who was Jewish, and could consider such a decision intellectually if not emotionally, Billy's mother was a devout Catholic and was ready to use her fists to keep away anyone who even contemplated pulling the plug.

I called Lori after her mother-in-law phoned, and told her what had happened. She was not surprised. The two were having their own problems deciding what to do with Billy.

"We both love him," Lori said. "But unfortunately we feel differently about what Billy would want."

I could hear the desperation and confusion in Lori's voice. Mary Gunn's faith was admirable, but I doubted she could will her son back to life. Legally, the decision about what to do with Billy was Lori's alone. And that was a lot of pressure for a young mother whose parents, first, and then her husband had always decided everything important in her life. She was reluctant to turn to anyone on this one. She knew it was a choice she would have to make—and live with—by herself.

My thoughts were mixed. A few months earlier, I would have thought that simply turning off the machines would take both Billy and Lori out of their misery. But since then Shawn Motayne had recovered, the jogger was improving and we'd just gotten enouraging news about Joe Cotter. So I wasn't ready to give up on Billy Gunn either. Maybe there would be a miracle for him, too, despite what the doctors said. As the helicopter lifted into the sky to take Billy to Connecticut, Lori wanted him to be at peace. Yet, as they floated through the clouds, she knew that unless she stepped in and ordered the doctors to take him off life support, that was as close to heaven as Billy would get for a long while.

After talking to Lori, I started on a follow-up piece about the woman who had been raped and thrown off the building. Detectives had arrested two young men, including sixteen-year-old Darron Decotea, who lived next door to the building where the woman was raped. Police said Decotea was involved in the rape but had not thrown the woman off the building. I interviewed his mother, Angela Decotea, a health care worker, who was sorry for her son but had no sympathy for what he'd done. "I wonder how he would like to know somebody did this to me or his sister?" she asked.

Decotea's mother also talked to Mike McAlary, who used his material to write a moving column about the dashed hopes of a woman who'd come from Trinidad to make a better life for her family. I admired his use of quotes, details and information to tell a heartrending story and told myself that over the next few days I would try to write something like that. Dr. Clarke told me that the victim had two brothers and three sisters who had visited her at the hospital. She was a divorced mother of four, including one son who was an investment consultant living in Manhattan, but she was estranged from most of her family. I wanted to do a profile of the woman in as much depth as all the pieces that had been written about the jogger. But I'd need to have either her or a family member cooperate.

On Sunday, May 7, my day off, the administrator at Kings County Hospital called me at home. If I could get there before eleven A.M., I could talk to the victim. I picked up a bouquet of yellow flowers at a nearby florist and raced to the hospital. After waiting outside the administrator's office for an hour, he and Dr. Clarke came down the hallway. I knew something was wrong. Clarke explained that the woman already had been visited by Donald Trump—who had pledged to pay her medical bill—a detective checking on her condition and a local Brooklyn minister who had appointed himself as her guardian protector. John Cardinal O'Connor was expected to bring her rosaries and spiritual counseling after mass at St. Patrick's Cathedral. The woman was tired and the Brooklyn minister had advised her to get some rest. Obviously, the archdiocese and the real estate mogul had more clout than the press.

I'd put an awful lot of energy into something that didn't come through, and still hadn't had my first cup of coffee. So, on my way home, I decided to treat myself to lunch at a café in the Park Slope section of Brooklyn. While reading the papers, I met a young dancer. She said I reminded her of someone she knew and, in an atypical attempt at trying out a line, I told her she reminded me of someone I'd like to know. She laughed and we chatted for a while. She walked me to my car and we exchanged phone numbers. I said I'd call her soon. I hadn't had a date in awhile and headed back to Manhattan thinking that maybe the trip to the hospital hadn't been a total waste.

During Esposito's absence, I tried to fill gaps he left in the paper's coverage. But I had no way to even come close. I couldn't deliver the kind of source-driven stories he had made his trademark. Instead, I tried to make sure we didn't miss anything on the sheets. I felt a lot of pressure, and woke up every morning afraid I had missed something. I believed I was only as good as my last story and whatever that story had been was never good enough.

My beeper seemed to be going off constantly. In one three-day stretch, I covered the death of the city's school chancellor, the shooting of a former city high school basketball superstar while buying crack and a Harlem kindergarten student found with an ounce of cocaine in class. All three were front-page stories. That week I truly grasped how the police beat drove the daily paper. Other crimes around that time further showed the depravity of the city. A mother dumped her newborn baby in a trash compactor. Dead. Another newborn was found in a courtyard. Dead. A groom-to-be and his best man threw a bachelor party that included a random shooting spree. One man dead. And all of this was coming at me one after the other.

In mid-May, I was having breakfast with Tom Plate at his favorite spot, the coffee shop at the Waldorf-Astoria, when a crime underscored a point he was making. We were talking about the difference between news reporting and opinion making. Just as Plate was explaining how as a young reporter he had grown tired of chasing ambulances and had switched to the editorial pages, I was beeped about a cop who had shot and killed his girlfriend and then put a bullet in his head in front of Police Headquarters.

At first, I was scared it was my friend Alex the security guard. He said he'd found salvation in God, but he was having tough times with his ex-girlfriend. As it turned out, the murder-suicide did not involve him. Who knows? Maybe the Lord was his answer. But recently he'd been getting carried away with his proselytizing.

Once he called around midnight to tell me I was destined to burn in hell unless I accepted Jesus. What did I care, I was already covering it in New York City. Alex was a great guy and all, and I was glad he had ensured his position in the hereafter. But his Jesus stuff was too much for me. We didn't talk much the rest of the year. I wasn't looking for God anymore. I was looking for another, more earthly comfort.

After work one Friday night, I went to pick up the dancer I'd met at the café in Park Slope. We were going to a movie, but we had a glass of wine at her apartment and never made it to the theater. Wynton

Marsalis was playing on her stereo and she curled her legs up next to me on the couch. I traced the sleek curves on her dancer's calves. She made the tension in my shoulders dissolve as she loosened the knot on my tie and massaged the back of my neck.

The evening was young, and everything about it promised good things. That's when my beeper went off. It was the desk. I called and got Joe Gambardello.

"What's up?" I asked, hoping it was just a question about the story I'd written that day.

"We've got an undercover shot making a buy on 116th and St. Nicholas," he said.

"How bad?"

"Pretty bad. Bad enough for you to go there and Alison to go to St. Luke's," he said.

"Shit," I mumbled as I hung up the phone.

I tried to show the dancer how upset I was about having to go. I really was. And at the same time I wasn't. As inconvenient as it was to be called away, I was starting to think of myself as a police reporter, and when big stories happened, I wanted to be called. I would have been angry if I wasn't. I apologized to the dancer and she said she understood, but I could tell from the look on her face that she didn't. How could she?

"I'll call you, okay?" I said.

"Okay," she said with a smile.

She was stretched out on the sofa as I pathetically walked out the door. *Beeperus interruptus.* If there were a police reporter's handbook, it would be referred to as an occupational hazard. Romance clearly didn't fit into my schedule. For diversion, I decided to stick with watching the Knicks and their battle through the playoffs. The cop survived the shooting. I never saw the dancer again.

I was driving through Chinatown the soggy morning of May 16, planning to pick up a few steamed pork buns, when Hap beeped. The night before, the cops had announced the third attack in a series of rapes of young girls in Brooklyn. With three rapes, the police were obliged to recognize a pattern and make a public announcement. Hap wanted me to go to Midwood, where the crimes had occurred, and find one of the girls.

The detective handling the case, Chris Jackson, told me that the rapist would follow the girls to or from school, carry them to rooftops, tape their mouths shut and rape them. The three girls were between the ages of ten and fourteen years old. Jackson was retiring soon and this would be his last case; he wanted to break this one before he left his job.

The police wouldn't release the names or addresses of the victims, so I didn't have much to go on other than the schools the girls attended. I met photographer Jeffrey Salter in the neighborhood and started following his Suzuki Samurai jeep, which added to the adventure of the pursuit. Salter's nickname was Salty Dog. He was always fun to work with, had a good way with people and could be as crazy as any crazed reporter on a story. I wanted to get this story so badly I didn't feel the rain pouring down as we waited outside each of the victims' schools. I was possessed with a single-mindedness that didn't allow room for perspective. The old bulldog had taken over; I was Jekyll turned into Hyde. Getting an interview with a child rape victim seemed like McAlary's column on Angela Decotea, the jogger case and men landing on the moon all rolled into one. No one was going to deny me this story.

"This is like swinging for the fences. It's a home run if we connect," I heard my adrenaline say to Salter.

"Let's do it," he said.

At one school, where parents were dropping their kids off and picking them up, a student said she knew the most recent rape victim. As I was explaining that we would never use the girl's name, the student, unaware of the dangers of cooperating with the media, told me what it was. We would protect the girl's privacy and not publish her name, but Salter and I could still use it to track her down. After several tries at wrong addresses, I finally reached the girl's apartment. She was home with her mother. Standing at a pay phone in the rain, running out of time before deadline, I told the girl's mother I was with the paper and asked if I could come over. She said she didn't know. I told her I'd be there in five minutes.

She came to the door, but didn't open it. I explained that I'd talked with Detective Jackson and thought a newspaper story might increase people's awareness of the case. Usually the paper included a composite sketch of the suspect with a story like this, and there was always a chance that a reader would recognize the suspect and call the cops. I didn't promise the girl's mother we'd run the sketch, but trying to convince her the story might be good for them was as gray a white lie as I ever want to tell, and I never mentioned to Jackson I'd used his name to get the interview. But it worked. The girl's mother opened the door. The dirty little secret about ethics in journalism is that at times like this, there are none.

The girl, ten years old with flowing black curls, sat on a couch in the living room and spoke in clinical, matter-of-fact detail about what happened. An honor student, she had been at the public library until four P.M. and was on her way home when a man grabbed her with his left arm, wrapped a cold right hand over her mouth and dragged her into a building. The girl chose her words carefully and tried to calm her weeping mother as she described what occurred next.

"He carried me up the stairs. When we got to the roof, he put tape on my mouth. He cut my pants off with a pair of little scissors, like the kind you trim a mustache with. Then, he raped me," she said. "It all took about ten minutes. He got up, put his pants back on and ran down the stairs. I lay there for another five minutes and then went for help."

The first place she turned for help was an apartment on the floor below the roof. She rang the buzzer and an elderly man came to the door. But the girl was too short for him to see her through the peephole, so the man didn't open the door. The girl then ran out into the street, where a woman bought her a Pepsi and called an ambulance and the police. Somebody else went to get the girl's mother.

"This man tells me, 'Your daughter is all right, but she just got raped,' " her mother said. "I was frantic and when I got to her, she was telling detectives what happened."

I wrote as fast as I could and wanted to get out of the apartment as soon as possible. I felt like an intruder and a fraud. I was also afraid that the girl's father or a detective would call and tell them to end the interview and cancel the story. Salter just sat to the side and, when the interview was over, asked if he could take a picture. He promised not to show the girl's face, and the mother consented. I couldn't believe it.

We went into the girl's room, where she had a barrel filled with stuffed animals, rock 'n' roll magazines scattered about and a dollhouse in a corner. It was a little girl's room. And also the room of a rape victim. The girl cuddled Bootsie, one of her three cats, and sat in her mother's arms with her back to the camera while Salter snapped a few shots.

When we got outside, I called Hap from a pay phone on the street. "We got the girl, the story and a picture."

"You're the best," he said.

"Coming in to write it, okay?" I said, indicating that I'd rather write the story in the main office than in the Shack.

"You got it," he said.

Back in the newsroom, Denis Hamill shook his head a few times, genuinely amazed that I'd convinced the girl's mother to give the interview. I was as nervous writing the story as I had been doing the interview. I was afraid I wouldn't get the right tone. Hamill said to lead with a description of the girl as she talked about what happened to her.

With help from Dee Murphy on the desk, I constructed a lead that had a little bit of everything: "The ten-year-old rape victim sat on the sofa in her Brooklyn home yesterday, reaching out to calm her shaken mother, who still trembled and sobbed when her daughter described the rooftop assault." The story ended with: "Yesterday . . . she said she just wanted to finish her homework and return to school so she can hand in her report on the economy and culture of Brazil. That's what she had been working on after school at the library."

The next morning, I opened the paper to page seven and became nauseous. The photograph was four by six inches but there was no composite sketch of the suspect. And without it, the story completely lacked any redeeming factor. I felt like screaming from a rooftop that I was sorry. When I walked up to DCPI, I got even dirtier looks than usual. Detective Joe McConville, one of the officers I got along with, shook his head. "Bad taste," he said. Inspector Mayronne was even blunter: "Why didn't you run the composite? There's people in Brooklyn Sex Crimes who gonna feel you used them." I could understand why and hoped Lieutenant Kelly or Detective Jackson wouldn't complain about the story.

I called Hap to find out why the sketch hadn't run and he blamed it on lack of space.

"But we had enough space to run the picture of the girl across the middle of the page," I said.

"Yeah. Even from the back, I could tell she was a cute girl. What do you think? Was she a virgin?" he said.

"Yo, that was one question I didn't ask. You probably want me to call back and ask her mother," I said. "Can we run the sketch in tomorow's paper? I'll do some kind of follow-up?"

"What would it say?"

"The schools, the fear, the cops, the neighborhood, the manhunt, the psychology of a serial child rapist. Anything that would give us an excuse to run the sketch."

"I don't want us to have the reputation of being a law-enforcement paper," Hap said.

"This has nothing to do with law enforcement; it's about civic responsibility, showing a little integrity. Doesn't any of that fit in anywhere?"

"I'll put you on the budget for a short on the psychology of a rapist. Slug it cRAPE18."

A few minutes later, Hap called back to tell me I'd put the wrong school in the profile of the little girl, and the principal was going bonkers. The paper had to run a correction. I cursed that story all morning. Not even a pat on the back from Forst—"The economy of Brazil. Nice touch"—could ease the guilt I felt over this one. When the paper's managing editor congratulated me on the story, I sneered at him, said, "Sick story," and walked away.

Following the afternoon meeting, Dee Murphy said cRAPE18 was being killed for space. So there wouldn't be a sketch the next day either. I'd given some credence to Janet Malcolm's generalizations about the press earlier in the year, but now I was beginning to really think that she was right about reporters being confidence men. I went to the Lion's Head that night, sat in a corner and drank a few too many Irish whiskeys. Instead of making the story go away, they just sent me into a world of dreams where little girls were being chased through Central Park by horrible men on bicycles.

The next week, I got a package at the office that contained a letter and a stuffed teddy bear with a red nose, brown eyes and a Christmas bow. It was from a reader, who had written "For the little girl" on the letter. "I am someone who was also hurt and did not want to go on," the letter said. "But I learned that by being happy and laughing I would hurt the person who hurt me. Every day you laugh, every day you learn, every day you plan towards a career which will help make your world better, you will be hurting that creature. Please start to fight back by knowing that you can help others through your courage. G-d help you, my dear little friend."

I called the girl's house and asked her father if he wanted me to send along the stuffed animal. I hadn't spoken with anyone in the girl's family since the article ran, but I wasn't surprised that he was livid and in no mood to talk. "She's got enough stuffed animals," he said. I tossed the teddy bear in the trunk of my car, figuring I'd find some other kid who wanted one. In the meantime, I wanted this story to disappear.

Everything would have been different if the serial rapist had been arrested, but he kept attacking girls. Eventually he shifted his activity to Queens, but he was still grabbing the girls off the street, taping their mouths, cutting off their clothes. I covered the crimes as they happened, and the paper started calling the rapist "the Schoolgirl Stalker," though the detectives more simply referred to the series as "the Tape Rapes." Chris Jackson's case folder kept getting thicker: pattern rape number four, five, six, seven. It was tormenting Jackson. The girls stared at him from the mirror while he shaved, and their screams wailed at him in his dreams. Jackson was scared he'd be haunted forever if he didn't catch the guy before he retired. He canvassed neighborhoods, cross-referenced fingerprints and pored through parole records looking for any recently released sex offenders.

The case stayed with him day and night, leaving him distracted and tired. One afternoon, Jackson fell asleep with his head in the pile of case folders on his desk. The other detectives treated him with the same kind of respect they had for any colleague going through tough times. They rounded up all the male dummies in the office, the ones used to help young rape victims explain what happened, and leaned them against Jackson's desk with their sex organs pointing at his face. The detectives took half a dozen Polaroid snapshots before he woke up. Even Jackson had to laugh.

The rapes kept happening. Eight, nine, ten, eleven, with each victim a heartbeat away from being a homicide. The faces kept coming to Jackson in the mirror. He kept hearing the little girls' screams in his sleep. He kept replaying the series in his mind, looking for clues.

Each time I thought of the girl I'd interviewed, my stomach became gnarled in knots of guilt. I tried telling myself to forget about the story, but I couldn't. Each time I opened the trunk of my car, the teddy bear poked its red nose in my face, reminding me not to pull anything like that again.

Joys of Summer

For four straight days, steady rain and cold wind brought coughs and the flu. Then almost instantly the temperature climbed to a seductive seventy-nine degrees. Despite what the calendar said, this was the official start of summer. The cover story of *Newsday*'s Sunday magazine that weekend was about the pleasures of ice cream, barbecues, swimming, boating and baseball. At one time my family enjoyed all the things the magazine story was about. We used to go to a small town in Massachusetts during the summer, where we had a big vegetable garden, and Dad joined my mother, sister and me on weekends. But this year I was staying in the city, where kids removed fire hydrant caps and sprayed the nozzles into the middle of the street, bringing relief from the sweltering heat and washing garbage into the gutter.

Sometimes a rainbow curved along the path of the water's arc, but almost as often a gunfight caused children to scatter. In 1988, the homicide rate had jumped 30 percent during the summer, and in 1989, the season arrived with a homicide in the Van Dyke Houses, a project in the Brownsville section of Brooklyn. While everyone was gathered in the courtyard, the adults gossiping and the children playing, a fight started between two teenage women over a puppy.

The little beige dog belonged to a friend of eighteen-year-old Paquita Braswell. Called Quita by her friends, she was a high school senior and hoped to get a basketball scholarship to college. She was big, strong

166

and a better ball player than a lot of the guys in the neighborhood. She also loved animals and had taken her friend's puppy, named Dawg, out to play.

Quita was teaching Dawg how to jump through the busted glass window of a project front door when fourteen-year-old Tomika Fleming was heading out of the building. Dawg jumped on Tomika's leg, and she kicked the puppy away. Quita yelled at Tomika, who told Quita she'd hang the puppy if it jumped on her again.

Things quickly escalated from what one detective called "a silly girl fight" into something much more dangerous. Tomika had a reputation for going out with men much older than she was, and Quita called her a slut. Tomika then said that Quita, who did not hide that she was a lesbian, was a lap-slapper. According to witnesses, Quita picked up the five-foot four-inch, 120-pound Tomika, pinned her to a park bench and told her not to bother her or Dawg again.

"The only reason you're fighting me is because I got a skirt on," Tomika said when she stood up. "I'll be right back. Stay here and you're one dead butch bitch."

Tomika went up to her apartment, changed into a pair of jeans and sneakers, braided her hair and came back down to the courtyard with a dagger palmed behind her right hip. The two of them squared off again. Quita knew that daggers slice through organs and do damage you didn't know had been done until you were on your last breath. They didn't look as murderous as guns but were just as deadly, and she saw the blade Tomika was hiding.

"I ain't fighting you with no knife," she said.

Tomika threw her knife to the ground. But as Quita came toward her, she picked it up again. A crowd had gathered and this time Quita, apparently feeling courageous and not wanting people to think she was afraid of the smaller girl, dared Tomika to use it.

"C'mon," she said. "Stick me. Stick me."

Tomika swung the knife up and around, winding up in an overhand motion like a pitcher, and delivered it into Quita's breast. Quita grabbed Tomika, tossed her over her shoulder and slammed her to the ground. Quita was about to pick up Tomika again to slam her once more when she stumbled back, feeling dizzy and bleeding from the mouth. As Tomika ran home to get rid of her bloodstained clothes, Quita staggered to a bench, lay down and lost consciousness. Her mother and girlfriend stood by and watched as she died.

By the time I entered the newsroom, I had everything I needed for a story; the who, what, where, when, why, and a photograph of the victim. I had "every lick and splatter," as Esposito would say. One thing was missing, though, but I didn't know it until Hap called me at the Shack the following morning.

"You did okay yesterday," he said. "But did you see the *Post*? They kicked your ass on this one."

"What did they have?" I asked bewildered.

"Take a look," he said.

I opened the *Post*. They had a picture of Dawg.

As the temperature started rising, the crimes I was covering seemed to be getting hotter, uglier and gorier. It was good to know there would always be a story to write and that it would always be on page three, five or seven in the paper the next day. But along with this sick pleasure came the creeping cynicism I'd been trying to fight. With so few good things to write about, it was hard to sustain any real optimism about the direction the city was moving.

Official New York quieted down, and with little news coming out of the mayor's race, those of us on the police beat felt a lot of pressure to fill the paper. On some days I wondered if we weren't hyping stories that wouldn't usually have gotten into print. One case in particular was about a black man accused of raping a white woman in Central Park on the morning of May 26. The suspect, a homeless ex-con from California, fit the woman's description of her attacker and the department's profile of a rapist. This had everything a tabloid could want— race, sex and crime in the park—and brought out a pack of journalists to watch detectives parade the suspect, thirty-two-year-old George Conner, to a van for the ride down to Central Booking.

"George, did you rape her?" I shouted as he passed.

"I don't even know what the woman looked like," he said as the cops stuffed him into the van.

Later that afternoon, Elaine talked to a detective who said the woman's story seemed funny. She was flighty, he said, and the cops had not been able to find the gun she said Conner had pulled on her. Something didn't seem right about this case. An inflection in Conner's voice and a shrug of his shoulder had made me doubt he was guilty. But I didn't have the courage to tell the desk, knowing this story had caused a tabloid feeding frenzy and would lead the television news that evening. When I called up the budget, cRAPE27 was on top, and in the morning a photograph of Conner, his hands cuffed behind his back, was on page three. The headline blared: RAPE IN CENTRAL PARK. Within a month, the cops let Conner go and arrested the woman for filing false charges. She admitted she had made the whole thing up. Turned out she'd faked rapes in other states in the past. Of course that story, the one exonerating George Conner, ran half the length of the original story, and it was way in the back on page thirty-eight.

I was developing a bad addiction to covering crime, and there was plenty to satisfy me. One story was so horrible that even New Yorkers shook their heads at the headline before snatching the paper off the newsstand.

Mom Throws Tot out Window

A Bronx mother, enraged because an air conditioner fell out the window, threw her 2-year-old daughter to her death five stories below, police said yesterday as they charged the woman with murder.

"The air conditioner dropped and the mother blamed it on the kids," said a police officer familiar with the case. "The mother was in an agitated emotional state and the little girl went out the window."

The girl, Rachel Sanchez, dropped between two clotheslines and landed in a puddle in an alley behind 2028 Grand Concourse near the air conditioner, neighbors said. She was taken to Bronx Lebanon Hospital, where she was pronounced dead on arrival, police said. A hospital official said Rachel died from multiple skull fractures as a result of the fall. . . .

Neighbors said that a few weeks earlier the woman had tossed two kittens and a dog out the window. Although I didn't have any pictures of the pets, I got that in the story just below the stuff about the baby being killed. The next day, more people asked why she threw out the animals than why she killed her daughter. "I don't know," I answered. "Maybe she wanted to see if kittens could fly."

Over the next few days, I kept thinking about the lady tossing pets out windows. For some reason, the spectacle of the airborne animals made me laugh, and that made me start worrying about myself. When I looked in the mirror, I saw the same expression I'd seen on Elaine and Alison a year before: tired eyes and a flat gaze. But at least it was good to know that at the bureau there were others who thought flight tests using kittens and dogs were funny. That made it easier to convince myself that I was still sane.

One person who helped me this way was Mike Koleniak, who still sat in Joe Cotter's chair. He usually got to work an hour or so before I did. I'd pick up coffee on my way in, and if nothing was breaking, we'd talk awhile before starting our days. One morning, Koleniak told me a story about his brother, a detective on the Lower East Side who'd arrested a nineteen-year-old New Jersey woman charged along with her boyfriend for killing a cabdriver. They shot him in the back of the head because they didn't want to pay the one-hundred-dollar fare. The case became known as the "Free Ride Homicide."

"While my brother was interviewing this girl in the squad room, he noticed she kept glancing at her watch. Then she asked him, 'How long is this going to be?' My brother's a polite guy, so he said, 'Oh, do you have somewhere to go?' And get this, she says, 'Well, I have school tomorrow. I have to go home and go to sleep.'

"Can you believe it!" Mike continued. "She blows away an innocent life and then wants to go home because she's afraid she will miss school in the morning!"

I was shaking my head, but Mike could see I wasn't as startled as I should have been.

"I know," he said. "It's enough to warp you."

And it was warping me and everybody else. Even one of the most efficient of the DCPI spokesmen, Lieutenant Raymond O'Donnell, appeared to be losing it. I called him one morning after he'd worked the overnight.

"Good morning. How are you?" I asked.

"Oh, we've just been sunbathing out here all night," Lieutenant O'Donnell said. "We've had baseball and football and basketball games on TV and I'm doing just hunky-dory in this glamorous city of glory and light."

"One of those nights, huh?"

"You could say that. But what can we do for you? How can we serve you?" he asked.

"Anything I should get going on this morning?"

"You've gotta be kidding. Tell me where to start. You want Brooklyn, Bronx or Queens? Or is Manhattan your preference?"

If the by-the-book, unflappable Ray O'Donnell was starting to come apart, that meant no one was safe. It seemed like the entire city had screws coming loose all over.

Around this time, a friend from high school, Tom Feuer, moved to the city. He was looking for work in sports television, and he took the bedroom my roommate had moved out of a few months back. Having Tom around, someone who'd known me when I played ball, drank beer and dated a cheerleader, made me aware of how much I'd changed. The expression on my face wasn't the only thing about my appearance that was different. For one thing, I was about twenty pounds heavier, most of which I had gained since coming to the police beat. When Tom invited me to go running with him, I was afraid I wouldn't be able to haul the gut I'd acquired up First Avenue, but Tom took it easy on me. Even though I didn't lose much weight, my mind seemed fresher because of the runs. And this was a great opportunity for Tom and me to talk about a lot of stuff, but mostly about sports and women. When the Knicks had gotten knocked out of the playoffs in the early rounds, I'd stopped reading the sports pages. Tom reminded me that batting averages and won-lost records were as important as homicide counts and clearance rates. I even started talking to him about Rose Arce, which told me I must have been interested in her a lot more than I'd been willing to admit.

Tom knew there was life beyond the criminal world of New York City, something I had apparently forgotten. He was surprised how obsessed I'd become covering the beat and could see that it was torquing my mind and wearing me down.

"Why are you doing this?" he asked one night.

I had a whole list of answers involving the ghosts of my father's past and wanting to write about the city where I was born. I could have told him that I wanted to report on issues that could affect others living here. But instead I said it was because this was my job, and to get ahead in my career I had to do it well. I sounded like a DCPI spokesman. I probably should have been more open, but I guess I didn't have it figured out enough myself to make him understand.

I was so wrapped up in the crime world that I also lost touch with my own family. My sister yelled at me when I forgot to call my dad on his birthday. She said he'd told her I didn't call and he was hurt by it. I thought of my dad sitting at home waiting for his son to call, and I felt like a jerk. Crime reporting was getting to my head and distorting my priorities, but knowing what was important and reorganizing things that way were not the same. The entire scope of my vision continued to be the story I'd be covering in the morning. And this wasn't helped any by the fact that the *News*, *Post* and *Times* would be there, too.

One friend told me she knew how to get my attention.

"I'll shoot somebody—and then I'll give you the exclusive!" she said.

Just when I thought things were as strange as they could get, I embarked on a mission of intergalactic exploration. I'd heard about a youth gang modeled on robots from a fantasy planet that stalked riders on the subways. They called themselves the Autobots and emulated Marvel comic book characters on a Saturday morning television show. These kids had been causing a lot of trouble, but the transit police refused to admit the group existed. The subways were already marred with every other kind of robber and rodent and they didn't want riders to be scared of anything else. Gangs were a symptom of problems that ran much deeper than the comic books. Many of these kids had had their families collapse, and with no support at home they did poorly in school. They turned to each other for confidence and identity.

I drove to Crown Heights, where a source had told me a group of them lived. A kid on the street directed me to a tenement where the gang hung out and where graffiti in a hallway proclaimed, AUTOBOTS ON THE MOVE. I found sixteen-year-old Dontay Smith inside a fourth-floor apartment. As if to prove he was an Autobot, he handed me a comic book with a strapping metal science-fiction figure on the cover. He opened it and pointed to the introduction, which said: "It seems you'd have to be living in Timbuktu not to know of the galaxy-spanning Autobot-Decepticon War unfolding in the pages of *The Transformers.*" According to the comic book, the Autobots and the Decepticons came from a planet called Cybertron, but Dontay told me that in real life, here on planet Earth, the Autobots' headquarters was located just a few blocks north of Grand Army Plaza. And the gang used the subways as the battleground for their epic struggle against the Decepticons, another citywide youth gang that was known to have more than one hundred core members.

This helped explain why subway crime had increased 18 percent in the first three months of the year and robberies were heading toward an all-time high. I went back to the office and wrote cGANG11. I turned in the story right on deadline, having learned that the less time editors had to mess with copy, the more quickly they read it and sent it over the link. I didn't want to have to answer questions on this story; it was too bizarre.

After I left the office that night, I glanced around the city, wondering what other King Kong, Batman and Superman impersonators were running around. Did any of the cabdrivers think they were Speed Racer? Were there dogs and cats convinced they were Snoopy or Garfield? I probably wasn't even really covering cops anymore. This had become Toon Town and it was my job to write fantasy fiction about comical intergalactic battles and transplanetary alliances.

The next morning, transit spokesman Al O'Leary called to say the story was wrong.

"Sorry about this," O'Leary said, "but your Autobots don't exist."

Just then, another line rang and I put O'Leary on hold. It was one of the Autobots.

I picked up O'Leary. "Sorry, Al. Gotta go. There's an Autobot on the other line." He must have thought I was joking. The Autobot asked if the cops were going to come after them. I told him not to worry about it because the transit brass still believed they were as real as their comic book heroes.

According to a confidential police department report I was able to get a look at, nearly a hundred gangs were flourishing from the North Bronx to South Brooklyn. Girl gangs and guy gangs, white, black, Korean and Chinese gangs, as well as multiracial bands. They had names like the Crazy Kids, Rock Steady, the Ching-A-Lings, Bitches With Attitudes, Partners In Crime and Heart to Deal With. There were also the Gucci Girls, the Albanian Boys and the Beat Down Posse. And right in the middle of the department's own report, listed alongside the Decepticons, which was regarded as the city's largest organized youth gang, were the Autobots of northeast Brooklyn and lower Manhattan. Even if the transit cops hadn't found the Autobots in their folders, the gang was right there in the secret files of the NYPD.

On a Saturday afternoon around this time, I was covering a story in Harlem about a thirty-year-old man who had killed his grandmother after she kicked him out of her apartment. He had lost his job and had been thrown out in the street by his mother. He also had a history of violence and had bounced in and out of jail and a few mental institutions. It was a terribly sad and brutal story. The murder happened in a four-story walk-up at 138th Street and Lenox Avenue, and while I was climbing the staircase to look for neighbors, I heard music coming from beneath an apartment door. It was a song by Tracy Chapman and it made me feel like I was in a movie and this was the soundtrack.

Last night I heard the screaming
Loud voices behind the wall
Another sleepless night for me
It won't do no good to call
The police
Always come late
If they come at all . . .

After I had talked to a few of the people who had been in the building when the murder happened, I met a woman on the stairwell who told me she was the young man's mother and the woman's daughter. She was on her way to the hospital to pick up her mother's things and to the precinct to help the cops hunt for her son, who had escaped. I offered her a ride to the hospital, hoping she would talk about the horror of having her son kill her mother. On our way out of the building, again I heard Tracy Chapman's voice filling the hallways.

Don't you know
 They're talkin' about a revolution
 It sounds like a whisper

While they're standing in the welfare lines
 Crying at the doorsteps of those armies of salvation
Wasting time in the unemployment lines
Sitting around waiting for a promotion

Poor people gonna rise up
And get their share
Poor people gonna rise up
And take what's theirs

I wondered about the revolution Tracy Chapman was singing about. Actually, she was singing about *talking* about a revolution. For years, I'd heard people talking about the revolution, in coffeehouses in college and in the newsroom and in bars in the city and on trains in

Mexico and Indonesia. I'd heard a lot more talking than planning. The people on the streets of New York weren't talking about a political revolution—not like the ones they teach in history books, anyway. They didn't want to overthrow their government, necessarily, but they did want to get more for themselves and their families. Moving to the beat of the sounds from under the door, I wondered if the crime happening all around us was the revolution unfolding. Maybe that's what the arming of the underclass with guns was all about. If power came from the barrel of a gun, there was plenty of that around. In a city where the politicians granted tax incentives to developers, the teenage criminals were doing their own bit to redistribute the wealth. Perhaps this was a revolution with bands of urban guerrillas like the Autobots and the Bitches With Attitudes fighting for independent material goals? Maybe this revolution was masquerading as crime.

On the drive to the hospital, I asked the woman if she'd have anything to tell her son if the police caught him.

"Just one thing," she said without pause. "Goodbye."

Before I dropped her off, she told me she had a daughter in her second year at Morgan State. I smiled, glad to know that.

Driving to Kings County Hospital on the morning of May 30, I couldn't count how many times I'd stood frustrated in the lobby, unable to get past the hospital police or public relations people. I was going there this time because a small-time drug dealer had shot and wounded his girlfriend and a cop. They'd both been taken to Kings County. When I got there, I immediately went to Dr. Kildare Clarke's office.

"You're here about the police officer," he said.

"Right. And the shooter's girlfriend."

"The officer is in intensive care, but the girlfriend is doing all right. Come on. We'll go see her."

With Clarke as my escort, all the barriers evaporated. We walked down the long, thin hallway toward the trauma and intensive care units. There were eight beds in each unit, and as we got closer I could hear the *ding-dong* of pumps monitoring the flow of IV fluids, the clicking of electrocardiogram monitors and the *whoosh-shoosh* of respirators over the muffled clamor of doctors' voices. Clarke took me right to the girlfriend's bedside.

Two gray-suited detectives questioning her must have assumed I was a visiting physician because I was with Clarke. I couldn't take notes, of course, so I had to remember everything in the room. The woman's leg was propped up on a cardboard box, her hair tinted orange and her fingernails polished hot pink. Her left knee had a bullet hole right through it and her shoulder had a graze mark. Clarke said she was one of the lucky ones. The police officer was in critical condition and surgeons were trying to repair his right lung.

I felt queasy and intrusive standing in the trauma ward. Filled to capacity, it was like a MASH unit in an urban war zone. The muscular, coal-black, naked body of a fifteen-year-old lay in one bed. His head was slightly tilted and his brown eyes stared into a curtain. Other than a tube coming out of his mouth, he looked normal, as if he'd been knocked unconscious during a football game. But he was gone on crack and was out forever. An attending physician snapped a crisp, clean white sheet over the teen's thighs, chest and face. He'd been shot in the head during a skirmish over drug turf. The doctor told a nurse the organ transplant team would arrive in a few minutes. I braced as he said that, but the nurse just quickly rolled the teen into the hall. They needed the bed. Clarke, too, could see what drugs were doing to the hospital and the surrounding neighborhood. He took me to his office on the way out and started talking about it.

"Quite a scene," he said. "Let's face it. How many in city government really care about these people?" He answered his own question: "Not a whole lot. The politicians would never end up at a place like this."

Clarke's office was the size of a walk-in closet. Two telephones kept ringing, and an old radio perched on a shelf played classic rock 'n' roll at a low volume. Clarke's desk was against a wall, and if he backed up his chair more than a foot or two, he'd bump into a hospital bed strewn with magazines, medical books, case files and insurance forms. He wore a white doctor's gown with a photo ID card on his lapel and had a stethoscope sticking out of a pocket and a beeper on his belt. A tall, thin man with a long chin and high forehead, his earth revolved around Kings County. The only indication that he had a life outside of this place was a gold bracelet with a simple KILDARE CLARKE nameplate underneath his left cuff. The bracelet was a gift from his daughter, one of three children. It would fall onto his wrist and glitter in the emergency room light when he examined a patient. Otherwise, it remained hidden.

The hospital was founded in the 1800s as an infirmary for the indigent. In 1989, it was the busiest in the city. More than 200,000 patients came to the emergency room every year, between five and six hundred a day. Yet the place was a hellhole. There were only three sinks for the eight examining rooms. The soap dispensers were empty, the equipment unsanitary and the supplies contaminated. This was in addition to careless record keeping, chronic understaffing and the swarms of flies that the doctors treated as housepets. In a way, Clarke, the man from Fat Hog Quarter, Jamaica, had never left the Third World.

"One thing we don't have back there are these horrible drug killings," he said. "In Jamaica, drugs are legal."

I couldn't stick around that morning, but I was so intrigued by Clarke's views that I asked him if we could talk more some other time.

A few days later, I returned to Kings County to see Clarke. This time, I wasn't concentrating on gathering facts for a story or racing against a deadline, so I was able to see more of what was going on. As I walked through the doors of the redbrick hospital and into the emergency room, I noticed that the hard, plastic chairs in the waiting room were filled with men and women who had nowhere else to go. Patients lined up at the intake window and asked the nurse how long they would have to wait before their number would be called. Few of them had the money or insurance to pay $995 per day for a bed, or even $88 for an emergency room visit. Some homeless people were sleeping on the floor near the candy and soda machines, and soft rock music—Linda Ronstadt's "Blue Bayou"—seeped through the heavy air.

Clarke was on the phone in his muggy office, trying to locate free beds elsewhere in the hospital. The more I spoke with Clarke, the more I respected his commitment. I often sensed that the reason Clarke could care so passionately about Kings County Hospital had a lot to do with where he was from. Because he grew up in poverty, the patients in the emergency room were not abstract figures to him. He looked them in the eye and saw himself, his parents, his brothers, sisters and children. Unlike most of the city's politicians and bureaucrats, medical school graduates and health care professionals, Clarke cared about these people because he considered himself one of them. His boyhood home had no electricity or running water. The bathroom was an outhouse. They had cows, goats and pigs. If he wanted to listen to broadcasts of cricket matches, he'd walk to his teacher's house and they'd hook a radio to a car battery.

He was connected to people for whom most of us could at best feel empathy. I couldn't know what it was like to be a member of an underclass, but Clarke helped me occasionally understand the struggle. Each morning, around the same time I got to the sheets at Police Headquarters, he received the bed census at the hospital. Mine would tell me there'd been five or six murders overnight; his would report a 2 or 3 percent availability of beds. Still, Clarke felt fresh outrage every day. Though he sometimes became angry and was often frustrated, he refused to become bitter.

While I was in his office, Clarke recalled the woman and the police officer who I'd come to see him about a few days earlier. The officer later died, and the man who killed him had committed suicide. Clarke went to the core of the problem and picked up where our conversation had left off that morning.

"Again, it's drugs, drugs, drugs," he said. Clarke had thought a lot about the ability of cops and courts to fight drugs. Every day and night of every week, victim after victim of drug violence or overdose rolled into his emergency room. They arrived by ambulance and, if they were fortunate, left on crutches or in wheelchairs instead of by hearse. "All because of this stupid drug problem," Clarke said.

To explain his frustration, he told me about a woman who had come to his hospital in December when her eighteen-year-old son was shot. She and his younger brother sobbed at his bedside. She was back six months later, this time to cry over her younger son, who had also been shot and killed over drugs. The killing would continue, Clarke said, until the government took the monetary reward out of the black-market narcotics trade by legalizing cocaine, heroin and marijuana.

"You should write about the legalization issue," he said.

I promised to check with my editors, and a few weeks later I did a story on Clarke's position on federal drug policy. Not only did I report his position but I also got responses to it from the mayor, the Brooklyn district attorney and Harlem congressman Charles Rangel, all of whom criticized Clarke. He couldn't have been happier. The week after the story ran, an editor from *The New York Times*'s Op-Ed page asked Clarke to write an opinion piece. Again he was ecstatic. Now he would have a chance to speak directly to the politicians in Washington through *The New York Times*. He phoned me almost breathless with the news. He was about to become a national spokesman for his cause.

Getting On

I stayed in touch with Kildare Clarke, and if reporters and sources can become friends, we became friends over the summer. I also began to develop a friendship with Lori Gunn. The challenges she and Clarke confronted made my work seem easy. From both of these people, I gained strength and endurance. Their lives became a ballast for my own questioning. If I found myself getting depressed or lazy, I'd think about Lori's determination to rebuild her life or Clarke's dedication to his emergency room.

In many ways, Lori's situation was the most difficult. She was terrified about being a single mother and remained tortured by Billy's condition. Her emotions were stretched, her body weak and her heart shattered. But she kept on going. Something told Lori she had too much to live for.

In early June, I saw a flier taped to a wall in DCPI announcing a softball game between a Brooklyn precinct and a local talk-radio station to raise money for the Billy Gunn Support Fund. Lori and Jennifer were getting by on Billy's base salary and a police department relief-fund check that made ends meet, but this extra money would help pay for Jennifer's babysitter, her nursery school and little things around the house. During the first weeks after Billy was shot, Lori had been inundated with friends and relatives offering help. They wouldn't let her lift a finger. The refrigerator was packed with food, the mailbox overflowed with condolence cards, and the phone rang every minute. However, around the time Billy was moved to Waterbury, all of that slowed down. The softball game would do more than bring in a few bucks (in the end it raised $1,500); it would show Lori that people still remembered Billy and cared about her.

I arrived around the second or third inning. The field was a few blocks north of Police Headquarters, and some of the top brass, including First Deputy Commissioner Richard Condon, and a couple of cops from DCPI were there. It was my day off, so I was wearing sweats and running shoes. The weather was on the cool side, but warm enough that the beer and soda concession was pretty profitable. Lori was a gracious host, greeting friends and officers and then retreating to the right-field bleachers with her parents, Mel and Sandy, and two sisters, Patty and Tammy, who went everywhere with her.

Lori was the guest of honor, but the star attraction was a Penthouse Pet of the Month who was signing seminude photographs. She sat at a table behind the backstop, and the officers lined up like they were waiting for a blockbuster movie. Lori's dad joined the Pet's line and asked her to sign a picture for Billy. She was signing so many photos for so many cops, partners, brothers, uncles, nephews and friends that I don't think she knew who this one was for. "To Billy Gunn," she wrote in loopy, cursive handwriting, "May all your dreams be sweet!"

I was standing with Lori when her father walked over with the picture. She saw it and laughed her public laugh.

"Too bad it won't do anything for him," she said.

This struck me as sad and funny. Most young wives wouldn't exactly relish their husbands' enjoying such a picture, but I could tell that Lori wished Billy could.

One of the unanswerable questions that nagged Lori was whether or not Billy could dream. During every visit in May and June, she would stare at Billy for hours and not pick up any signs. Each time she would leave not knowing if he had even known she'd been there. Billy was at the New Medico Coma Rehabilitation Center, a colonial home with columns in the front and modern technology inside. It was such an improvement over the dismal snake pit of a room Billy was in at Kings

County that it made the two-and-a-half-hour drive seem worthwhile. But even this hospital was depressing. Billy shared a room with three other men. No matter how much they cleaned, a slight smell of urine would not wash away. The room was stiflingly hot and Billy always seemed to be in a pool of sweat. Lori would spend much of her time there lovingly wiping his brow with a cold, damp cloth.

The nurses would prop Billy up in a recliner before Lori arrived. His eyes were open. He was clean shaven and appeared awake. He wore sweat suits and Nike sneakers big enough to cover his swollen feet. And instead of the Inspector Clouseau hat, a blue NYPD baseball cap covered the indentation on the right side of his head.

Each morning she visited, Lori would greet her husband.

"Hi, honey. How are you today?"

No response. Not a shake or a shiver. Then she'd tell him what day and year it was, and what the weather was like. His eyes were the same walnut brown as Jennifer's, the same eyes Lori had fallen in love with on their first date. Sometimes they darted in her direction when she walked in, but that was more likely a reaction to the shifting light than a response to Lori's arrival. When she whispered to him, those deep brown eyes met her words with a flat, blank stare.

The patient in the bed next to Billy was a middle-aged man who had overdosed on cocaine. He'd had a heart attack and was in a coma. Lori would often marvel at how tragically comic it was that a drug user and a drug fighter had ended up side by side in the same state. Billy seemed like a Cabbage Patch doll to Lori, but she still loved him like she always had. As she walked through the hallways, she wondered if Billy would live the rest of his life like the other coma patients. She couldn't think about that. She encouraged Billy to keep fighting and come back to her. She brought cassette tapes of Jennifer speaking. When Billy was shot, Jennifer knew only one word. It was from a book on animals. Billy had leaped for joy when he heard Jennifer say "turtle" for the first time. Now Lori brought him tapes of Jennifer speaking her first full sentences—"I love you, Daddy. Come home, Daddy." Each tape marked a new phase in her development. Eventually she was singing —"You are my sunshine, my only sunshine. You make me happy when skies are gray." Lori watched him closely, looking for a sign that he was aware of what was happening, but nothing changed his artificially controlled pattern of breathing or the blips on his heart monitor.

Lori tried everything to communicate with Billy. Each morning, she'd wake up wondering if he'd make his breakthrough, and each evening, she would return from Waterbury depressed that he hadn't changed at all. As she walked in the door, tired and psychologically ravaged, Jennifer would be jumping up and down. But Lori would have no energy to play. She was often short-tempered and confused. There were many days when Jennifer's babysitter, a French woman named Anna, helped Lori through what could have been endless nights. She and Lori didn't talk, but they understood each other. Lori didn't have to explain what she was thinking or how she was feeling. And Anna didn't have to ask. Anna had lost a husband, too. Her husband had died in a fire, and she knew that sometimes Lori just needed to sit down and cry.

Her emotions were raw. She'd be out shopping or driving down the expressway and everything would be fine. The next second, she'd be sobbing uncontrollably. Her tears would come without warning. Anything could trigger them. A child riding a bicycle could make her break down, because teaching Jennifer to ride a bike should have been Billy's job. A song on the car radio would remind her of a night she had shared with her husband, and she'd cry because they'd never have a night like that again. The body in the rehabilitation center was not Billy's. It was the body of a man wasting away, not the vibrant, masculine marathoner she'd married and given a daughter to. She wondered if his mind was trapped inside.

Until this happened, Lori had been like a lot of other young American women. She'd been raised by caring parents and had left the shelter of her home for a home where she was protected by her husband. She didn't resent this at all. She liked being looked after, and being dependent on others did not bother her. Lori Gunn did not consider herself a feminist. She didn't want to be a Superwoman, just a loyal daughter, good mom and loving wife. She was comfortable in those roles, never having felt any great desire to explore the trails cleared for her generation by the women's movement. She picked up copies of

Good Housekeeping and *People* magazine and got part-time secretarial work so she wouldn't have to bother Billy for money to get her nails and hair done. But with him gone, Lori started seeing things differently.

She found herself fighting the urge to lean on her parents and sisters. Except for Anna, Lori didn't have many people she felt comfortable turning to for help. Friendship, once something that meant a bunch of couples hanging out over a barbecue in the backyard, took on new meaning. A friend for Lori was someone who still called her four months after Billy was shot. As time passed, some of the people Billy had considered his closest friends on the police force were not there anymore. Oddly enough, the people who spent the most time looking after Lori and Jennifer were cops Billy hadn't really thought of as friends. Some of Lori's friends drifted off, too, and for the first time in her life, she realized that the only person she could rely on was herself.

She was beginning to have independent thoughts about a lot of things, and she was taking care of chores and family business she had never dealt with before. She had to worry about mortgage and car payments, taxes and insurance. She had to mediate problems with neighbors and deal with the press and the police department and the doctors. Lori also had to pick a preschool for Jennifer and figure out how to be a mother *and* father to the little girl. Although her parents, sisters and a few close friends, including PBA president Phil Caruso, offered advice and assistance, Lori chose to confront these new challenges alone.

Her heaviest burden was Billy. His condition remained unchanged. The drive to Waterbury and back three times a week was taking its toll. Lori started to think about her responsibility to Jennifer. She wanted her daughter to have as normal a childhood as possible, and that included a mother at home. Lori had begun to think about the unthinkable: whether she should turn off Billy's life support. They'd never discussed what they would do if one of them ended up in a coma. Billy never wanted to worry about things like that. After dinner, when Lori and her mom would talk about morbid things like where they wanted to be buried, Billy and Lori's father would sneer at them and disappear into the living room to watch a ball game. But Lori was sure that Billy, like her, believed in euthanasia. She believed he thought there were times it was better to be dead than alive. One time, when they had been watching television, Billy was shaken up by a show about a paraplegic cop. "Man, take my gun and shoot me if I'm ever like that," he had told Lori. She remembered that, but didn't know if he'd seriously considered his comment or had just been reacting emotionally.

The choice to let Billy live or die was Lori's alone. As his wife, she held the power to turn off the life support. Billy's mother felt strongly that he should be given a chance to survive. Lori promised to delay making a final decision, but she told Mary Gunn she wouldn't hold off indefinitely. Searching for guidance, Lori longed for modern science to tell her whether Billy could feel, think, see, smell, dream, do anything at all. What if all he could feel was discomfort and sense was frustration? What if he stared all day into a blinding light? She asked herself if a life feeling only pain could possibly be better than no life at all. She didn't have an answer.

Faced with these new responsibilities, Lori started feeling constantly fatigued. When she was weighed by a doctor, she couldn't believe what the scale showed. She had always felt she was a few pounds overweight, around 110 or 115 pounds on her five-foot frame. But the doctor put the big weight at 50 pounds and slid the small weight along the scale until it balanced at a total of 95 pounds. Lori hadn't weighed less than a hundred pounds since junior high school. She thought she had cancer and nearly fainted, thinking that if she died, Jennifer would have no one. The doctor did a full examination, checking her heart and lungs, taking blood and urine, but he couldn't find anything wrong with her physically. He suggested she see a therapist. Lori didn't believe in psychiatry and wanted to deal with her problems by herself. But that was difficult because she still couldn't forget about Billy. Not for a second. She tried to separate his situation from her own, but she couldn't.

"There were times I would rather have had him dead, at peace, than have seen him every day, suffering," Lori recalled. "At night, I would tell myself that if there was a good God, he would take Billy. But that wasn't going to happen. Billy would not die. His life, if that's what it was, wasn't going to amount to much. But this was Billy. This was the only husband I had, the only father Jennifer would know. If Billy had been dead, I could have said at least my husband is in heaven, at peace. But I had no solace. Nothing to make me feel good. I was consumed by my thoughts about Billy. It was torture, a nightmare. I couldn't laugh or smile. I thought I had no right to have a pleasant emotion. If I started to enjoy myself, I would hurt because Billy couldn't enjoy himself. As soon as I started feeling good things, I'd wonder if Billy was having a respiratory disorder, cramps, a cavity or an itch he couldn't scratch. If I'd be having a good day, I'd wonder if he was having a spasm."

The worst times for Lori came on special days, holidays and anniversaries. Those were terrible. Jennifer was about to turn two years old. A year earlier, Billy had decked the house with Alf, the television extraterrestrial, for her party. With him in a coma, Lori didn't know what to do. Finally she decided that Billy would want Jennifer to have a party. She hired a clown and invited all of her and Jennifer's friends. Their home in Massapequa Park was bustling with the shouts of two-year-olds, and the clown was blowing up balloons and doing magic tricks, when the white push-button phone on the kitchen wall rang. It was Mary Gunn calling from Waterbury, where she was with Billy. She had been invited to the party, but had gone to see Billy instead.

"How's the party?" Mary Gunn asked.

"It's good. The kids like the clown. How's Billy?" Lori said.

"I told him there was a party for Jennifer and a tear came out of his eye and rolled down his cheek," she said.

Lori nearly collapsed into a kitchen chair and almost dropped the phone. Guilt swept over her. She was speechless and the rest of the party was ruined. Mary Gunn couldn't know if it was really a tear or if Billy was just sweating in the overheated room. Lori couldn't figure out why her mother-in-law would say something like that. It was bad enough that Billy couldn't be at Jennifer's birthday party. Did she want to mess up the party for everybody? After hanging up the phone, Lori went off by herself to cry. She felt completely alone.

But she wasn't. Some people still cared. Certain cops had not forgotten her hardship, and there was an announcement for another benefit for Billy in a week or so. This would be a Ten-thirteen Party—a party cops threw when one of their extended family needed help—at Avanti's, a Queens disco. Hundreds of police officers, politicians and other friends and supporters would be there. Lori was nervous about going, but her mother told her to think of it like a night out, like a big family gathering. She bought a new black dress with frills on the arms, and was excited when a limousine came to pick her up. At Avanti's, she climbed out of the limo and entered the disco. At the top of the stairs, she saw an ice sculpture of Billy's shield number—1054—and she knew it wouldn't be like any night out she'd experienced before. All the television sets around the bar and over the dance floor showed pictures of Billy and his shield. Reminders of Billy were everywhere she looked, so Lori spent most of the evening in the club's backyard, out by the buffet.

As she slid swiftly through the crowd, she paused to smile politely at people she didn't know, and to say hello to ones she did. The cops all told her to hang in there, that she'd pull through, that Billy had their prayers and that he was a great guy. Rudy Giuliani, Republican candidate for mayor, had already come, asked for their support, promised safer streets and more cops if he was elected, and had gone. Lori appreciated everything being done for her, but felt distant at her own party. Without Billy, she didn't belong to this society of cops and their girlfriends and wives. Lori didn't feel she fit in with the cop crowd anymore. She didn't know where she belonged.

At the end of the party, a police officer reached into a bucket of raffle tickets and pulled out a number. "It's Lori Gunn's ticket," he said. "She won the television set!" Lori shuffled up to the officer; her expression, like her black, frilly dress, showed muted enthusiasm—potentially full of excitement but still hostage to sadness. She said thanks and half an hour later went home in the limousine with a new Sony by her side.

The next morning, Lori couldn't figure out where to put the new television. She already had televisions in the living room and bedroom and didn't have room on her kitchen counter. Then she realized she didn't care about the television set. She didn't need another one. Her life was static. She remembered what the doctor had said and thought he may have been right, that what she really needed was therapy.

                    *   *   *

On June 15, I wrote about the rape and murder of a twenty-four-year-old mother killed while her three young children cowered in their bedroom listening to her screams. The woman's husband, Tony Serrano, Sr., the super in the building, was out when the crime occurred. But I interviewed him the next morning, and he gave me a Bronx phone number where his seven-year-old son, Tony Jr., who'd been home during the attack, was staying with relatives. As I left the apartment, wondering whether or not I had the nerve to call the boy, I saw Rose Arce.

"Hey," Rose shouted from her Toyota Tercel. "What are you doing here?"

"I was going to ask you the same thing," I said.

"I'd never tell."

"Well, Tony Serrano is inside if you need him."

"Junior or senior?"

"Senior."

"No problem," she said and drove off.

If Rose knew about Tony Jr., she might've talked to him. I didn't really want to prod a seven-year-old into telling me the details of his mother's vicious murder. But it wouldn't look good if the *News* had Tony Jr., and we didn't. Besides, no way, no how, no chance was I going to let Rose Marie Arce beat me on another story. I called the Bronx number from a pay phone on East 97th Street and interviewed Tony Jr. He said he'd been scared because the man threatened to cut his mother's eyes out before he killed her. He seemed rather detached from what he was recounting, as if he didn't yet understand what had happened, but I still felt uncomfortable and wanted to hang up as soon as possible.

In the morning I saw that Rose had talked to the kid as well. Our stories were gruesome and horrible—classic tabloid copy. We both reported the murder through Tony Jr.'s recollection. The structure, facts and quotes we used were nearly identical.

Beginning the first day we'd crossed paths in Queens nearly a year before, Rose and I had been living parallel lives. We wrote about the same crimes, shared similar ambitions and knew a lot of the same people. And ever since the Inner Circle dinner I'd become increasingly intrigued by her. The morning the schools' chancellor died in May, she'd showed up at the hospital at four-thirty A.M.; as usual, a few minutes before I arrived. My attraction then was undoubtedly a combination of the early hour, the tight black pants she wore and her consistent ability to write, report and look better than me. But it had grown.

On the morning that the Serrano stories were in the paper, I was pleased when Rose called me at the Shack. We agreed that even among the rest of the butchery, this story was exceptionally wicked. I wanted to talk to her longer, maybe even ask her out, but the timing wasn't right. I had to run out on a story.

Two weeks later, after working late the first Saturday in July, I wasn't tired and didn't feel like going back to an empty apartment. I kept driving downtown, and ended up outside the Lion's Head. It seemed as good a place as any to find some company. I had finished my second front-page story in a row that evening, yet I had a bizarre sensation that if this was all there was to it, I was wasting my time in journalism. I'd always wanted to prove to myself, and to my father, that I could make it as a reporter in New York. Now that I was getting there, it seemed a hollow goal.

I pulled up a bar stool and ordered a Diet Coke. I'd never been a drinker like the guys Pete Hamill wrote about. Alcohol only sharpened whatever emotion I was feeling, and I didn't want to get any deeper into the loathsome self-pity I was already in. I was having some kind of mini–existential crisis. I had spent too much time during the past year trying to cultivate sources and not enough building friendships. Some of that was the nature of the police beat, but it also reflected my own twisted priorities. I was getting good at writing news stories, but the rest of my life was not happening.

I ordered another soda when a song I'd picked—"Handle with Care," a tortured love ballad by the Traveling Wilburys—came on the jukebox, and Rose, Elaine Rivera, Julie Shpiesel and a fourth woman I didn't know walked past on the street. They peered through the window to see if there was anybody inside they wanted to hang out with, then kept going west on Christopher Street. I turned back to my soda. About ten minutes later, they came back and invited me to join them in the dining room. We ordered a pitcher of Prior Dark, and Rose and Elaine started telling stories about wild murders they'd covered before moving to New York. Neither of the two other women were police reporters, and they giggled nervously as Rose and Elaine exchanged tales about the sordid things they'd seen and written about. Their excitement refreshed my interest in reporting.

Around two A.M., Julie and the other woman went home, and Rose, Elaine and I headed across the street to a restaurant called Boxers for more beer and some food. As we crossed Sheridan Square, Rose bought a copy of the early edition of the Sunday *Daily News*. She had a big follow-up story on the Serrano murder in the paper. She'd talked to Tony Serrano, Sr., again, and written about how the rape and murder of his wife had caused the family to split apart. When she finished reading her story, she passed it to Elaine, who sat between us, and Elaine passed it to me. Actually, I was more interested in Snoopy and *Doonesbury*, but I read Rose's story and saw that she had done a really good job. She seemed pleased with it.

Occasionally Rose and I glanced at each other over the guacamole and chips. It was an uncomfortable glance. We'd spent so much time competing, it was odd being friends. Elaine thought the two of us made a pretty funny pair.

"Look at the both of you. You have so much energy," she said. "You're like little kids. You compete against each other for other papers and soon Rose will come to *Newsday* and you'll compete at the same paper. You guys are exactly alike, reading the Sunday paper on a Saturday night. Ah, how can I keep up with all your youthfulness?"

The week before, Elaine had celebrated her thirtieth birthday with a party she proclaimed to be the start of La Revolución. So she wasn't really the ancient warrior she made herself out to be. Still, Rose and I smiled at her comment, knowing that in some ways she was probably right.

At three A.M., Elaine and I took Rose to her car. As we walked up Barrow Street, where my parents had lived when I was born, Elaine was ogling at the opulence of the Village and talking disdainfully about the people who lived there. I could have taken this personally, but I really wanted Elaine and Rose to accept me as a friend, so I didn't say anything about my past. I didn't want them to think I was a spoiled rich kid.

Rose was driving back to her apartment in Brooklyn and I was heading uptown, so I offered Elaine a lift. When I dropped her at her apartment I must have said something inappropriately formal, like "Have a nice day tomorrow and I'll see you at work next week." Whatever it was, it must have seemed defensive.

Elaine looked at me and said, "Don't put up so many walls. People will still like you."

"Okay, I'll try not to," I said.

"All right. G'night," she said.

Elaine's comment had surprised me. I drove home that night hoping that she, and especially Rose, who I was more taken with than ever, really would like me.

On July 5, I got a phone call with some of the best news I'd heard in awhile. It was about the ten-year-old girl who had been raped seven weeks earlier, the one I'd interviewed in her apartment. The story had continued to bother me because the paper had run it without the sketch of the suspect. Chris Jackson, the detective who had been tormented by the case, reached me at home.

"We got him!" he said.

I called the desk, drove straight to the Brooklyn Sex Crimes Unit and rode with Jackson and a few other detectives to Brooklyn Central Booking. A *Newsday* photographer met us there. Even though Jackson had been up all night and needed a shave, he was smiling bigger than I'd ever seen. The photographer snapped a picture as Jackson walked the suspect, Lorenzo Rojas, a twenty-one-year-old busboy with a wife and four-year-old daughter in his native Mexico, to his cell. I slapped Jackson on the back and went to the Shack to write the story.

To get rid of the anxiety I'd felt since the original story, I had to write this one through the eyes of the ten-year-old victim. I called her home and talked to her father. He was still angry about the first article, but was relieved that for now the trauma for his daughter, his wife and himself was over. We talked for a while and he told me how his daughter had reacted when she heard about the arrest. I wrote this story with more self-assurance than the first one, and with a hook neither the *Post* nor the *News* could match: the little girl.

The story ran on page three the next day with a thumbnail head shot of the suspect. "Seven weeks after she was raped on a rooftop, a 10-year-old girl picked a 21-year-old busboy out of a lineup and identified him as the man who attacked her on her way home from the library after school, police said yesterday," it began. I closed the story with a quote from Jackson. "I just wish we'd gotten to him before some of the girls were raped," Jackson said. He added: "This case is closed, except for the paper work."

I couldn't imagine a greater sound than the jail guard slamming the cell door on Lorenzo Rojas. The *clank* of the steel bars made me want to thrust a fist in the air. Three weeks later, Chris Jackson retired after twenty years on the police force.

It was rare that a story closed itself out like that. Most of the time, they lingered in my mind, each murder running into the next one. To the victims, these were among the most traumatic moments of their lives, but to a cop reporter, they came one on top of another without reaching any kind of resolution. In fact, these stories were starting to seem so routine that I felt a need to broaden the range of what I was writing about, to include some of the other law enforcement agencies in town. One afternoon, I was talking to Esposito, who was still on his book leave, and he offered to put me in touch with a few of his sources at the Drug Enforcement Administration. He suggested that I call the press office at the DEA, which occasionally hooked up reporters with good stories. And when I did, they asked if I wanted to cover a big drug raid.

On July 21, I went with a local television reporter to meet the head of the regional DEA office, Robert Stutman, at the agency's midtown offices at four o'clock in the morning. It was still dark when I got to West 57th Street. Agents' cars were parked all over the place, and inside, more than a hundred agents and cops, including Iron Mike and his team of Bronx narcotics officers, had gathered in a conference room. They were preparing to hit twenty-one locations simultaneously throughout the city and parts of New Jersey. The drug raid was named "Operation Bury the Hatchet," after the drug kingpin Roberto "the Hatchet" Rodriguez, who led a $200-million-a-year operation connected to the Cali and Medellín cartels in Colombia.

Before we went out, one of the lead agents and the DEA press liaison, Bob Strang, briefed us on the case. They gave us background information and also tried to put their own spin on the story. "It's a snapshot of coke and crack distribution in New York," Strang said, describing the case as "a dynamite conspiracy that starts in Colombia and ends up on the streets of Upper Manhattan and the South Bronx." I jotted down an organization chart of the drug ring and quotes the DEA had picked up on wire taps that caught the Hatchet making deals and planning parties.

Shortly after five A.M., we rolled out of midtown Manhattan in a convoy of cars, and an hour later we were outside the Hatchet's suburban New Jersey home. A call went over the DEA scanner to all twenty-one units: "Take 'em down now.... Take 'em down now." I stood on the perimeter as the cops and agents, wearing bulletproof vests and carrying automatic weapons and shotguns, slammed a battering ram through the Hatchet's front door. There was a thunderstorm of noise, with cops shouting *"Policia! Policia!"* and guns swirling everywhere and lights flashing. The raid had happened so fast I didn't have time to be scared. I followed the agents up a flight of stairs into the Hatchet's bedroom, where they pulled him out of bed. He was lying naked with his girlfriend.

"Hope we didn't interrupt anything," one agent said in Spanish as he dragged the Hatchet from the peach-colored sheets.

My blood was still pumping when I called the desk after we returned to Manhattan. That kind of reporting was thrilling and action-packed, but it was like eating puffed wheat: nothing was left when you were done chewing. The access from the DEA had made the story possible, but there was a trade-off. It was understood from the beginning that Stutman would be quoted high up in both the lead story and the sidebar I wrote on the operation. There was also an unspoken agreement that as long as he liked the coverage, the door would remain open for me at the DEA. A lot of top-level source-based reporting was done this way, with reporters and sources engaging in highly charged, potentially volatile relationships. These alliances held as long as they remained mutually beneficial. That, of course, meant they were governed by Italian Rules, in which anything went as long as you didn't get caught. And then we'd work something out.

I was in the Shack one Saturday morning when Rose came down to fill in for the *Daily News*'s regular Saturday cop reporter. She couldn't get into their office because the door was locked and she didn't have a key. So she asked if she could use our phone to call the sheets in to her desk. There wasn't much going on and I didn't mind company— even if it was the competition. Besides, if I kept Rose in my sights, she couldn't beat me on any more stories.

I'd bought some little explosive "pops" at the candy store when I picked up the papers that morning. The pops were a few grams of powder wrapped like a tiny Hershey's kiss in white paper that exploded when you threw them against a wall. I tossed them at Rose while she tried to read the sheets to her editors. I guess that was part of the mating dance. Whatever, I showed I had a playful side beneath the company ties, and by the end of the day, I was no longer too intimidated to ask her out to dinner.

On our first date, we went to Chinatown. While I waited for her outside the restaurant, I knew this would be different from the time we ended up out drinking with Elaine, and I was nervous about how the evening would go. During dinner, Rose told me that she was taking care of a friend's cat, who did nothing all day and night but play hockey with everything in her apartment. After our second date—dinner at an Italian place—she invited me home to meet this furry gray terror. We watched Oscar paw-handle a bottle cap from the kitchen to the bedroom and back. Then we flipped on the eleven o'clock news.

This seemed to set a pattern for our dates. Somehow there always seemed to be an underlying news-story theme. One night, we met at Tompkins Square Park. A year after the riot, there were still protesters who wanted the park left open for the homeless to sleep in at night, and residents who said it was populated mostly by drug dealers and anarchists. The mayor had ordered the cops to evict anyone who put up a tent or laid down a mattress. Strolling around the park, Rose and I bumped into a police inspector I knew. He'd recently been put in charge of the local precinct and I'd done a profile of him the week before.

"I don't believe I know your wife," he said.

"I'm not his wife," Rose quickly said. "We're colleagues."

"And friends," I added.

Rose and I walked from the park toward the East River, past the tenements and through the Lower East Side projects. Already I knew that Rose was a mature, aggressive and resourceful reporter, but that night, when she kneeled down to speak to a group of project kids and played with their dolls and jacks, I saw another side of her that made my whole insides smile. She was smart, pretty and passionate, and with the sunset reflecting on the water, I didn't want to be anywhere else with anyone else. I hadn't felt that in a long while.

Rose and I didn't look like we belonged together. You never would have matched us if we'd been standing on opposite sides of a room. She was tall, dark and attractive, of Peruvian parents. I was a blond, blue-eyed Jew of average height. She still teased me about my Brooks Brothers button-downs, gray flannels and power ties. She even felt that now she could do something about this, and bought me a couple of hip white shirts, patterned ties and slacks with buttons in the front. I appreciated her attempts to make me look more presentable, and we were getting along great.

But it wasn't long before something happened that could have abruptly ended our relationship. Rose accepted an offer to come to *Newsday*. This concerned me much more than it did her. I'd never dated anyone at the office, but Rose's attitude was that we spent so much time at work we should make it as interesting as possible. I was cautious but liked her too much to end things over this. We decided to keep our relationship a secret from everyone except a few close friends. It certainly added an intrigue and an intimacy to the newsroom. On Rose's last day at the *News*, she invited me to a goodbye party her colleagues were throwing for her at the Lion's Head. Afterward we went back to my apartment.

"Thanks for sharing your special evening with me," I said before going to sleep.

"That sounds like a line from a book," she said.

"Naw, I heard it in a movie," I told her. But it was really from my heart.

The next week, she started at *Newsday*. I was jealous as hell when she made a big splash with a front-page byline just ten days after coming to the paper. But we were having fun.

Things were going pretty well at the Shack, too. Everyone was in good spirits over the report we got on Joe Cotter's condition. He was out of his coma and undergoing intensive rehabilitation. It looked like he might pull through. He'd told his wife he wanted to come back to work, but that didn't seem likely. Still, Anne Murray and Ginny Byrne reminded us that Joe usually kept his word.

The big news was that Hap Hairston left *Newsday* to become a city editor at the *Daily News*. He'd gotten me into some things I wasn't proud of, like the story on the ten-year-old rape victim, but he'd also taught me a lot. The day Hap left, a few of us took him out for a drink. After a round or two, I bought him a Stoli on the rocks and pressed it into his gut. He dropped his heavy arm on my shoulder.

"You're the best," he said.

"No, you're better," I said.

"You know why I like you? Because you're one bad motherfucker."

"If I'm bad, you're the worst. Just when I'm starting to learn stuff from you, you take off like this."

"Come to the *News*," he said.

"Are you serious?" I asked, but Hap was pulled away before he could answer. I didn't think much of it; I thought he was just kidding around.

A few weeks later, I saw Hap at the Lion's Head and he asked again if I'd come to the *News*. This time, he offered more money than I was getting at *Newsday*. I was flattered but didn't say anything about it to my editors. They found out anyway because Hap apparently told Denis

Hamill, who told Forst. When Forst asked me about Hap's offer, I proceeded with a combination of arrogance and innocence that almost resulted in a really dumb decision.

At first, I was intrigued by this newspaper poker that the big names in the business played. Forst and the paper's associate publisher, Steven Isenberg, who knew me from the editorial pages, took me out to dinner. Within seconds, Isenberg started talking to Forst as if I weren't at the table.

"Mitch can't be serious," he said.

"Maybe he is," Forst said.

"He can't be that stupid," Isenberg said.

Forst shrugged and Isenberg listed a thousand and one reasons, from corporate strength to personal loyalty, why I'd be a moron to leave.

I showed up at the newsroom early the next morning. Tom Curran was the only editor around.

"How was dinner?" he asked.

"I didn't even make it through the salad," I said.

Curran laughed. "It's good to be put in your place sometimes."

Around this time, I was beginning to have second thoughts about being a reporter. I was kicking around the idea of doing some kind of youth services work or going back to school to become an architect and build better public housing. I was disappointed by the lack of altruism in reporting. But the more I thought about these other professions, the more limited each one seemed. Plus, I had to pay the rent. If I was going to stay a reporter, I wanted to cover the community I was living in. *Newsday* gave more space and had a greater commitment to writing about New York than the other papers in town. For the time being, I was in the right place.

The paper had become the center of my world. I was dating Rose and reporting stories six, sometimes seven, days a week. I couldn't imagine there was anything else, but I tried to remember what my sister had said about not calling my father, and did manage to spend some time with him. One night, we went to see Spike Lee's movie *Do the Right Thing*, about the territoriality and distrust between blacks and whites in the city. The whites in the film were Italians from Bensonhurst, a little northwest of Sheepshead Bay in Brooklyn. This was my dad's old neighborhood, which was a mix of Italians and Jews when he was growing up there. The movie's storyline was familiar to him. When he was a kid, one man on his block was always battling with the neighbors. If the man got really angry he'd make his ultimate threat: "Fuck all of you. I'm going to move—and sell my house to a nigger."

After the movie, Dad and I went to dinner near the theater. We were eating pasta and salad and having some wine when I told him I'd decided journalism and life were the same thing. He smiled and kind of shook his head in a way that reminded me he'd been around both a few decades longer than I had.

"Don't you think so?" I said.

"Well, no," he said. "Life is life and journalism is journalism. And sometimes the two intersect."

My father was usually able to set me straight about things. But no sooner had I heard what he said than once again I was buried in the newspaper, working on a series *Newsday* was preparing on crime. This finally gave us a chance to use the 1988 homicide list I'd fought to obtain earlier in the year. Due to Alice McGillion's successful stalling, the list lacked the dramatic impact it had once promised. But it filled four full pages of the August 14 edition and still graphically displayed the number of lives the city had lost in a single year.

As a whole, the crime series was comprehensive. A dozen reporters worked on a week-long package of articles that covered everything from hit men to police-response time. My story, which was about the crime stats and the leather-bound ledger where the detectives logged the names of victims, and the list of these names ran on the same day. The story's headline was chilling: HOMICIDE, THEY WROTE, 1,896 TIMES. The series also included a poll showing that half of all New Yorkers, around four million people, had been victims of crime in the previous twelve months. The poll also said what anyone following the police beat already knew: The majority of the people asked (69 percent) considered crime, including the drug plague, to be the city's biggest problem.

Poverty, housing, the environment, political corruption, unemployment, AIDS and economic development were so far behind that they hardly made the graph.

As the mayoral primaries drew near, Rudy Giuliani seemed to have the Republican nomination locked up. The Democratic candidates, engaged in a close battle fraught with the issue of race, pulled out all the stops. They spent money, called in favors and shook hands until their palms were raw. Would Ed Koch be able to stay in City Hall for a fourth term? Or could David Dinkins become New York's first black mayor? All the politics and strategy, speeches and advertising, however, would mean nothing. The election would come down to a gun in the hand of a troubled eighteen-year-old on a hot summer night in Brooklyn.

"They Got the Wrong Niggers"

I fumbled to answer the phone when it rang early on the morning of August 24. I'd been out late the night before, but managed a "Hello" that sounded like I'd been awake for hours. Still, I didn't recognize the voice on the other end. Denis Hamill never called me at home.

"Yeah, it's Denis," he said. "What do you make of this thing with the baseball bats?"

"What thing?" I said.

"A black kid was killed over here last night."

"How'd it happen?"

"On *Good Day New York*, they're saying a mob of whites chased him and his friends and one of the whites pulled a gun and popped him a coupla times," he said.

"Christ, this sounds like another Howard Beach," I said, recalling the 1986 crime in which a gang of whites chased a black teen in front of a speeding car.

"Sounds worse," he said. "We oughta get out there."

"All right," I said. "I'll drive."

I frantically dialed the public information office. Before I could call any editors, I had to find out what was happening from the cops' end. A police spokesman read the sheet with the same detached precision as always. I scribbled everything he said on the back of an overdue Con Edison bill.

The incident happened at nine twenty-five P.M. in front of 2007 Bay Ridge Avenue. The victim, sixteen-year-old Yusuf Hawkins, lived at 485 Hegeman Avenue in East New York. He was shot twice in the chest. Hawkins was with three friends, all black, and they'd gone to Bensonhurst to look at a used car. After getting off the N train at 20th Avenue and 64th Street, they walked to Bay Ridge Avenue, also known as 69th Street, stopping in a candy store on the way. Just as they turned left onto Bay Ridge Avenue, they were surrounded by at least ten whites who were wielding baseball bats. After the shots were fired, the whites fled. Police later found seven bats and four .32-caliber shell casings near the scene.

I tried to ask if there were any suspects or a motive, but the spokesman cut me off. He said all further questions would be handled by the mayor and the police commissioner at a press conference.

Hamill came right down when I buzzed his intercom. He was wearing a white sport jacket with a spiral notebook sticking out of a front pocket. I still wasn't sure how the neighborhoods fit together in Brooklyn, so Hamill, who'd been born and raised there, directed me south along Ocean Avenue and right toward the 62nd Precinct in Bensonhurst. It was a few minutes after nine A.M. and the press conference would start in less than half an hour.

The precinct was in a state of pre-press-conference chaos when we arrived. Print, television and radio reporters checked their watches and waited. A cop was guarding the staircase to the second-floor squad room, where detectives were interviewing suspects and witnesses. A blue and white police department barrier protected the precinct captain's office, which was serving as a kind of situation room for top brass. All the ranking bosses had been there since dawn.

Inside the office, First Deputy Commissioner Condon was conferring with Spin Doctor McGillion. The Democratic primary was less than three weeks away, and Koch's chances could be helped or hurt by his handling of a major murder case. The facts were clear. Yusuf Hawkins and his friends were completely innocent. All they wanted was to see a used car. But in a city divided into islands by the color of a person's skin, blacks were not safe in Bensonhurst. The mayor's advisers suggested he be straightforward. But nobody had to tell Koch he should step carefully around the circumstances of the murder.

When Koch entered the briefing room, I noticed a terrifying calm on his face. He stood coolly beside his black police commissioner as Ward paraphrased what I'd already written on the Con Ed bill. Then Ward added an element we hadn't heard yet. He said the killing was a case of mistaken identity stemming from an argument between a pair of ex-lovers. A young white man had been jilted by his girlfriend for a black guy. She was having an eighteenth birthday party and had invited the new man in her life. Her ex-boyfriend and his buddies staked out the party, waiting for this guy to arrive with his friends. When they saw a group of blacks coming, they ambushed the wrong group. Four neighborhood youths were likely to be arrested that afternoon, Ward said, and others later. Detectives were still looking for the gunman and hadn't recovered the .32-caliber pistol.

Koch and Ward steered around the race issue, until Hamill raised the question. A hush came over the room. Ward replied that, yes, racial slurs had been used. When a reporter asked what slurs, Ward said he couldn't get into that.

Balding, jowly and maybe thirty pounds heavier than when he was first elected in 1977 by a coalition of Jews, minorities, ethnic whites and liberals, Koch was still Fast Eddie, perhaps the quickest tongue in American politics. And he went into maximum constituency control. Of course it was a horrible crime, he said, but not everybody in Bensonhurst was a racist. He blamed the murder on a small group of hoodlums.

Perhaps I was hatching my own political conspiracy theory, but the press conference seemed like an attempt to take the color out of the case. They wanted to present it as a bitter love triangle, not a race killing. When Ward likened the case to the Broadway musical *West Side Story*, I felt the subtle hand of Alice McGillion. But it was too late to rein in the truth. Once the presser ended, a reporter asked McGillion if she'd confirm the slur used was "nigger." She did, and that started a stampede for the phones.

I felt a brief surge of anger and the same bitterness and frustration that overcame me when I wrote about Juan Iribarren. My heart ripped and my gut seethed. But unlike the slashing in January, this story gave way to my professional instincts; there was a lot of reporting to do.

The line at the precinct pay phone was six deep, so I ran down the station-house steps and called the desk from the street. By eleven A.M., a team of *Newsday* reporters had been deployed throughout East New York and Bensonhurst, and the daily budget had eight story slugs pertaining to the killing. Laura Durkin told me to go with Hamill to the scene.

Fifteen minutes later, we were standing at the intersection of 68th Street and 20th Avenue. Already there was a feeling that this murder was a modern-day lynching and that Bensonhurst, because of its attempts to keep out blacks, could be Little Rock's Central High School or Bull Conner's Birmingham. Almost all the reporters and television crews there were focusing on the neighborhood as well as the facts of the case. But I couldn't think about that yet. I had to get the who, what, where, when and why. There'd be time for analysis later.

A columnist-reporter team from the *Daily News* had been on the street for a couple of hours already. Mike McAlary and Mark Kriegel had half of their notebooks filled. Luckily I had time to catch up. I asked McAlary where the girl lived, but he said he'd worked to get that information and wasn't just handing it over.

"Why did you go to the press conference? You can get the official stuff later. Richie could've told you that," he said.

I nodded and turned back to the street. I didn't know any of the cops or detectives on the case, or for that matter, anybody in the neighborhood. I had to keep my ears and eyes open, make like a human vacuum cleaner and inhale whatever I could.

The center of the action stretched along 20th Avenue from 68th Street to Bay Ridge Avenue. A rust-colored circle of dried blood remained by the maple tree in front of 2007 Bay Ridge Avenue where Hawkins had fallen. Faint yellow chalk lines marked the spots where detectives had found other evidence. One of the people on the corner told me the girl who'd had the birthday party was named Gina Feliciano. She lived with her mother and older sister in an apartment over a candy store on the southeast corner of 68th Street and 20th Avenue.

The guy she had once been involved with was Keith Mondello. He was eighteen years old and lived over a dental supply store across 20th Avenue from Gina. Their bedroom windows faced each other, and though they were lovers at one time, now they were sworn enemies.

The candy store beneath Gina's window, Snacks & Candy, was the hangout for the 68th Street Boys, as Mondello and his friends called themselves. The store had a big white sign with its name in peppermint-striped red and white lettering above huge plate-glass windows. It was a regular neighborhood hangout that sold newspapers, cigarettes, magazines, overnight film developing and ice cream. Its owner, a man named Sal, whom everyone called Squid because of a tattoo on his arm, was the Pied Piper of the local youth.

Many of the 68th Street Boys had just finished high school or, as Mondello had, dropped out. Now they found themselves in a tight employment market, and were discovering that life beyond Bensonhurst was no block party. The municipal and industrial jobs that had sustained their fathers were not as available as they had once been. Some of the kids worked part-time. They all lived at home and were rooted in their closely knit community.

A black Mercury Cougar parked in front of the candy store was cordoned off by police and surrounded by reporters, cops and locals. It was Keith Mondello's car. The cops had already talked to him and would charge him and three others in connection with the killing that afternoon. They didn't think he'd been the shooter. But they believed the murder weapon was in the trunk of the car, and they needed a warrant to open it. The car attracted a crowd all day and remained in front of Snacks & Candy until police towed it away at dusk. It was like a temporary landmark, and anyone from the neighborhood who came near the Cougar had the opportunity to become an unofficial Voice of Bensonhurst. The same faces filled television screens and print reporters' notebooks with babble about blacks not having any business being there in the first place. The pay phone next to the candy store turned into a landline for reporters.

The first post-press-conference development came out of the police department. The cops released the names of the three other 68th Street Boys who'd been arrested, and the desk beeped me with this information. I was also asked to get bios to go along with the names of the teens. After half a dozen people said they didn't know "nuthin' 'bout nobody," two young men agreed to talk about their friends.

Hamill and I walked with them to a pizzeria a few blocks down 20th Avenue. They were eighteen or nineteen years old, both about five ten and slim, with smart-alecky faces. One was wearing a pair of shorts and a SAL'S AUTO WRECKING AND SALVAGE T-shirt, the other faded jeans and a white T-shirt. Both had silver-dollar-size crosses dangling from their necks. For the price of a couple of slices of pizza, they broke the neighborhood code of silence and became our best local sources of the day.

"You're not going to use our real names," the one in the faded jeans said when we sat at an outside table.

"How could we?" I said. "You haven't told us your names. How 'bout we call you Victor and your friend Tony?"

"Yeah," Victor said. "Okay, what do you want to know?"

"Why'd this happen?" Hamill asked.

"Everybody's saying it was between Keith and Gina, and it's sorta like that. But-choo gotta know Gina," Tony said.

"What about her?" I asked.

"She's from 'round heah, but don't act like it. Nobody would want to hang 'round wid her . . ."

"Except Keith?"

"Naw. That's bullshit that they went out. They mighta, a few years ago, have hung out or sumpthin', but there wasn't nuthin' between them. Keith's got a girlfriend. He could have whatever girl he wanted," Tony said.

"Yeah, Keith don't mess wid no Gina," Victor said. "She's a hoowah."

"A what?" I asked.

"A hoowah—W-H-O-R-E—hoowah," Tony explained. "She's also a crackhead. She's been on drugs since junior high school. Dropped out of Utrecht in ninth or tenth grade and spends all her time going down Coney," Tony said.

"Did she go down there a lot?" Hamill asked, picking up Tony's reference to Coney Island.

"She's down there almost every night—you know, spandex pants and halter tops, tight boots and miniskirts," Victor said. "Sometimes she takes off Friday night and you don't see her until she's red-eyed and wasted on Monday."

"Yeah," said Tony.

I couldn't confirm that any of these accusations against Gina were true; in fact, they could have easily just been the result of anger over Gina's having spurned their friend.

"This whole thing's 'cause of *her*," Victor said, avoiding her name like it was a curse.

"How's that?" Hamill asked.

"She wanted to get back at Keith," Victor continued. "She told him her nigger and spic friends were coming to her party. Said they'd be packin' and people was going to get hurt. Keith just put the word out they was comin'."

"What about the other guys?" I asked.

"These kids were just there," Tony said.

"You know them?"

"Yeah," he said, touching his cross. "Everybody knows everybody here. We played roller hockey together and everything. These are good kids."

"They were into rap, too," Victor said. "They was playin' it all the time. How could people say this was racial when they listened to dat music?"

Victor and Tony said we should look for a tall black guy who'd be around later. They said his name was Joe and he could tell us what happened.

"If it wasn't racial, what was it?" Hamill asked.

"It would've been nuthin'," Tony said. "Except . . ."

"Except what?" I asked.

"Except they got the wrong niggers," he said.

Hamill and I had heard enough. And "Victor" and "Tony" were about done with their pizza. No matter what these guys said, it was clear to me that the killing was motivated by racism. Still, I wondered if some of the guys in the pack had just been dragged along. Were all of them racist killers? Or could some of them have been regular teens in the wrong place at the wrong time?

Walking back to 68th Street, I remembered when I was fourteen years old and had gone out with a group after an eighth grade school play. A man in a corner grocery store had sold me a Miller High Life, and I was feeling tough. When we were by the piers in the West Village, someone said, "Let's go roll some fags." This scared me, and one of the guys I was with showed me a knife. He said he'd take care of things if there was trouble. Ten minutes later, he climbed into a parked van and sat behind the wheel pretending to drive. Soon a man walked up and told him to get out. The boy emerged with the knife in his hand. The man raised a trash-can cover as a shield, but the boy slipped the knife into the man's gut. I remember seeing him run down the street, gripping his stomach, bleeding on an orange T-shirt. The man died at St. Vincent's Hospital and detectives were all over the school for days.

A headline in *The Villager*, a local paper, said a youth gang had murdered this man, who, I recall, someone later said was gay. If the comment by the piers had ever been reported, this could have turned into a major bias crime. I'd only been with these guys to have a good time, but the cops wouldn't have seen it that way. Within a few days, they arrested the guy who stabbed the man and were looking for the rest of us. Eventually I talked to my father, and we went to the Sixth Precinct with a lawyer. I gave a statement and that was it. Yet thirteen years later, in Bensonhurst, I understood how the press could paint with a deceptively broad stroke. Though Yusuf Hawkins's murder was hateful, I wondered if all the kids in the white mob had actually been out for blood.

Gina, too, remained a mystery. Who was she? What had her role been? Had she instigated this or was she an innocent victim? Gina's mother was Italian and her father, killed in Vietnam before she was born, was Puerto Rican. She was an outcast, alienated from the local in-crowd that Keith Mondello epitomized. "I'm a lunatic, he's a psychopath," she would later tell *New York* magazine. "We just hit—collided like two fists." But little was known about her that first morning. The only thing that was certain was that for some reason, Gina and Keith had it in for each other.

While Hamill and I walked around, we began to suck up bits and pieces of the events that immediately preceded the shooting. At around seven-thirty P.M., Mondello and more than thirty friends armed with bats and at least one gun began waiting outside Gina's building. Less than two hours later, they would see the blacks coming.

Down the street from Gina's building, the subway station's stone-washed outer walls were covered with graffiti; short green awnings gave it the look of a multitiered pagoda. The station was a gateway between Bensonhurst and the rest of the city. The only way outsiders could rise into the middle of the neighborhood was through the turnstiles or the steel-barred flywheel of the 64th Street station.

For nearly a century, Bensonhurst had represented the heart of white, working-class New York. Near the water and not far from the city, it grew into an isolated community of well-kept one- and two-family homes and apartment buildings. In the forties, Bensonhurst was about 50 percent Jewish and 50 percent Italian. Half a century later, most of the Jews had moved to Manhattan or Long Island. Many of the Italians—even the successful ones—had stayed. By 1989, they numbered about 150,000 and gave Bensonhurst the highest concentration of Italians in the city. These people took pride in how little they had changed over the years. Men drank espresso in cafés along the avenues and spoke in their native dialects. Mothers made tomato sauce with family recipes and bought sausage from their favorite local pork stores. Instead of leaving, families bought bigger houses down the block or fixed up the ones they owned. With new aluminum siding, cramped porches, ostentatious steel gates and satellite dishes too large for roofs, the houses, like their inhabitants, suffered from too much inbreeding.

When Yusuf Hawkins, Luther Sylvester, Claude Stanford and Troy Banner emerged from the subway, they didn't know how different this neighborhood was from the one they'd left. Earlier that evening, they'd been at a friend's house watching movies on a VCR. The first was *The Naked Gun*, a slapstick comedy starring Leslie Nielsen as a blissfully unaware detective. Then they slipped in *Mississippi Burning*, a film based on the murders of civil rights activists Schwerner, Goodman and Chaney outside of Philadelphia, Mississippi, in 1964. They didn't watch all of it, because Banner was excited about buying a car. They weren't too concerned about missing the end of the film because, as one would later say, they knew how things had been back then in the Deep South. And the owner of the car had told Banner he could see it as soon as he wanted. Besides, the film was history, and the car, a long, blue Pontiac, was waiting for them in the future.

After getting on the wrong train, they had to double back to make the connection to the N train. During the ride they joked and played around. Yusuf, a gangly youth who was usually quiet and meditative, was in a surprisingly animated mood. He shadowboxed with his reflection in the subway car windows and boasted that someday he'd beat Mike Tyson. When the four friends arrived in Bensonhurst around ten past nine, they were not sure which way to turn onto 20th Avenue. Nor did they know that Bay Ridge Avenue, which they were looking for, was also named 69th Street. The only other time they'd been to Bensonhurst was for a school leadership convention. They were apparently unaware of the neighborhood's reputation as being "closed."

They were a little disoriented, but not afraid, when they reached the street. They stepped into a dimly lit, narrow newsstand next to the station that sold English and Italian newspapers, soda and snacks. Before continuing their trek, Hawkins bought some candy and Claude Stanford picked up some film and batteries he had promised he'd get for his mother.

As Hamill and I retraced the teens' steps, we found a woman who'd seen the four when they got off the train. The woman said they'd asked where Bay Ridge Avenue was and continued along 20th Avenue. Troy Banner had a piece of paper with the car owner's address in his pocket, and Hawkins was holding a Snickers bar he'd bought at the newsstand. They passed the huge tan façade of P.S. 205 and, as they walked by 68th Street, didn't notice the youths in front of Snacks & Candy. It couldn't have taken them more than ten minutes to walk the four blocks.

By the time the first wave of whites had turned from 68th Street onto 20th Avenue, the blacks were three quarters of a block away. Two young women were standing by a pay telephone with their small children at the corner of 69th Street and 20th Avenue, and Banner stopped to admire one of the toddlers. He told his three friends to wait while he checked street addresses to see which way they should turn. The first address he saw was 2007 Bay Ridge Avenue. Before he had a chance to check the next one, the whites had the four blacks surrounded.

At first, the blacks thought the whites were chasing someone else. They tried to move aside, but the whites didn't leave. They raised the bats above their heads, threatening to swing. Luther Sylvester was up against a tree. Banner and Stanford were surrounded. Hawkins was backing up, looking for a way out, when one of the whites shoved him against the building's wooden door. "Is this him?" one of the whites asked, wondering if Hawkins was Gina's new man. Another apparently didn't care. "Fuck the bats!" he screamed. "I'm gonna shoot the nigger!" Then: *Pop! Pop! Pop! Pop!*

A blue flash sparked from the gun with each shot. Two of the 71-grain, 7.65-millimeter-diameter bullets ripped through Hawkins's white windbreaker at a speed of 950 feet per second. One tore into his heart. He stumbled fifteen feet to his left and collapsed facedown across the roots of the small maple tree near the curb. As the whites sprinted off, throwing bats over fences and behind woodsheds, Hawkins bled on the sidewalk.

The next morning, I stared at the spot where Hawkins had fallen and tried to re-create the scene in my head. I tried to imagine the terror in the eyes of the blacks and the panic among the whites. I envisioned bats flying and people screaming. Police officers inside a mobile command vehicle on the corner were not speaking to anybody, and the suspects and witnesses were under guard or under wraps. Just when there didn't seem to be anybody around who knew anything else, I noticed a woman talking to reporters in a vestibule across 20th Avenue.

Speaking in broken Spanish, thirty-two-year-old Elizabeth Galarza said she'd heard the shots from her apartment and had come running to the fallen teenager. He was breathing when she got to him. His feet, in white sneakers, were splayed to the sides. He was lying on his back.

"Don't worry, baby. Take small breaths," Galarza said she told him. She had been trained as a nurse and didn't want Hawkins to waste energy talking.

"I checked his pulse," she said. "He was still alive. I screamed at the crowd to call 911, get paramedics immediately. I held the boy's hand. He stared up at me. His eyes were terrified. I told him not to try to talk. I told him that I was going to ask him some questions. I told him to blink once for yes and twice for no. I asked him if he understood. He blinked once meaning he did. I asked him if he was scared. He blinked once. I asked him if he felt like he was slipping away. He blinked once. I asked him if he knew why he had been shot. He blinked twice. Then his eyes closed . . . and his hand went limp."

He'd been clutching the Snickers bar.

The first two paramedics, unit No. 32-Young from Maimonides Medical Center, got a call for a "teenager in traumatic cardiac arrest," according to the Emergency Medical Services spokeswoman. They arrived within five minutes of the shooting, but there was hardly any life left in his body. Yusuf Hawkins was pronounced dead at Maimonides Medical Center at nine forty-eight P.M.

When I called Laura that afternoon from a pay phone by the subway station, I gave her the quotes from Galarza and a brief outline of what we had from Tony and Victor. I expected her to tell me to hustle back to the office to write.

"Okay, Snookie," she said when I finished. "That's good stuff. You'll dump to Drury and stay out there. There are supposed to be some politicians coming to the neighborhood later. So keep an eye out for them. Okay?"

It wasn't okay. I almost dropped the phone. I didn't know what to say. I wanted to come back and write the main story. I had it all in my head—a feel for the streets, a vision of where Hawkins had died. I'd taken notes on Snacks & Candy and made a map of where everything had happened. Back in March, I hadn't minded when they assigned Drury to write the story about Robert Machate's killing. I wasn't good enough then. But I'd had five months to develop my reporting, improve my writing, and learn to control my emotions on deadline. I thought I'd proved I could handle the pressure.

"Are you sure?" I asked Laura.

"Yeah. We need somebody out there," she said.

"There's not much happening."

"Something could happen."

"Is there anyone else to cover?" I asked.

"No, Snookie."

Don't Snookie me, I was thinking as I slammed the receiver.

Drury was their star and their best hard-news, deadline writer. But I couldn't understand how he could write the story without having been to the scene. After a summer of racing from one grisly homicide to another, which apparently I was good enough to do, I'd been reduced to Drury's legman on the biggest story of the year. In the editors' view, it was just a case of getting their best wordsmith on the keyboard. In retrospect, I can see why they wanted him putting the feeds together, but that afternoon I took it as a real vote of no confidence. I told Hamill I had to stay in the neighborhood and couldn't give him a ride back to the office.

"Who said?" he asked.

"The fucking desk," I told him.

Cursing editors was common practice among reporters, but I'd tried to maintain good relations with them. More often than not, they saved me from myself on stories. But there I was, cursing them all.

By the time I got back to 68th Street, the cops had towed the Mercury Cougar and opened the trunk. They found two bats, a mop handle, a table leg and a *Playboy* magazine. But no gun. A tall black guy stood out amid the all-white crowd on the corner. He was the guy Victor and Tony had called Joe. His full name was Russell Joseph Gibbons. I told him I was a reporter and that I'd heard about him from some of his friends.

"They said you've lived here awhile," I said.

"Yeah," he said. His tone was clipped. "What do you want to know?"

"Well, how long have you known these guys?"

"Long time," he said.

"How long?"

"I've lived here seventeen years. I'm twenty-one now. That's nearly my whole life," he said. "I've never had any problems here."

Gibbons said that growing up in Bensonhurst was like growing up in any community. It was what he knew. He said he was sorry Hawkins had been killed, but he couldn't forget that the guys arrested for the murder were his friends. After ten minutes, he said he had to get home for dinner.

"Okay," I said. "I'll see you around."

Twenty-four hours after Hawkins had been killed, everything was dark and quiet, except for the glow from the police command van. Before returning to Manhattan, I stopped by the 62nd Precinct. The detectives assigned to the case had gone out or gone home. I was about to leave when a large black man with James Brown–styled hair entered the precinct.

There was no mistaking Al Sharpton. The Reverend Al, a self-styled activist, was a swagger in a sweat suit with a Martin Luther King, Jr., medallion hanging around his neck. The most quotable man in the city after Ed Koch, Sharpton was an opportunist, but he had a following. Although he'd earned some respect during the Howard Beach case, Sharpton had lost a lot of credibility when he stood beside Tawana Brawley, a black teenager who faked her own racially motivated rape and perpetrated a highly publicized hoax in 1987. Sharpton probably viewed the Bensonhurst murder as a way to restore his reputation. After securing the trust of Yusuf Hawkins's mother and father that afternoon, Sharpton was looking for the other three blacks. But Banner, Sylvester and Stanford had already left the precinct by then.

A few hours earlier, the white suspects had been taken out of the station house, too. They'd been walked down the steps wearing bullet-proof vests to protect them from potential snipers. Now Sharpton was on the phone in the precinct lobby organizing a march into the heart of whiteness for Saturday afternoon.

On my way home, I stopped at the Lion's Head. I was so into the story that I whisked past the book covers and met Rose, who was at a table with Hap Hairston and a bunch of reporters, in the back. Before going to my apartment, Rose and I bumped into McAlary and Kriegel and traded tales about who we'd interviewed and where we thought the story was moving. By the next morning, names none of us had heard before—Gina Feliciano, Keith Mondello and especially Yusuf Hawkins—were rolling off our tongues like they were people we'd known all our lives.

*   *   *

While I was in the shower at seven A.M. on Friday morning, my phone rang and my beeper went off at the same time. I wanted to get a jump on the second day of the Bensonhurst coverage, but Gina Feliciano beat me out of bed. Dripping a trail of soapy water across the floor, I grabbed the phone and the beeper. Tom Curran was using both to find me.

"How fast can you get to Bensonhurst?" he asked.

"Why?"

"Gina's been coming to her window all morning. We have a photographer there, but we need a reporter," he said.

"I'm on my way," I said, hanging up the receiver and reaching for a shirt. Despite Rose's efforts to improve my wardrobe, it had been months since I'd taken any time picking my clothes before work. I had a new fashion style. I'd put on anything that was clean.

I screeched my car to a stop on 20th Avenue, across from P.S. 205. Jon Naso, the *Newsday* photographer, was standing across from Gina's apartment. He said she'd stuck her head out the window earlier and returned a few times, but hadn't been back for the last half hour. I wished I'd camped out there overnight. A quote from Gina, no matter what she said, would have led the paper. She was the most talked-about woman in the city. I rang her doorbell, but a detective's voice told me to go away.

"I just want to ask her if there's anything she wants to say," I called through the door.

"She doesn't want to say anything," the detective said.

"Can I ask her that?"

"No!" he said. "Now, I'm being a gentleman about this. You understand. She's not speaking to or seeing anybody."

That's when I heard a beep from my belt, but the number it registered was my home phone. I called and Rose answered.

"Guess what?" she said. "You're wearing my beeper."

"Uh-oh!"

In the morning flurry, I'd grabbed her beeper off the night table. Rose was assigned to cover Hawkins's family that day. So whenever the desk beeped her, they were going to get me in Bensonhurst. And when they beeped me, they'd get her in East New York. So much for keeping our newsroom romance a secret.

Without an interview with Gina, I had to come up with another angle for a story. There were a few Hispanic and Asian residents in the predominantly white neighborhood, but Russell Gibbons and his family were the only blacks living there. The only other blacks who came around were cheap labor and home-care workers. It seemed ironic that the whites would let blacks take care of their elderly parents but not play with their children. A story on blacks in Bensonhurst seemed like a natural second-day feature. I interviewed a few black workers and went to Gibbons's apartment. He was not home, but his mother, Diane Gibbons, invited me in. I could tell from the way she talked that she was scared for her son. He may have thought he fit in, but when she first heard about the shooting, she thought some crazy local who didn't know Russell had killed him by mistake. I filled my notebook with quotes from Diane Gibbons and the blacks who came, from Bedford Stuyvesant and East Flatbush to care for the elderly or distribute fliers for a local printing shop.

Before I could go ahead with this story, I had to run it by the desk. The editors liked the story enough to put it on the budget, but Gina was still the tabloid focus for the day. The cops were taking her from her apartment to view the suspects in a lineup at a nearby precinct, and the press waited in front of her building, eager to get a look at her. But when Gina came out, she had her head shrouded by a zippered blue sweatshirt and all we could see was a pair of knobby knees beneath a short skirt. Two detectives guided her into an unmarked car, and her mother, Phyliss D'Agatta, quickly followed.

"How is she? How's Gina doing?" a reporter asked her mother.

"She's all right," D'Agatta said, and decided that this was the time to set one thing straight: "My daughter doesn't date blacks. Maybe Hispanics. But no blacks."

After Gina and her mother drove off in the car, Murray Kempton, a *Newsday* columnist, and I headed to the same pizza place that Hamill and I had gone to the day before. The seventy-one-year-old Kempton had spent a large part of his career writing for the *Post*, and had covered stories like this one before. He suggested a twist to this case that at first seemed unlikely but later turned out to be true. "The saddest part of this whole episode is that poor Gina's new boyfriend probably wasn't coming to the party at all," Kempton said. He ordered a cappuccino at the pizzeria and started talking about the neighborhood. "No matter how much societies change, places like this are still built on people's fear of outsiders," he said. Then he remembered something he'd heard at a conference in the 1950s: "A neighborhood is a place where when you leave it you get beat up." That would be the lead for his next column.

The afternoon was warm, and Bensonhurst seemed to be returning to normal. Teenagers were blasting Public Enemy's "Fight the Power," from the soundtrack of Spike Lee's movie *Do the Right Thing*, and old ladies were sitting on stoops as kids played basketball in the P.S. 205 schoolyard.

When Kempton and I returned to the newsroom, the place was on high energy. One of the clerks, Renee Lolya, said that only she really knew how to talk to Gina. Renee had grown up with a lot of Ginas. "You just gotta see her and say, 'Like, Gina, what kinda mousse you usin' in your hair? You know, I got dis gel the other day and it really holds.' She'll get into it." According to Renee's theory about Gina, city history was being made because an eighteen-year-old girl didn't have the right kind of hair mousse. If she had, Renee explained, maybe Keith would have liked her more and none of this would have happened.

I banged out a few quotes to send Drury, who was again writing the main story, and was working on my sidebar about the blacks of Bensonhurst when everyone in the newsroom gathered to watch Chief of Detectives Robert Colangelo on the evening news. The Dapper Detective, his pompadour coiffed and combed, was appealing for help locating a nineteen-year-old named Joseph (Joey) Fama of 71st Street and 18th Avenue, Bensonhurst. Fama was wanted for questioning in connection with Hawkins's murder. It was obvious from Colangelo's urgency that Fama was the suspected gunman.

"To Me, He Sounded Like an American"

Nothing short of a Soviet bombing of Rockefeller Center would have taken Bensonhurst off the front page. The first five suspects were to be arraigned on Saturday afternoon, and Al Sharpton's march through the neighborhood was scheduled for the same time. I was assigned to cover the arraignment, which meant going to the courthouse and calling the desk with the specific charges, the bail agreements, courtroom color and quotes from prosecutors and defense lawyers. I didn't have to be there for a few hours so I was relaxing in the Shack with a cup of coffee when the phone rang.

"I'm trying to reach the reporter Mitch Gelman," the caller said.

"What is it concerning?" I asked.

"Yeah, tell him it's Russell Gibbons trying to get him."

I put my hand over the receiver and tried to figure out what he was calling about. "One second," I said. I was pretty sure he was furious, because the article in that morning's paper had referred to him as "a white-black."

"Russell. What's up? The story okay?"

"Yeah," he said. "I'm not calling about that. I saw it. I know you talked to my mother. It's okay. Can you come out here?"

He said he wanted to give me some information about his best friend, Charles Stressler, who had been arrested and charged along with the other suspects in Hawkins's murder. Gibbons asked me if I

218

would mention in whatever story I wrote that Stressler's best friend was a black. After checking with the Saturday editor, Barbara Strauch, I figured I had enough time to see Gibbons and still make the arraignment. We met at a McDonald's where Stressler used to work. Gibbons wanted a letter from the manager for Stressler's lawyer to use as a character reference in court. I ordered some food, and we sat down at a table near a window.

"So, what did you want to tell me?" I said.

"All right, but you can't put my name on this," he said.

I nodded.

"I was there. Until right before everyone left to go around the corner after the four kids, I was with them," he said.

I nearly choked on my iced tea. What was a black man doing in the middle of a white mob?

"Have you talked to the cops yet?"

"Not yet."

Then he told me who had been there, where they were standing, why they had come together, when they got to the candy store and what they did. His story filled in a lot of blanks.

It all really started two nights before the shooting. Late Monday, some black and Hispanic guys Gina knew had a run-in with Keith Mondello and his crowd. Gina's friends had been playing music and goofing off in front of her building. Mondello told them to leave, and after a little argument, they took off. The next morning, Gina told Sal the Squid that her friends were coming to her party. She boasted that they were bringing guns and trouble. Squid told Keith, and the two of them got the word out that Gina's spics and niggers hadn't had enough.

Keith reached out not only to the guys from around the schoolyard, but also to some people he knew over on 18th Avenue. Gibbons explained that that group, which included Joey Fama, was older and tougher than the 68th Street Boys. According to neighborhood lore, the young thugs from 18th Avenue were connected to the Mafia. Gibbons also said that he and Stressler brought the bats, but the guys from 18th Avenue brought the gun.

At around seven-thirty P.M., people started arriving at the candy store. Strains of "Happy Birthday" filtered down from Gina's apartment, but it didn't seem like much of a party. Only Gina, her mother, an aunt and a few others were there. Gina's own sister, Dawn, refused to go. And the only black or Hispanic within blocks was Gibbons—but he was with the mob on the street. The crowd outside numbered between thirty and forty, at least four times the size of the party.

Gina poked her head out the window a few times to mock Keith and his friends. "You're all jealous because the black guys are getting all the white meat," she said at one point. Later she shouted, "It's because you guys are all dead in bed."

The guys outside postured, flexing their muscles and stretching their teenage egos. "It was like a bunch of guys with bats," Gibbons said. "We passed them around, took practice swings. Guys were calling back and forth stuff like, 'Hey, let me see your bat!' And, 'Yeah, that's a good bat.' We were just hanging out, talking, you know, like always, about sports, women, cars. The usual stuff." Then around nine o'clock the mood of the crowd changed. Their adrenaline had peaked and they began to doubt that Gina's friends would show.

"It got to the point where a bunch of us didn't think anyone was coming," Gibbons said. "We thought it was just Gina trying to make fools of us. So, we all started to drift off. I had my radio with me and was sitting on some steps in the schoolyard when somebody yelled from the corner." Everyone heard the call: "They're here!" one of the whites screamed. "They're here!"

Stressler ran with the others while Gibbons gave his radio to a woman sitting on a stoop. But before Gibbons could put the radio down and join the mob, the shots had already been fired. Though Gibbons didn't actually see what happened, Stressler later told him that the whites, responding to the rallying cry, moved around the corner in waves. Mondello and Fama were in the first wave; more followed. The four blacks had just turned onto Bay Ridge Avenue. And as some of the whites tried to figure out if they were actually Gina's friends, Gibbons said, Fama stepped forward and fired his pistol four times. The black kid fell and the white guys split.

"That's it," Gibbons said.

I'd been listening to him for about twenty-five minutes, waiting for him to finish his story before I asked the most obvious question: What was a black man doing with group of white guys who intended to beat up a group of black guys for coming into their neighborhood?

"They're my friends," he answered. "We do everything together. If I was in trouble, Keith Mondello would come to my side. I was there for him."

"But what about beating up the blacks?"

"I didn't think anything would happen. It usually doesn't. Words are exchanged, then the whole thing is over," he said. "It's more a macho thing than anything else. Except this time, one idiot had a gun. I didn't do anything in the end."

Maybe so, but I still suggested he get a lawyer because I knew that the cops would be coming to talk to him soon. So would the defense lawyers for the whites, who would do whatever they could to try to make this seem like less of a race crime than a battle over turf.

When I dropped Gibbons off at his house, three guys from the neighborhood rode by on bicycles.

"How's it going?" one of them called out.

"All right," Gibbons said.

"You want to go riding?"

"Not today."

"All right, hang in there," one said.

"We love you, man," said another.

Of all the insane parts of the Bensonhurst story, this one seemed the craziest—and I couldn't even report it, because I'd promised Gibbons I wouldn't use his name. He was a product of Bensonhurst, and liked it there even though there were people in his neighborhood who would kill someone just for having his skin color. In order to be accepted in his neighborhood, Gibbons had become like the people there, even if that meant taking part in a mob that was waiting to attack others of his race. That couldn't have been what Martin Luther King meant when he prayed that someday "the sons of former slaves and the sons of former slave owners will be able to sit down together at the table of brotherhood." When Gibbons later testified at the murder trial, Yusuf Hawkins's father would call him "an Oreo cookie in a tall glass of milk." Gibbons had known that was true for a long time, including the morning we talked.

I drove straight from Gibbons's house to the Brooklyn courtroom, where five young men were arraigned for allegedly participating in the racial slaying of Yusuf Hawkins. And at the march on 20th Avenue, whites confronted hundreds of blacks with racist chants and obscene gestures.

The TV footage from 20th Avenue was almost unbelievable. The marchers, including Hawkins's brothers, Freddy and Amir, and Al Sharpton, were accosted with shameless disdain. The whites contorted their faces into bestial glares and held signs saying JOEY FAMA FOR MAYOR. They chanted, "Niggers go home," and waved watermelons at the marchers. The white thugs spat at Hawkins's brothers and flashed middle fingers at Sharpton. The only reason mass violence didn't break out was the presence of hundreds of cops in riot helmets and on motorcycles. The white protesters seemed wild with hatred, terror and fury, as well as confusion and certainty. I wondered what they were afraid of. I figured retaliation was inevitable, and half-expected a posse in a Nissan Maxima to roll down 20th Avenue and paint the neighborhood red with 9-mm. automatics. I went to bed that Saturday night waiting to be called out to cover the first shots of a citywide race war.

Sunday and Monday were supposed to be my days off, but I couldn't pull myself away from the story. On Sunday, I put some notes on Gina into the city queue. The next day, I wanted to try something a little off the news and called Spike Lee to see if he would go to Bensonhurst. He was from Brooklyn, his movies were about Brooklyn, and his production company, 40 Acres and a Mule, was located in the borough's Fort Greene section. A receptionist said that Lee answered only those press inquiries that came in writing. I called the paper and asked a clerk to fax a note to Lee, and a few minutes later, he called.

When I arrived at his office, he was in his studio, an airy room with high ceilings, posters from his movies, drafting tables and an old movie projector. He was wearing a T-shirt with a saxophone and the word SOUL across the front, and he had a diamond stud in his left ear. Lee was already considered one of the country's hottest moviemakers, as well as a leading voice of black America. When he noticed that I was taking notes on what he was wearing, he paused in our conversation and said, "They're Nikes—Air Jordans."

Lee hadn't actually said he'd go to Bensonhurst with me when we spoke on the phone, so I had to talk him into it. But first I had to win his trust. I figured the only way to do that was to start talking. Twenty minutes later, we were stuck in traffic discussing *Do the Right Thing* on the Brooklyn-Queens Expressway.

"When we shot the film in the summer of 'eighty-eight, I wasn't being a fortune-teller," he said. "To me, it was a cautionary tale. It was not science fiction. It's what's happening today. In the movie, Sal, Vito and Pino were from Bensonhurst. I did not choose them to be from Bensonhurst by mistake."

We pulled up near Gina's building, and Lee's expression changed. When we were in his studio and driving to the neighborhood, he showed his anger, but once out of the car, he hid his emotions as a crowd of white teens quickly formed around him. The same people who had yelled at the black marchers on Saturday were now asking Lee for his autograph.

"Yo, Spike!" they called out. "You're the best."

As we walked along 20th Avenue, we were followed by a dozen or so of Lee's fans. As he smelled the aroma from the loaves of Italian bread in the Realmuto Bakery, he told the entourage behind us to leave him alone, but they wouldn't go away.

"It's like in the movie," he said. "To them, I'm a celebrity. They all listen to rap and watch basketball. They want me to bring Michael Jordan and Flavor Flav down. We're not niggers to them; we're athletes, rappers, movie stars."

Then he turned onto Bay Ridge Avenue and stood at the corner where the four blacks had been surrounded. His eyes panned from the corner to the maple tree and back again. He walked to the spot where Hawkins had fallen, and his goatee appeared to stretch with the tension that crossed his lips.

"If I wasn't a celebrity, I'd just be another nigger to them," he said. "They wouldn't have recognized me at night. They coulda shot me, too, just like they shot Yusuf Hawkins."

By then, a few photographers and other reporters had picked up our trail.

"Where'd they go after they shot Yusuf?" he asked.

"They scattered," I said.

We walked to 21st Avenue and back to 68th Street, past Russell Gibbons's house and the P.S. 205 schoolyard. A group of white teens were talking to *Newsday* reporter Rita Giordano and listening to Public Enemy when they noticed him. "Yo, Spike!" one said. "Spike! How ya doing? How 'bout an autograph?" Lee glanced sharply at the group, and the teenagers were taken aback. "Why's Spike so mad?" one asked Giordano.

"The sad thing," he said as we approached Snacks & Candy, "is they don't even know they're racists."

Lee crossed to the front of the school and began talking to an Italian man who didn't recognize him. Lee didn't waste time with introductions and both of them started talking about what was on their minds.

"It didn't have to be Yusuf. They were standing there waiting to kill the first black who came by," Lee said.

"It could have happened to a white guy, too. It was about Gina," the Italian said.

"I say it was because they were pissed off because it was like, 'This black stud is boning my ex-girlfriend,' " Lee said. "I don't buy this we-all-get-along-around-here crap."

"These are good kids. Not racists," the Italian said.

"What about the watermelons the other day?"

"That was stupid."

"The chanting?"

"That was stupid."

"And the bullet?"

"Yeah," the Italian said. "That was stupid, too."

"Yeah," Lee said.

Before we left, he dashed into a Korean greengrocer located under Keith Mondello's window. He bought a cranberry seltzer from the same place the whites had grabbed watermelons over the weekend. Kids surrounded him as he walked to the car. One told him he was great, and another said he should come back and make a movie there. When we were in the car, a teenage critic stepped from the crowd.

"It's like, Spike, a word of advice. I think you're a really good director, and I love your movies. But you can't act," he said. "Don't put yourself in your movies. Next time, stick to directing."

Lee looked to one of the critic's friends. "Do you know this guy?" he asked. "Do me a favor. Take a baseball bat and hit him with it. On the skull."

That was my exit line. I pressed the gas and we were gone.

I got more reaction to that article than any other I'd ever written. The national wires picked it up, and *Life* magazine picked one of Lee's comments from the article as a quote of the year. The story even got slammed in "Apple Sauce," the *Daily News*'s gossip column, which called it "a publicity stunt." Then the *News* asked Lee to write a guest column about Bensonhurst and teased it on their front page. This led my friends on our gossip page, "Inside New York," to run an item headlined: ONE PAPER'S 'STUNT,' ANOTHER'S 'EXCLUSIVE.'

On Tuesday, everyone seemed focused on the search for Joey Fama. There'd been rumors that Fama, whose family had mob ties, was already hiding out in some small town in southern Italy, but local cops insisted he hadn't gone far. They pressured the Brooklyn mob to help find Fama, turning up the heat on the gangsters and pledging not to let up until the kid was found. Inspector Richard Mayronne offered his own theory. "This guy's not too high on the food chain," he said. "He'll turn up."

The next afternoon, Yusuf Hawkins was buried. Thousands of mourners went to his funeral at a small brick church next to a weedy lot in the Brownsville section of Brooklyn. A few hundred people crowded into the sanctuary, and the rest listened to the service from outside. Security was provided by black Muslims wearing white shirts and red bow ties. Police sharpshooters were staked out on surrounding rooftops to protect the perimeter. When Koch arrived, he was greeted with shouts of "Koch must go!" and the masses mocked Police Commissioner Ben Ward, calling him "Uncle Ben." They also booed Governor Mario Cuomo, an Italian who'd failed to go to Bensonhurst in person to address the bigotry. Republican mayoral candidate Rudolph Giuliani tried to sneak in quietly, but he, too, was jeered. "First time out here, Rudy?" someone yelled.

Yusuf Hawkins had become a martyr in a war of racial politics. Prior to the service, Jesse Jackson reportedly stood over his body as it lay in a silver casket and predicted, "This boy is going to make David Dinkins mayor." Moses Stewart, Hawkins's father, was incensed that Jackson saw his son's death in political terms. But there was no getting around the fact that the funeral, which was attended by the Reverend Louis Farrakhan of the Nation of Islam, Al Sharpton, Spike Lee and an avalanche of local black leaders, had become the most monumental stop on David Dinkins's campaign trail.

Dinkins refused to blame his opponent Ed Koch for the city's racial problems, at least not directly. "I have never charged any single individual with responsibility for this tragic circumstance, or for Howard Beach or other sad occasions like this," he said after the funeral. "But I have said the tone is set on high, and I believe that."

The primary elections were less than two weeks away, and Giuliani had the Republican nomination sewn up. As a result, all eyes turned to the race for the Democratic nomination. Dinkins focused his campaign on bringing the city together, but Koch was uncharacteristically reserved. The mayor's silence led editorial writers around town to criticize his lack of leadership. "[Koch] has always had a troubling propensity for sending the wrong message," *The New York Times* wrote. "What New York needs now is healing. Mr. Koch has failed, so far, to promote it." And the *Daily News* wrote: "Mayor Koch must do more."

Meanwhile, the police were doing everything they could to find Joey Fama. They kept his house under twenty-four-hour surveillance, appealed to the public for leads and continued pressuring the mob to give him up. Nothing seemed to be working when, at two-nineteen A.M. Thursday, Fama walked into the police station in Oneonta, New York, a town 150 miles upstate. He was wearing faded dungarees, a gray sweatshirt and a tam-o'-shanter cap. Fama had been hitchhiking for seven days. He was unshaven, appeared disheveled, and was down to his last fifty-three dollars.

"My name is Joseph Fama. I'm wanted by the New York City Police

Department for murder," he told the desk officer. "I'm sick and tired of running."

I was sent to do a profile of Fama. When I got to Bensonhurst, 18th Avenue was already set up for that night's annual Feast of Santa Rosalia festivities. Streamers were stretched from streetlight to streetlight down the block past Fama's house. In the evening, the avenue would pulse with children's shrieks and smell of peppers and sausage, bracciola, keg beer and soft fried dough sprinkled with powdered sugar. But that morning, the food and game stalls were empty and the avenue was quiet.

The Fama's neighbors told me that Joey's father, Rocco, had left a few hours earlier in his pickup truck for work at a Manhattan construction site and that none of the other Famas were home. At a pizza place around the corner, Joe Pollari was tossing dough. "I know Joey Fama, sure," he said. "He'd come in here a coupla times every week. He'd order the same thing every time, the Panelle Special for two seventy-five and a Coca-Cola. Always a Coca-Cola. The Panelle, fried dough sandwich stuffed with ricotta, that was his favorite food. Always, 'Hiya, Joe,' he'd say. And always, he'd say, 'please,' always, 'please.' This is the first feast he's gonna miss for years."

I also found a group of teenagers who knew Fama. They were corner-kids, the local *cugeens*, who smacked their lips at women and dreamed that someday they'd trade in their skateboards for big cars. None of them would let me use their names, but they gave me enough to form a superficial sketch of Fama. He'd been an altar boy and had followed his father into construction work. Fama lived at home and spent his paychecks trying to look sharp and have a good time. He liked new shoes, Sergio Tachini suits and local dance clubs, but was best known as a roller-hockey player. He didn't have any real close friends and was always going home to shower and wash the construction dirt from his fingers. On the day Hawkins was shot, Fama had gone to work at six-thirty A.M., just like always. One friend remembered that he'd stopped for a dental appointment on the way home and left his house after dinner. After the shooting, he returned home and the next day went to work before disappearing to elude the police.

That wasn't much to work with, so I drove to New Utrecht High

School, where Fama had gone but didn't graduate from. I hoped to find somebody who knew more about him, but no one seemed to be around. I slipped through a side door into a building with long hallways and high ceilings. I'd never been there before, but the place seemed instantly familiar. Maybe because my father had gone to high school there. I discovered an office of gray filing cabinets filled with old grade cards. As I pulled open the drawers, I forgot about Joey Fama and started looking for my father's student files.

I remembered the stories he'd told me about growing up in the old neighborhood, about the big house he'd lived in on 80th Street and 18th Avenue and about playing stickball with his friends in the street. One time, Dad told me about the line drive he hit when he was seventeen years old in a championship game between neighborhood teams. The center fielder had robbed him of a sure home run. Decades later, he still remembered the schoolyard glory that center fielder had taken away. In the middle of my biggest story ever, I became obsessed with finding my father's old grades. I thought that perhaps if I found them I'd be less driven to prove myself to him. There I was, rummaging through my father's past, when a school maintenance worker walked into the office.

"What are you doing here?" she asked.

"I'm a reporter," I said. "You know that killing they had last week? Well, the cops arrested the shooter today and I'm looking for his school records."

"Well, you better look somewhere's else, 'cause you're not supposed to be in here," she said.

"It's okay. Just pretend you didn't see me here and ..."

"I think you better just leave so I don't have to call the police," she said.

Another maintenance worker, a really big guy, came by and asked what the problem was.

"No problem," she said. "I see he's leaving."

Sliding out the same side door I came in, I thought, *Yeah, journalism is journalism and life is life, but sometimes they intersect in the oddest places.* I drove back to the Fama's house and arrived just as

Rocco Fama pulled up in his truck. He had on black work pants, a sweat-stained blue T-shirt and a tan corduroy cap. He looked tired.

"I know it's a tough time for you, Mr. Fama, but can I come in and maybe talk about what's been going on?" I asked.

"I'm feeling very sick," he said, his eyes drooping over a well-groomed mustache. "I'm sick over all this. It is so much confusion."

One of his neighbors yelled from the corner, "Yo, Rocks, you doing all right? Hang in there, Rocks." Fama went inside, and a few minutes later peered out between lace curtains. He nodded to the teens, who called to him. "Don't worry, Rocks," one of them said. "Joey was just protecting the neighborhood from the niggers." In the paper the next day, I wrote the best profile I could with the information I had and ended it with that quote.

Although Hawkins was buried and Fama had been arrested, our coverage of the Bensonhurst murder was not finished. Rita Giordano, Rose and I were asked to write a reconstruction of the events leading up to the murder and its aftermath for the upcoming Sunday edition. All three of us had been so intensely involved in the reporting of this story that this assignment simply seemed like the next logical step. We pooled all of our notes. Before Giordano could weave them together into a narrative tale, we discovered that we'd forgotten about a few things as the story had grown, like how it all started. I asked Inspector Mayronne what type of car Hawkins and his friends had wanted to see. He said it was a Pontiac G-2000. I looked in *Buy-Lines Press* for the classified ad that had captured Troy Banner's attention.

There it was:

PONTIAC—UNDER $1,000
1983 G-2000, 5sp, aircond, p/steering,
brakes, am/fm; excel cond in/out, needs
engine work $500   718-256-4281

The owner, Nick Hadzimas, said the car remained unseen and un-sold. The blue Pontiac was still parked in front of 1965 Bay Ridge Avenue. Hadzimas, a twenty-five-year-old Greek immigrant construction worker whose English was not good, had bought the car a year earlier. He'd driven it to and from sites and was ready to buy a new car. A friend placed the ad in the circular for him—two weeks for twenty dollars. Hadzimas told me he remembered the phone call he received in the early evening on August 23. "The man seemed in a hurry, and said he wanted to see the car that night and I said okay," Hadzimas said. "I was waiting, one hour, two hours, three hours. Then I fell asleep on the couch. Nobody came. I thought maybe the guy changed his mind, didn't want the car."

Later that night, two detectives woke Hadzimas up and told him about a teen shot dead and a white gang with bats. "I couldn't believe it. I didn't even know that it was a black man calling," Hadzimas recalled. "To me, he sounded like an American."

No matter what Moses Stewart wanted for his son's death, Yusuf Hawkins had become a powerful symbol. On Primary Day, *Newsday* ran one of its most powerful pieces about the Hawkins murder, one that reminded people that this was a human being who had died. The story quoted a letter from one of Hawkins's junior high school teachers. She had been shocked when she read in the paper that her student had been killed. He'd only just graduated. She characterized herself as a tough teacher who began giving out assignments on the first day of class. Most students resisted this, she wrote, but not Hawkins. He did his work and participated in class. He wrote for the school newspaper, had won an award for physical excellence and always had something worthwhile to say. "Yusuf," she remembered, "was going to be somebody."

That night, after the polls closed, a friend and I went to a party in Brooklyn to watch the early returns. They were inconclusive at first, but at eleven P.M., while we were stuck in a traffic jam on the Brooklyn-Queens Expressway, Koch came on the radio. In a modest, almost gracious manner, he conceded the primary to Dinkins. At that very moment, the traffic started moving as if it had been preordained. We headed for the Dinkins victory celebration at the Penta Hotel, across from Madison Square Garden.

The ballroom was standing room only. Jesse Jackson was at the microphone and the place was wild with energy. Arms pumped with campaign signs and people batted balloons. They were dancing, singing, hugging and drinking. The mood spread across the city. Horns honked in Harlem. Fists were raised in East New York. Already, everything, everywhere seemed better.

Dinkins strode triumphantly to the podium. Blacks, whites, Hispanics and Asians, gays and straights, women and men, rich and poor, yuppies and unionists, Catholics, Protestants, Muslims and Jews cheered in unison. Dinkins was neither brilliant nor eloquent, but he said a lot with a few words. When he mentioned that Koch had called to congratulate him, just the mayor's name triggered boos and hisses.

"No. No," Dinkins said sternly. "Remember me? I'm the guy who brings us together!"

It was as if a two-ton weight had been lifted off the city. I joined a group of reporters in a corner of the ballroom. They were fantasizing about the end of the Koch era. One of them drew a tombstone on his hand and wrote A.M.—R.I.P. He told everyone that it translated to: "Alice McGillion—Rest In Peace." Her departure was just one of the great things we expected.

The official festivities wrapped up around one A.M., but I wasn't tired and stayed out until three A.M. drinking and dreaming with Elaine and a few others. Driving home, I hummed Bob Dylan's "The Times They Are A-Changin'," even if I was a little premature. The general election lay ahead, and Rudy Giuliani would be a tough opponent.

As I climbed into bed, I recalled what Jesse Jackson had said earlier that evening. "The killing of Yusuf Hawkins was the crucifixion," he had preached. "The election of David Dinkins will be the redemption."

Yes, I nodded before falling asleep, Hawkins's teacher could rest easy now. He had become somebody.

Never Say Die

When the Bensonhurst story started to quiet down, I remembered I'd been carrying around four Polaroid photographs that a transit police officer had given me a month earlier. They were so startling I could hardly believe I'd forgotten about them. The photos were of a group of prisoners lying on their backs in a holding cell. Their hands were cuffed to horseshoe-shaped rings more than two feet off the cement floor. The cuffs stretched their arms from their shoulders and cut into their wrists. It looked like the men were going through some ancient Chinese torture, except it was clear that the photos had been taken in New York. Most cops believed prisoners deserved to be treated like this. Some even called them mutts and mopes and figured nobody cared about them once they were in custody. Well, one cop did, and he had sneaked a camera into the holding cell so he'd have evidence that this was going on.

At first, I couldn't imagine why this guy would risk his ass like this, but that was because I didn't know Helmuth Ruppe. He had spent most of his nineteen-year career on the Deuce, the street name for the stretch of 42nd Street from Seventh to Eighth Avenue. He worked from midnight until eight A.M. with all the pimps, hookers, drug dealers and teenage runaways. Ruppe was six feet, four inches, 275 pounds, with a full red beard and thick arms. People on the street called him Red— like "Yo, Rayyid, what's happenin'?"—as he ambled past porno shops and triple-X-rated theaters banging his fist into his hand, flashing his smirk and bantering with crackheads and whores. What made him successful on this beat was his ability to work with these people. Ruppe used criminals to catch criminals. And with all his friends feeding him information, the Roopster, as some other cops called him, could be in a hundred places at the same time.

The people on the Deuce were not normal. They included Harry the Hooker, Mary the Pross, and a topless dancer known as Daisy because she'd let anybody pick her up. There were also transvestites, like Carmen, Suzie Q. and all their girlfriends (the young Latin American men made the best transvestites because they were small and had less hair than whites). They were the biggest gossips and Ruppe's best sources. They loved him because he treated them like ladies when he visited them in Sally's Hideaway, a lounge on West 43rd Street that was their hangout. He told them they were charming and brushed his beard against their cheeks as he whispered in their ears.

The Deuce was like a small town, and Ruppe laid down the law. But he couldn't arrest everyone, so he went by a simple code: As long as someone wasn't hurting children or old people, they could go about their business. Ruppe and his "friends" were like kids who had never grown up. They thrived on excitement and being on the edge of survival. Ruppe's friends knew he liked them, but they were also sure he'd arrest them in a second if they broke his code. He made more arrests than any other transit cop, but he knew how to treat prisoners as he brought them down to Central Booking. He always made sure they had a pack of cigarettes or a sandwich, or if they were one of his transvestite friends, he gave them time to pick up a pair of sneakers so they wouldn't have to go to jail wearing pumps. Ruppe believed that no matter what, his prisoners deserved their dignity, and when they were released, they always remembered him for it.

The department's recent double-cuffing order went directly against his principles. Under that policy, whenever a cop brought a suspect into the District One holding cell, he was required to shackle the prisoner to the horseshoe-shaped rings. The suspects stayed that way in the Columbus Avenue station beneath 59th Street and Central Park West for up to ten hours before being taken to Central Booking. For weeks, Ruppe's friends complained to him about it. They held him personally responsible because he was the only cop they knew. Ruppe was also mad because the district's captain had moved him to a new post, away from the Deuce. The captain thought Ruppe was making too many arrests and driving up the district's overtime budget, and wanted him in a lower-crime area. Banned from the beat he loved and angry with the double-cuffing policy, Ruppe took a camera to work, snapped the photos and passed them to me.

I knew Ruppe was pissed off at the district captain, so I couldn't go with the story on his word and the pictures alone. On the morning of September 20, I went by district headquarters. I stopped the first transit cop I saw and showed him the photos. He wasn't surprised at all and confirmed that it was policy to double-cuff prisoners, and had been for a few months. That was all I needed. I went back to the newsroom, laid the pictures on top of my computer terminal and began to write. I knew this was a legitimate story, but still hadn't grasped its significance.

Esposito was just back from his book leave and was working on the desk as well as running the police bureau. Hap's job was still open, and Esposito wanted to show Forst he was serious about taking that spot as city editor. Laura Durkin was a candidate, too, but she was about to take maternity leave. The choice then was between Esposito and Tom Curran.

Esposito looked at the pictures and nodded. "These are great! I'm going to push them for page one," he said, then disappeared into Forst's office for the four o'clock news meeting.

After the meeting, Curran suggested I try working into the story a doctor affiliated with Amnesty International as well as someone from the Civil Liberties Union. When I called DCPI to find out how the NYPD felt about the transit police policy, Sergeant John Clifford said it was not NYPD practice to double-cuff its prisoners. It was nice to finally agree with my old nemesis on a police issue. A comment from Al O'Leary, the transit spokesman, was also important because the story was about something going on in his department. He told me that double-cuffing was the practice in District One, but that "no complaints have been received by the department about its holding areas."

I thought I owed Richard Gollinge, the district captain, a phone call before he saw the story in the paper. Esposito reminded me that police officers had been known to put bullets in their heads after being surprised by news stories that could threaten their careers. When I couldn't reach Gollinge at his office, I got his home number from the operator. A little girl's voice was on his answering machine, saying something like, "I'm sorry, my daddy is not home. He's out catching bad guys, so please call back later." I shook my head when I heard that. If everything Ruppe said was true, Gollinge's idea of catching crime suspects also involved stringing them up. Finally, he got one of my messages and called me at the paper. Gollinge wasn't defensive at all about the double-cuffing and confirmed it was his policy. He said he'd ordered it for the prisoners' own safety, claiming that in the past they had used glass and fists to harm each other and steal each other's personal items.

"It was my decision to issue the directive," Gollinge said. "Everything I did I feel is justified and reasonable. It was for the safety of the prisoners."

"How so?" I asked.

"This is one of the busiest transit districts," he explained. "We get a large number of violent and emotionally disturbed people."

"You feel it was justified, then?" I asked.

"Everything I do I feel is justified and reasonable," Gollinge said.

Curran worked with me on the lead. We pumped it with facts and shock value. Under the headline TA COPS' CRUEL CUFF POLICY, it was one of the stories being considered for the front page, but as can always happen in the news business, the story was overtaken by a much bigger event. The night before that issue went on sale, a plane crashed at LaGuardia Airport as it attempted to take off, killing two people. This occupied the front page for days. In the morning, as we scrambled to put together our coverage of the disaster and the rescue, Esposito joked that the crash of USAir Flight 5050 had saved Captain Gollinge's career.

I was so involved with plane crash stories that I didn't have time to follow up on the transit police's cuffing policy. The editors checked me into a Queens hotel where the National Transportation Safety

Board team was examining the crash. This was actually a good break; it allowed me to focus entirely on one story rather than worrying about every siren and gunshot in the city. I could also run at a nearby park in the mornings, because my assignment was primarily hanging out in the hotel bar at night, schmoozing with the federal investigators.

While I was at the hotel, there was a major shake-up at One Police Plaza. Police Commissioner Ben Ward announced his retirement effective October 22, claiming that chronic asthma had "sapped [his] strength." However, nobody missed the coincidence of this coming less than two weeks after his boss lost the primary. Koch appointed First Deputy Commissioner Richard Condon to fill Ward's job. And a few day later, Condon selected Alice McGillion to take the post he was leaving. That shocked a lot of the superchiefs and borough commanders of the macho, male-centric New York Police Department. Not only was McGillion a public-relations person who'd never been a cop, but she was also a woman. A.M. was not about to rest in peace just yet.

Now that McGillion was her own boss, she seemed more relaxed and easier to deal with. As Condon probably had intended, her promotion also sent a positive message to the small minority of women who worked in the police department. She was the highest-ranking woman the NYPD had ever had and represented the kind of break from business-as-usual that Condon had to exhibit if he hoped to stay on under a new mayor.

When I returned to the Shack after the plane crash stories, I found a little surprise waiting for me. Someone had taped a tiny set of thumb-cuffs to our office door. Above them was the headline from the double-cuffing story and the note, "GELMAN—You better be watching your back. Signed, Your Friends at the Transit Police Department." It was obviously a joke, and Mike Koleniak had to fess up the next day because his detective brother needed the thumb-cuffs back. Another surprise was that the story about the double-cuffing hadn't been ignored during the plane crash. While I was away, Norman Siegel of the New York Civil Liberties Union had issued a complaint, which prompted the transit police chief to order an end to this policy.

This was what it was all about. A cop with a conscience and a newspaper that was willing to run a tough story had forced the department to clean up its act. I read and reread the fax of the directive O'Leary sent me about a hundred times.

A few weeks later, Ruppe called me at the Shack.

"I got something for you," he said.

"Roop, I don't do crack no more," I said.

"Nooooooo, this is serious," he said. "Meet me at the Waterfront Crab House in Queens at ten o'clock tonight."

I got there a few minutes late and Ruppe was sitting on a stool. Wood-paneled walls were covered with boxing memorabilia, including gloves signed by Rocky Graziano, Sandy Sadler and Willie Pep. There were barrels of peanuts on both sides of the room. Ruppe was nursing a cognac.

"You want a drink?" he asked.

"What's on tap?" I said.

"You drink that gorilla piss?"

"I don't care. Get me what you're having," I said.

"No. I don't think you're ready for that," he said.

Then he put me in a choke hold, laughed and told the bartender to bring two mugs of gorilla piss, one for each of us.

"So what you got?" I asked.

"Look at this," he said, pulling out a T-shirt from a bag beneath his stool.

The shirt was a present for me from the transit cops at District One. They'd nicknamed their district Fort Shackle and had made shirts with that name over a caricature of a suspect labeled MUTT who was double-cuffed to a wall with his eyes bugged out and a ball and chain dangling from an ankle. Ruppe had something else to tell me. He was putting in his papers to retire. He was fed up and bitter. "The job isn't what it used to be," he said. Especially since they'd taken the Deuce away from him; losing his beat was like losing a love. Ruppe had earned enough overtime and put in enough years to take home an annual pension he and his wife could live on. But even if he wouldn't admit it, he would miss police work. It seemed ironic that Ruppe's creative crime-fighting and belief in principles above pieties had landed him on the fast track right out to pasture.

At Ruppe's retirement party, his colleagues gave him a card that ranked him fifth behind other illustrious lawmen: J. Edgar Hoover, Dick Tracy, Bat Masterson and Dirty Harry. They also had a plaque that proclaimed him MR. 24-7-365, for his round-the-clock dedication to the Deuce. His favorite retirement gift, however, was a little piece of his old beat. Two transit cops asked one of his friends on the Deuce for this special present—a street sign from the corner of 42nd Street and Eighth Avenue.

As I walked into the Shack one morning toward the end of September, I dropped my bag on a chair and grabbed the phone that was ringing (I no longer carried my leather briefcase, but instead had an old, gray vinyl bag that was easier to lug around and looked less yup-puppish). It was Tom Curran, but his urgent tone somehow gave me the impression he'd just gotten out of a conversation with an angry Don Forst.

"You see the stories on the ballerina in the *News* and the *Post*?" he asked.

"How could I miss them?" I said.

"You could have missed ours."

"We had something, didn't we?"

"A short on page two made replate," he said, referring to the final edition.

Curran was talking about a late-breaking story we had nearly missed the night before. We had earlier deadlines than the *News* and the *Post* because they were printed in the city and we used the paper's Long Island presses. They had detailed coverage, while all we had put together was a small story.

> A short order cook was arrested last night and charged with killing his girlfriend, dismembering the dancer's body, boiling the flesh off her bones and stashing the remains at the checked baggage office of the Port Authority Bus Terminal, police said.
>
> A friend of the victim and the suspect allegedly saw the Swiss woman's decapi-

tated head in the couple's Lower East Side apartment about a week after the killing, but never reported it to police, authorities said.

The victim, identified as Monika Beerle, 26, a modern dancer who had moved to New York from Switzerland, was allegedly beaten and stabbed Aug. 19 by Daniel Rakowitz at their third-floor apartment at 700 E. Ninth Street.

Rakowitz, 28, killed the woman after they had an argument, police said. . . . Rakowitz was charged with second-degree murder [and] police said other charges were pending. . . .

The story went on to quote Ronald Fenrich, who had recently switched from head of Brooklyn detectives to the same job in Manhattan when the former chief was transferred. Fenrich had said Rakowitz had cut up Beerle's body in the bathtub and flushed her boiled flesh down the toilet. It was disgusting, but it was also tabloid heaven. It had blood and guts, a twisted psycho-killer and a beautiful, young victim. In any year, in any place, this story would stand out.

"All right," I said to Curran. "What do you want me to go after today?"

"Everything," he said.

I inhaled a mug of Community Affairs coffee and headed out, trying to think of something that would put us ahead on the story. The obvious thing was a photograph of the ballerina, because no one had had one the night before. But finding one this late was a long shot. The inspector I knew in the local precinct was on vacation, so I did what I always did when I didn't have any other leads: I went to the scene of the crime.

It was raining on East Ninth Street off Avenue C. Inside the tenement where Beerle and Rakowitz had lived, nasty graffiti had already appeared on the walls of the dank third-floor hallway: HOME OF "THE FINE YOUNG CANIBALS," and *SHE DRIVES ME CRAZY . . . SO I KILLED HER*. A neighbor pointed out their apartment. It was the one with IS IT SOUP YET? scrawled on a door dusted with fingerprint powder. Another slogan said, WELCOME TO CHARLIE GEIN'S SPAUN RANCH, a misspelled reference to Charles Manson's Spahn Ranch and Ed Gein, the real-life model for the Anthony Perkins character in *Psycho*.

Unlike most murder locations, the door wasn't sealed with a police sticker. I guess the detectives had come and gone. Inside, I found a two-bedroom apartment that looked more like a cheap flophouse than a place anyone would pay $605 a month to live in. Pots were strewn all over the kitchen, and the whole place smelled like a farm. I later learned that Rakowitz had kept a pet rooster, which he said was possessed by evil spirits. In Beerle's room, the floor was littered with clothes, ceramic figurines, cassette tapes, sexually explicit novels, a book of German poetry and a collection of watercolors. One pink ballet slipper was perched on a chair.

After searching everywhere and coming up with nothing, I tossed Beerle's soiled mattress against the wall and found her whole life hiding under her bed. There were photographs, résumés, letters, addresses, programs from past dance performances, all neatly packed in a clear plastic bag. My heartbeat quickened. I was shocked and thrilled, and felt like a thief, a sneak, and a damn lucky reporter. Just then, a television crew entered the apartment. I stuffed the package underneath my blazer and snuck past the TV crew out to my car. The photographs showed a young woman with stringy blond hair and a lithesome body. Half of a 35-millimeter contact sheet was of Beerle practicing pirouettes in a white leotard. That must have been her light, traditional side. The rest of the roll pictured her in a black, long-sleeved bodysuit doing kinky things with inner tubes. In one eight-by-ten close-up, Beerle had blood streaming from her polished lips. The most erotic image was on the cover of a program from a 1986 modern dance tour through Switzerland. In it, Beerle, her face contorted with passion, was peeling lingerie from her shoulders, leaving her breasts thinly veiled by a white lace bra.

Her résumé was also in the package. It was just the kind of short sketch that would have been in the program if she'd made it to Lincoln Center:

> Monika Beerle, born May 11, 1964, is
> from Switzerland where she has received a

certificate for teaching and choreography
from the Sigurd Leeder School. She has
toured her own work around Europe as
well as presented it at the Martha Graham
School, where she is currently a student.

And there was a letter from a friend awaiting her arrival back home:

Dear Moni,

How do you do in New York? We are expecting you with tension
to see your new dance! Did you receive your contract? Please
send it back fast! Your rehearsal time [for the Tapeo Dance Festi-
val] is Thursday October 13th—12 p.m. Be there Wednesday to
confirm.

We'll see you soon, Good bye.

I stuck the package under my car seat and went back inside to finish
my reporting.

Rakowitz, a drifter and son of a Texas cop, had lived in New York
for five or six years. He told anyone who'd listen that he wanted to get
rich selling marijuana. Even in a neighborhood known for its characters, he was considered as eccentric as the best of them. With his long
hair and dirty blond beard, Rakowitz looked like Jesus, but claimed he
was the Antichrist. He talked of Satan worship, carried his pet rooster
on his shoulder and cooked chicken to feed the homeless in Tompkins
Square Park.

Rakowitz and Beerle had met in the park one day earlier in the
summer. He must have found her alluring, and perhaps she found him
intriguing. He had an apartment near the park, but not enough money
to keep it. She paid the back rent, moved in and took over the lease.
One neighbor from down the hall said Beerle had been living with
Rakowitz for about two weeks when he went berserk. Rakowitz had
bragged their sex was wild and exciting, the neighbor said, but then
Beerle had told him she wouldn't fuck him anymore, and Rakowitz
turned on her.

"In our last conversation, we were sitting on a stoop nearby, and he
told me he killed her," the neighbor recalled. "Then he cooked her

head, ate part of the brain, cut up her body and fed it to the people in the park. I said, 'Danny, if you did that, the police will get you.' And he said, 'I'm just kidding. Oh, James, you know I talk crazy stuff.' I wanted to believe he was just talking nonsense, but he was crying when he said it."

On the way to the newsroom, I stopped at a Blimpie's sandwich shop near the office. Blimpie's had real sentimental value for me because the No. 1—turkey, cheese and spiced salami, with extra onions and vinegar—was the same sandwich I'd get when I went out for lunch during elementary school. As I was watching the rain, my beeper went off. It was the desk, letting me know that Chief Fenrich was trying to reach me with new information on the case.

He was as cool, precise and emotionless as ever, speaking of these insane acts as if he were going over a shopping list. "There were rumors in the community that found their way to detectives," he said. "The rumors were that people had seen body parts in an apartment on East Ninth Street and that the suspect cooked them and fed them as soup to homeless individuals." I scribbled down everything he said. Rakowitz had made a videotaped confession, and the medical examiner's office was waiting for dental records from Switzerland so they could positively identify Beerle's skull.

"Chief," I said, hoping to hook him into a quotable tabloid phrase. "Have you ever seen anything like this?"

I wanted some snappy rejoinder like "Only in the movies" or "It's the goriest in recent history," but that wasn't Fenrich's style. He paused and recited some more facts. "What happened was that a relationship that started as girlfriend-boyfriend and became a tenant-landlord relationship as well turned sour," he said.

Uh-huh. I thanked him for the call and finished my Blimpie's No. 1.

At the office, I was pretty pumped up knowing I'd gotten Forst this exclusive art on the victim—about as erotic as a U.S. tabloid can get and still be legitimate—and enough new reporting to put together a strong package for the next day. The rest of the Boiled Ballerina Pak spread across pages two and three, then jumped to page thirty-one, where there was another photo of Beerle, this one in her black bodysuit arched over an inner tube.

I realized while I was writing why this story had made me a little nostalgic. The log-on code I'd selected when I joined the editorial pages was 25E9, the address of the building I'd grown up in. This was the same street where Beerle had been killed. As I laid my notes and the photographs on my desk, I realized that in covering this story I'd come back to the place where I'd spent so much time as a kid. I was back home, writing about the city I'd grown up in. I also discovered that I'd covered enough crime by this point that the extraordinary circumstances of this murder didn't even turn my stomach. And I don't know why, but Monika Beerle never became a person to me. I'd been in her room, been through her things, talked to people who knew her. But her death never angered or saddened me. She was first a story to chase, then a character to write about.

I hadn't realized how desensitized I'd become until Rose and I had dinner the next night with a close friend of mine who was finishing law school in Portland, Oregon. I'd known Scott Snyder when we both lived in Los Angeles. We'd played Little League baseball together. I'd listened to him strum on the dulcimer and read his poetry during high school. Scott also went to college at Berkeley, and when the workload would get too heavy, we'd escape to a Warriors-Knicks game or sneak up to Lake Tahoe for a couple of days of skiing. That night we met at a Spanish restaurant and were joined by Scott's fiancée, Melissa, and another couple, both local magazine writers. As we dug into the paella and drank sangria, Scott asked me what I'd been doing while he and Melissa had been out seeing museums and catching tourist sights.

"Been writing about the boiled ballerina," I said.

Scott hadn't seen the paper, so I took this as a great opportunity to mention every gritty detail of the murder and its aftermath. I laughed loudly as I told the story. Rose continued eating as did the other couple. Then I noticed Scott and Melissa glaring at me. They were shocked by what I was saying—and by how casually I was saying it. I had become so sick I didn't know sick when I saw it.

Scott and I were living in two different worlds and weren't able to talk to each other the way we used to. While he'd been studying and writing about the laws and values we'd spent so much time discussing in college, I'd let my emotions harden to the point that this horror story about a young woman mutilated by a psychopath seemed like a comedy. Scott had always been something of a conscience to me. That dinner and the way Scott and Melissa had looked at me began to show me that every day it was getting more difficult to fight cynicism and indifference. The curses I'd sworn to resist were taking over.

Once I understood this, instead of turning myself around, I started losing the energy I brought to the beat. I was finding it harder and harder to get excited about covering "the crime of the day," and the little bit of sympathy I felt when I saw the list of unidentified dead black males on the sheets was slipping away. Some mornings my head felt like a rock when I woke up. This wasn't from too much booze or beer; I was hung over from the constant contact with crime. If the beeper went off or the phone rang, I felt like calling a bulldozer to lift my head off the pillow.

The best aspirin was a tip on a story. On the morning of October 17, my beeper went off at six-thirty A.M. The number was Esposito's home phone followed by a 10-13, which was part of a code system he'd set up. This was code for a cop needing emergency assistance.

"You've got a dead cop in midtown," he blurted out when I called. I had no time to think. "I want every lick and splatter. And call photo as soon as you find out who the cop is."

"Okay," I said.

"I called you at home a few minutes ago. There was no answer. Where are you?"

"At Rose's."

Until then, I don't think Esposito had figured out that Rose and I were involved. Some reporter.

"Hmmm," he said. "When did this happen?"

"You were away for a while," I said.

"We're going to have to have a talk about this girl thing. It can screw up your reporting."

"I heard you had a few 'girl things' in the past."

"Uh, what did you say? . . . I think we're losing the phone connection. Wha-wha . . . Did you say something?" he said.

"Nothing. Just that I hear there're a few newsrooms around town where it's no longer safe for you to enter," I said.

"Maybe. But no lawsuits."

"And what's that about how someone used to keep clean shirts in his desk at the Shack?" I asked.

"Uh, yeah. Back to the story. You gotta rock 'n' roll on this one," he said as he hung up.

Esposito was running hard for the city editor job. Curran, who'd been an editor a long time, was the logical choice, and he had the inside track. But Esposito wanted the spot, and I felt obligated to help him whenever I could because he had done so much for me when I was breaking in. There wasn't much I could do, but I could put whatever enthusiasm I had left into the stories he assigned.

While I was out covering the police officer who had been killed, I was missing a ceremony at Police Headquarters in which Lori Gunn and Jennifer were accepting an award for Billy. He was still in a coma but had received a plaque from the New York's Finest Foundation for exceptional valor. Later I called Lori from home to explain why I'd missed the ceremony. She'd heard about the officer by then and started asking me questions about him.

"Was he married?" she asked.

"No. Single," I said.

"How old was he?"

"Twenty-three."

"So young," she said.

"Too young," I said.

"I guess you'll be writing about his funeral," she said.

At first, that struck me as an odd thing for Lori to say. "I might cover it," I said. "But the paper could send someone from the Island, since he lived out there."

"I can't get myself to go to any cop funerals," she said. "Since I know that is something that is waiting for me, it scares me. All those blue uniforms and white gloves make me shake sometimes. Maybe I should be there to support the widows, but I'm not a widow, I'm not, and I can't get myself to go."

I guess it wasn't such an odd question after all.

*   *   *

There is a point in any young reporter's career when it is time to do more than just write daily news stories. You are expected to address broad themes and important issues, not simply tell what happened. In the middle of October, I was still having trouble getting excited about stories, but one did capture my attention. At first, it only interested me intellectually, but as time went on, it grabbed me emotionally as well. And this story, if I could pull it off, was my chance for that break-through. I began by writing a regular news story about the death of eleven-year-old Raheem Clark, but I discovered that this was an oppor-tunity to expand on the crime beat.

Raheem had been riding a mountain bicycle at three A.M. on Friday the thirteenth when he was shot with a bullet intended for someone else. The cops said that he had been in trouble before and may have been delivering crack for one of his older brothers the night he was killed, but this kid seemed too young to be a hardened criminal. Ra-heem lived in a crumbling redbrick tenement in the Mott Haven section of the South Bronx, an area that had the lowest per-capita income in the country. When I parked my car outside Raheem's building at around nine A.M., I had to leap over a stream of water from an open fire hydrant to get to the sidewalk. I made my way through a lobby covered with graffiti and climbed a stairwell that smelled of urine and booze to the third floor. I knocked on the door and someone peered through the peephole. "Go away," a female voice said. I shouted that I was a reporter and wanted to write something nice about Raheem's life. The door cracked open.

"It's a newsman," one of Raheem's aunts or sisters said as she let me in.

Raheem's mother sat on the far side of the kitchen table. Cock-roaches darted across the chipped Formica top, past a bottle of Pepsi in a paper bag and down the rusted table leg to the floor. Jacqueline Clark wore a faded denim skirt, black tights, white boots and a soiled black work shirt. Her Afro was short and natty, and her face seemed to be filled with as much guilt and anger as it was with sorrow. The kitchen ceiling was cracked and pipes bled water down the walls. One of Raheem's older brothers, a sixteen-year-old who was strong and thin and wore a black baseball cap tilted to the side of his head, glared at me suspiciously.

Raheem had lived with his mother, three brothers and two sisters, aged eight to sixteen. When he dropped out of school in the fifth grade, he was maintaining a family tradition. His mother, who had had her first child when she was seventeen years old, never finished junior high school, and his brothers weren't exactly on any honor rolls. When Raheem's mother was pregnant with him, she and his father got into an argument and he fired a gun at her. The bullet grazed her skull. She never reported the shooting to the police, but Raheem's father was convicted a short time later for attempting to murder a man. He served time in prison and was then deported back to his native Dominican Republic.

Meanwhile, Jacqueline Clark received $322 in welfare payments and $230 in food stamps each month, which was hardly enough to support six children in 1989. Growing up in this environment, all Raheem cared about was food. He bought pizza, Big Macs, french fries and take-out Chinese with whatever money he could get. His five-foot, 158-pound frame earned him the nickname "the Fat Kid."

After interviewing Raheem's family, I asked if they had a photo we could publish. Jacqueline Clark looked but couldn't find one. Raheem's grandmother, Annie Barnes, thought she had a picture at her apartment I could use, even though it was a couple of years old. She agreed to ride over to her place with me to get it. Barnes was a strong woman. She'd been a counselor and dietitian at a psychiatric institute for twenty-three years. Although she had two other daughters who were making it, she could never accept the tragedies that befell Jacqueline's crew. And she had had a special feeling for Raheem. On the ride across the Bronx, she told me that the week before Raheem had given her a brass ring with a silver butterfly on it.

"He said he'd gotten it from a bubble gum machine and told me, 'Now, Grandma, you keep this and give it back to me when I get married.' I asked him, 'Do you have a girlfriend?' He laughed. Oh, he had a deep laugh. He was like a man-child, bigger in size and older in his ways than other kids. 'No. No,' he told me 'bout having a girlfriend. But someday he said he would."

The next morning, I was shocked to see that the reporter from the *Daily News* and I had done very different stories, showing opposite sides of the same boy. I had thought it was important to show what Raheem's family situation was like and how circumstances like that could lead a boy to trouble. But the *News*'s story basically said Raheem was young, bad and dead. Their tone was set in the headline THE LITTLE BIG SHOT. What bothered me most about the *News*'s story was that it did nothing to explain how a kid Raheem's age ended up out riding a bicycle, possibly delivering drugs, at three A.M. on the streets of Mott Haven. Despite the intentions of the city's education, social-services and legal systems, no one had been able to save Raheem. That, to me, was the tragedy of this story, and I wanted to find out more about it.

Tracing this aspect of Raheem's life involved going into the city's welfare, public education and law-enforcement bureaucracies. Not surprisingly, the people at these agencies did not completely welcome a reporter probing into their business. The Human Resources Administration told me I couldn't talk to the caseworker assigned to Raheem's family because of confidentiality laws. The principals at the schools he attended would say only that he had a poor attendance record and had been transferred into a special education program at one school and subsequently moved to a neighborhood program for troubled youth. After that program failed, Raheem's mother brought him to family court. There the judge referred him to the probation department, where he was slotted as a PINS kid, social work jargon for "person-in-need-of-supervision" and sent to the Pleasantville Diagnostic Center, a home for wayward kids in Westchester County.

At Pleasantville, Raheem constructed his own fantasy universe with his father as a mythic figure at the center. According to a counselor I spoke with, "this universe was nurtured by all the deviant behavior, drug dealing and prostitution he saw in his neighborhood. All the characters bore a resemblance to the indestructible villains he saw on television cartoons. And in the fantasy, everyone, including his father, lived defiantly yet survived." These counselors worked with Raheem, but he kept running back to the streets. When he went AWOL for the fifth or sixth time, they gave up on him. Back home, he grew more impulsive and violent. His next contact with official New York was an arrest for allegedly extorting five hundred dollars from a bodega around the corner from his apartment.

While awaiting disposition of the case, Raheem's great-aunt, Lillian Pettaway, a religious lady, made one of the last attempts to help him. "I talked to him about Jesus," Pettaway recalled. "I told him the Lord loved him and asked him if he knew the song 'Jesus loves me, this I know, because the Bible tells me so.' He didn't respond. Just said, 'Yep.' " Apparently, that wasn't the way to get to Raheem either.

A few weeks later, Raheem became Homicide Case No. 1714, the fifty-eighth person killed in the Mott Haven section of the Bronx in 1989. As I delved into his story, I was reminded of Shawn Motayne, the ten-year-old who was shot in the head in Flatbush and made the miraculous recovery at Kings County Hospital. These two boys had grown up in very different circumstances, yet nearly met the same fate. Shawn was blessed with a good family and a strong faith, and Raheem had been surrounded by turbulence and instability since the day he was born. I wanted Shawn's perspective on Raheem's life. If nothing else, he could describe how it felt to be shot at at that age. And we could show readers how another victim had survived.

Shawn's family had moved to New Jersey, but I reached his mother at her job in the city. She told me to call Shawn at their new home that night. This was my first time talking to Shawn, and he sounded bright and energetic. It had been six months since he was struck down on his way to pick up the laundry in Flatbush. He still came to Brooklyn to play on his dad's soccer team, but said he liked Jersey fine. His head was a little tender and itched sometimes. The most difficult part of his rehabilitation, he said, was dealing with the students at his new school.

"They keep calling me 'Scar-head' and 'Split-head,' " Shawn said, noting that the bullet had left a mark on his skull. "My mother told me to tell them about the shooting. So I told them I was shot, and they said I was lying. They said that if I'd been shot in the head, I'd be dead."

I was surprised when he said he'd already heard about Raheem on the radio. He said he had wondered why an eleven-year-old's mother had let him stay out that late. Having lived in East Flatbush, Shawn understood how kids like Raheem could get into trouble. But even if they didn't court violence, the streets were dangerous places for children to be. Shawn still remembered the evening he was shot—the shouts and the men with guns. He was trying to put the shooting behind him, but some nights he'd wake up in a cold sweat after dreaming about men in full-length leather coats and gunfire. The cops never made an arrest in his case, but Shawn was not bitter, because the Bible taught him to forgive those who make mistakes. He was more concerned about his future than his past. He wanted to be a doctor or a lawyer so that he could save people's lives or put criminals in prison. In the meantime, he just wanted to finish the sixth grade and keep playing soccer.

While Shawn could get on with his life, the only thing left to do with Raheem's was write about it. I had all the material I needed to make Raheem's story dramatic, and Esposito and assistant managing editor Rich Galant, the number two editorial guy after Forst, had given me time to concentrate on it. Galant believed this piece went beyond daily tabloid fare and wanted it in the paper. I had never tried writing anything this long and was terrified I wouldn't be able to string it together. I worked up four leads, structured it ten different ways and stayed late rearranging drafts. One night, I brought it home and actually worked on the story in bed.

During that time, I was a miserable person to be around. I was rude to friends and ignored Rose. I had been upset earlier in our relationship because I thought Rose was too into the newspaper thing. One night, we'd even gotten into an argument about this.

"Rose, talk to me like a girlfriend, not a journalist," I had said.

"You forget your girlfriend is a journalist," she'd responded.

The next morning, the argument was still simmering and had continued on our way to buy the newspapers. She said something that burst my self-control and I threw the whole stack of dailies into the air. They came fluttering down in front of the newsstand. It was a weak attempt at releasing my frustration over being trapped in that world. Somehow I blamed this on her.

But while I was writing about Raheem Clark, it was clear that I was into this stuff as much as she was. I couldn't get my mind off this story, nor did I want to. Late one night, I even drove to the North Bronx to get a recent photograph of Raheem from a relative who lived in the Edenwald Houses. This was particularly stupid because at the time this was where an ongoing drug-gang war was taking place. Also that week, Rose and I met some of her friends for a movie. But when we learned the film was sold out, instead of joining her friends for dinner, I left to go home and work on the story. Rose was understandably angry.

Although my writing had come a long way since I'd bungled the brief on the unidentified parking lot attendant during the first few weeks on the beat, I still had a lot to learn. I worked with Esposito on my early drafts. He hadn't edited many large stories, and we were kind of like a comedy team, sitting at his terminal trying to act like we knew what we were doing. Finally, I moved what I thought was a sufficient draft to Galant. I nearly croaked when he sent it back with a list of suggestions almost as long as the story. He wanted a new lead, tighter writing, more focus on the larger implications of the boy's death and a quote from a prominent sociologist on the state of inner-city youth in the nation. It took a few more days, but I completed a publishable version.

The most poignant part of the story, which took up two full pages in the paper, was the ending: Raheem's funeral. As a gray-bearded preacher delivered the eulogy, Raheem lay in a metallic-blue casket dressed in a white seersucker suit. His hands were clasped and resting on his stomach. The color of the casket matched his shirt, tie and pocket handkerchief. White carnations rested in the folds of his elbows. Ten aisles of folding chairs were filled with Raheem's family and friends. His brothers were there—teenagers with jagged, razor-cut hair —as were his mother, his grandmother and his great-aunt, who looked prim and proper in her black dress and a pillbox hat.

"Raheem's name will live on because he was a victim, but more because he was part of a family," the Reverend T. Metz Rollins said. At first, his voice was soft, then it rose slightly. "And more because he was a flesh-and-blood young man. We must care. And we must be angry. Because, brothers and sisters and friends and relatives of Raheem Clark, as long as there is a sense of anger over the loss of one person, there is a sense of hope for the future of others."

After the service, the preacher told me he'd been in the Bronx for seventeen years but had never buried as many children as he had in 1989. "Whenever I hold an infant at baptism, I wonder if the child is going to make it to Communion," he said. I nodded and we stood on the sidewalk and watched the pallbearers carry Raheem's child-size casket from the funeral home and load it into the hearse.

Despite the cynicism I'd developed, as I watched the hearse roll off toward the cemetery I noted with some surprise how involved I had become with this story. Like all crime reporters, I'd done a pretty good job recently of distancing myself from the people I wrote about. I tried to think of them as victims, not people. Maintaining your psyche was easier if you saw them this way. But taking the time to write more than just a news story about Raheem's death forced me to see that this wasn't always possible. I had to believe that by telling his story—even if it had only a small effect—I'd make other people see what was happening. And maybe that would make someone try harder to keep children from getting into the paths of bullets.

At the end of the month, Rose and I took off to the Bahamas—as far from the crime beat as we could get. As much as I loved being with her, sometimes our dedication to the paper was too much. Even at the beach, there wasn't much room to expand our relationship. I feared that the same thing that had brought us together would force us apart. Still, being away from New York with Rose was great. We walked on the sand, took boat rides and gambled at the casinos. It was a lovely week and it ended too soon.

At the airport, we saw by the headlines at the newsstand that the city was in the final days of the mayoral campaign. Dinkins led Giuliani in the polls, but few thought he'd win easily. The campaign had been waged more on contrasts in image—skin color, manner and party affiliation—than on the candidates' positions on the issues.

As a crime reporter, I was not part of the election coverage and chose to watch the returns on November 7 with Dr. Clarke at the hospital. I wanted to see what was really going on in the city that night, and felt Kings County was the best barometer of that. I entered the lobby and stepped carefully through a maze of homeless men and women wrapped in ragged blankets. Outside the emergency room, I saw Clarke hurriedly walking from his office to the trauma unit.

"Can you believe it?" he said, waving me toward him, his Jamaican accent harsh with exasperation. "Thirty-two patients have been admitted without beds for any of them, and there are a hundred and five patients waiting to be examined. Soon, I will have to park them in the hallways."

The place looked and sounded like a Civil War hospital. Bodies were lined up side by side in the male and female treatment rooms, and patients covered with pale blue sheets were hallucinating or lying comatose. They tried to catch Clarke's ear. "Doctor ... doctor ... doctor ..." they called. Like stricken animals, they begged to have their pain relieved. But their voices trailed away as the sounds of Linda Ronstadt and James Taylor oozed through the air.

Clarke stepped up to one man, who appeared to be in his forties. He was sitting on the side of a bed waiting for treatment. The man was semiconscious and had a seven-inch gash in his head. His face and neck were covered with blood. Clarke pulled on a pair of latex gloves and asked what had happened. The man had fallen on the sidewalk while trying to escape a group of teenagers who were mugging him. They ran away when he crashed to the pavement.

"Let's take a look," Clarke said. He stretched the wound open, shaved around the gash and injected the man's head with Novocain. Clarke then used a curved needle to carefully stitch the gash closed. He pressed the needle into the man's scalp, gripped the thread, pulling it through with a pair of tweezers. With each stitch, the gold bracelet his daughter had given him fell to his wrist and glimmered slightly.

"You'll be all right," Clarke said when the wound was fully sutured.

Another man was running around the emergency room corridor. His right hand was shredded and blood was dripping on scuffed high-top sneakers. He reeked of whiskey and peered through drug-crazed eyes. The man was yelling that he'd put his hand through a glass window. Another doctor and two security guards tried to get him to stand still.

Clarke asked him to calm down and take a seat, but the man only snarled: "You're a doctor. I'm a crackhead. That don't mix." Finally, the security guards wrestled the man onto a stretcher and he passed out.

It was nine-twenty P.M. and Emergency Medical Service paramedics were rolling more patients up the cement loading dock into the E.R.

"Oh-my-God, they're still bringing patients here," Clarke said as he hustled back into his office. "I have a feeling it will be a long night." He paused. "I've been having that feeling a lot lately."

In his office, Clarke flipped on a little Casio pocket television and put it on the cluttered bed. The latest returns had Dinkins at 52 percent and Giuliani at 46 percent, with about half the precincts reporting. Clarke predicted the margin would widen before the night was over. "You see," he explained in a bit of physician philosophy, "Giuliani had an inability to show strength with empathy. That is a combination you need to heal." Instead of stretching, Dinkins's lead narrowed to 2 percent, but it still held.

At his election headquarters, Dinkins stepped before his balloon-tapping, confetti-tossing supporters. "How far we have come since the days when my father was young," he said. "November 7, 1989, is a day that will live in history. We passed another milestone on Freedom's Road." The cameras panned the ballroom, where hundreds cheered a new leader and reveled in hopes of a newly invigorated city.

But at Kings County Hospital, two paramedics pushed a stretcher up the cement loading dock and rolled it into the trauma unit. A fifteen-year-old with three bulletholes in his body lay motionless on the white sheets. The paramedics didn't know why or how the teenager had been shot, only that they'd picked him up on a Flatbush corner famous for two things: cheap crack and fatal gunfights. From the trauma unit, politics seemed like nothing more than a meaningless diversion.

Another Record

Lori Gunn had started therapy and was slowly learning to deal with her life. She still traveled to the rehabilitation center in Waterbury at least three times a week, though Billy wasn't getting any better. His muscles were atrophying, and each time she saw him, his legs were curled closer to his chest. The right side of his head looked like someone had planted a bowl in his skull. The wound's ridges ran three inches deep, from above his right eyebrow to the back of his head, and the crater, about six inches in circumference, had a scar down the middle. His hair hadn't grown back there, but Billy did have his mustache again.

He seemed to relax when she petted his forehead. He breathed through a tracheotomy tube in his neck, and a catheter carried his urine into a plastic bag. Lori laughed when she remembered making Billy go on a Slim Fast liquid diet a few weeks before he was shot. Now, when he'd spend the rest of his days being fed intravenously, it seemed pretty silly. She'd look at him and kiss him on the cheek. Her nose would squish down like a button and she could tell he needed a shave. Then she'd say softly into his ear: "Billy, this is Lori. If you can hear me, close your eyes. Close your eyes and keep them shut if you can hear me." Some days he'd close his eyes and she'd talk to him. Other days, his brown eyes just darted whenever the light shifted.

Lori played tapes for Billy: James Taylor, Waylon Jennings, Bruce

Springsteen, Randy Travis and special mood tapes she'd bought for him, *Tropical Rain Forest* and *Ocean Spray*. When football games were on, the nurses turned on the television and put earphones around Billy's head. But when someone scored a touchdown or made a tackle, Billy didn't react. The Billy who used to slam his fist into his hand while watching the Jets was not the Billy lying in the bed.

Lately Lori's life had fallen into a rut, and she was getting depressed. She was losing hope of getting clues from Billy. She yearned to know if he was aware of anything and was drained from not being able to find out. The doctors were little help. One told her Billy had the intellectual capacity of a lower life-form. He compared him to a frog. Lori tried to imagine talking to her husband like he was a frog. It didn't help. What did a frog know? Could you train one? Did a frog feel joy or pain? She didn't know. She would go to sleep at night thinking about the man detained inside her husband's deformed skull and wonder if he was trying to escape. She prayed that Billy was unconscious and didn't know what was going on. Still, when she looked into his eyes, she feared he was inside. If so, he was not ready to give up the fight. And neither was she.

There were only two ways for her to get away from Billy. She couldn't pull the plug anymore. He was off a respirator and it was too late for that. She could either cut him loose by ordering doctors not to resuscitate him if he stopped breathing, or set herself free by getting a divorce. She meditated on these options. A lawyer Lori had seen just after Billy was shot had told her about a firefighter who lay in a coma for years. Eventually his wife left him. Lori was haunted by that story. She didn't want Billy to be that firefighter nor did she want to be that wife. Some days she cursed Billy for leaving her stranded, but other days she was overcome with love. As long as he was alive and that brain was connected to a heart that was beating, she would stay his wife.

In early November, I saw Lori and her parents at a police officers' football game in Brooklyn. The game raised a few thousand dollars for the Billy Gunn Support Fund. Lori enjoyed the celebrity that came with being the wife of a wounded police officer, but even that had its pressures. "It's like people I hardly know come up to me and tell me their problems," she said while shivering in the grandstands. "As if I don't have enough of my own. I don't mean to be bitchy. I'd like to be more supportive. But what do they think I'm made of? Some kind of unbreakable plastic? They come up to me at functions and things and tell me their crises." Whenever she was at functions like this, she felt she had to fit some image of the quiet, stoic woman with the fortitude to smile through the tough times and live for a better day. But she wasn't always like that.

Lori's memory of Billy as a person was fading into myth, and she didn't know if it was fair to her or Jennifer to cling to the dream that someday he'd return. "It would have been easier if he were dead. Then, we'd have our pleasant memories of him, mourn him and get on with our lives," she said awhile later. "By his not being dead, he was a part of our lives every day. It was like there were two Billys, the old one and the one that was left." She began taking down Billy's photographs so that people walking into her home wouldn't be greeted by a shrine to Billy Gunn. But she kept his clothes in the closet. As she watched Jennifer grow, Lori realized that time was passing and she wanted to prepare to go back to school or get a job. Without Billy, she had to discover herself.

One afternoon, I checked in with Lori after I'd covered a story about two police officers who had been killed. I didn't call to talk to her about the cops, but every time a cop was shot I couldn't help thinking about how she was doing.

"Could you hold on one second? I'm sorry," she said.

I could hear Jennifer crying in the background.

"Do you want your hair braided or not?" Lori asked.

"Okay," Jennifer squeaked.

"Then come here and behave yourself while Mommy talks on the phone," Lori said and picked up the receiver. "She's been acting up today. I don't know. Maybe something's wrong with her."

"Sounds like she's acting like a two-year-old," I said.

"Yeah, but I'm in no mood for a two-year-old today," she said.

On days like that, instead of feeling sorry for Billy because he was missing Jennifer growing up, she cursed him for not being there to help her. Lori often felt stranded without a husband, especially today,

258 I CRIME SCENE

she said, because tomorrow was their anniversary. In the morning, she and her father drove to Waterbury together. In Billy's room, she found a dozen roses that her father had sent ahead. They made her cry.

The Sunday before Thanksgiving, she visited a recently married friend who was living in a Manhattan high rise. "We went to Sarabeth's Kitchen, this place with lace napkins and all that. I had a nice time and will have to do this more often," she said. "But the people in the city are weird, though. You can't get normal things there. Like, if you just want a cheese omelet, you can't get regular cheese. You have to get Gruyère cheese or goat cheese. And I don't understand why the women don't wear pumps."

For a few hours, at least, Lori was able to leave her problems behind and talk about things like shoes and clothes and cheese. She was happy her friend's marriage was working out but remained confused about her own. Lori and Billy didn't have a conventional marriage, but in many ways their bonds were deeper than ordinary couples'. Certain needs were still fulfilled while other desires were left unsatisfied. For Lori, marriage had become something other than living together and having someone to sleep with and wake up beside.

She had discovered that she could give and care with a capacity she hadn't dreamed of. Her need to be needed, by both Jennifer and Billy, was constantly reaffirmed. She still had a long way to go before she'd be able to fully accept what had happened to Billy, but she was also growing out of her old self and into somebody different. "When I lost Billy, I lost part of myself, too," she said. "I also found a part of myself that I wouldn't have found with Billy." If things had gone on without that bullet from Ralph Richardson's gun, Lori knew she would have remained sheltered. Watching this unfamiliar woman emerge from inside her was exciting and scary, but more often than not, Lori liked her new self just fine. She had become more independent, decisive and confident than she'd ever imagined. Whether she was peppering Billy's doctor with questions, challenging her parents on money matters or choosing a school for Jennifer, she was being herself, someone she'd never been before.

The only truly terrifying part of her changes was a thought Lori kept in the back of her mind but would never utter. What if by some miracle Billy did come back and didn't like the woman she'd become?

November 23 was the best kind of New York day. Clear and crisp, but not so cold that the wind bit too hard. The Cop Shop was quiet. Koleniak, Jim McKinley (who'd replaced Don Terry at the *Times*) and I were drinking coffee and hoping nothing would happen.

Jim told a story about an old Dodge Dart he'd bought for four hundred dollars to help him get around on stories. The car was so wrecked he figured nobody'd ever bother it. But one morning, he found a hooker and a john screwing in the backseat. He said, "Excuse me, but I have to go to work, too." And the hooker grew angry. "Wait a minute," she said, as if she were finishing up something and he'd just have to understand. From there, we started talking about the women in our lives. Jim and I had girlfriends, which somehow seemed more complicated than Koleniak's wife and three daughters. As we were rattling on, an unmistakable face appeared in the doorway. My heart started beating faster.

Joe Cotter was home.

I reached out and hugged him and gave him a kiss on his cheek. He had lost a lot of weight and was wearing a new blue blazer. Joe showed his crooked teeth behind a wide smile. His mind was quicker than his mouth and he talked more softly than he had before. But I heard every word.

"Is Richie here?" he asked.

"No," I said. "But let me call him."

I got Esposito on the line and told him someone wanted to say hello. I handed the receiver to Cotter, and they talked for a few minutes. Cotter muttered something about the place being much dirtier than when he'd left it. After he hung up, I introduced him to the new people at the Shack as the "dean" of police reporters. He told them he wasn't a dean at all since that's what they called you when you were all washed up. With Anne Murray as his escort, and his wife, Pat, by his side, Cotter headed up to visit Alice McGillion.

"Oh, Joe, while you're upstairs could you check the sheets?" I asked.

"Of course," he said.

The morning had gotten even better. Esposito and the paper's gossip columnist concocted an item that made us chuckle at the Shack the next day.

Welcome Back . . .

Eyes misted over and even crusty crime reporters and cops applauded spontaneously when New York Post veteran police reporter **Joe Cotter** showed up at police headquarters the other day after being in a coma for several months. Cotter came by with his wife, **Pat,** to pick up the overnight crime sheets, and meet with police brass. A police reporter for 41 years, Cotter walked in, looked around and said, "These kids keep the place much dirtier than we used to." He then went on to chew out New York Newsday reporter **Mitch Gelman** for contributing his share in turning their little police HQ enclave into something more closely resembling a pigsty. Gelman, for the first time in his life, said he was happy to be chewed out, and that, "You could look into those Irish eyes and see the human spirit live forever." Cotter is known as the guy who'd crawl into police headquarters around 4 A.M. and get all the scoops before other reporters heard the first strains of the alarm clock. Before Cotter went into his meeting with police brass, he asked his wife, "Is my hair combed? Both of them?"

Ben Ward's retirement party was jammed with cops who blustered from one end of the hors d'oeuvres table to another, angling for favors and promotions. Ward received dozens of awards and testimonials and seemed touched, triumphant and gracious that night, except when it came to the press. Recalling Calvin Coolidge's remark that the business of America is business, Ward commented that the business of the press is business, and added that the business of Ben Ward made good press. Ward may not have been a smooth talker, but in a lot of ways, he was right.

Even though Ward had spent most of his tenure putting his foot in his mouth, he had broken a color barrier. That made it easier for Dinkins to select anyone of any race as Ward's successor. The selection of a new police commissioner would be Dinkins's highest profile appointment. This would be the person who would stand next to the mayor during crises and would symbolize law and order in an increasingly lawless city. Dinkins needed someone he could trust as well as someone whom the people of the city would respect.

As the jockeying for this job went on, crime continued. An eighty-one-year-old Salvation Army volunteer was robbed by two men who grabbed his collection pot and ran off with the donations. Not exactly *Miracle on 34th Street.* A fifty-five-year-old woman, dubbed the "Coke-Dealing Granny" by the cops, was babysitting five grandchildren and wearing a pink housedress when police raided her Upper West Side apartment. Wonder what kind of Christmas they had? And a black man fatally stabbed another black man who was mugging a white straphanger on a train in Harlem. Millions of New Yorkers hailed the unidentified "Subway Samaritan" as a hero.

By mid-December, Dinkins had narrowed the field of candidates to four: Richard Condon; Henry DeGeneste, executive director of the Port Authority Police Department; Joseph McNamara, former city cop and chief of the San Jose Police Department in California; and Lee Patrick Brown, chief of police in Houston, Texas. After they met a screening panel, DeGeneste was the first to go. Condon was next; Dinkins wanted his own man running the NYPD. The choice came down to Brown and McNamara, two men who could not have been more different.

McNamara was a swashbuckling former city police captain who'd gone west. His father had been a city cop and his roots were in New York. McNamara was also a national figure, having written several bestselling police novels. And he had a personality as big as his Hollywood grin. On the other hand, Brown was a behind-the-scenes man, erudite, professorial and measured in everything he did. He was a self-described law-enforcement professional who was respected for having turned the Houston Police Department into a first-rate force.

Esposito decided that if Brown got the nod, I was to write his profile. Another reporter began researching McNamara's career and background. Dinkins pledged to make his choice on Monday, December 18, and at a public appearance the Saturday before, I asked him if a plane ticket to Houston would be a good investment. "Houston's always nice to visit," he said.

Acting on his instincts, Esposito sent me to Houston, along with my notes and a tiny Tandy computer and modem. I picked up a car at the airport and checked into a room at the Hyatt Regency. Despite the time difference, I wasn't tired and walked around downtown Houston that night. It was clean and quiet. Pennzoil Plaza was a long way from Times Square. I was excited about being sent to another city to report a big story, but I was also terrified that Dinkins actually would pick Brown and I'd screw up the assignment.

In the morning, I arranged to use a desk and telephone at the *Houston Chronicle*, and before I was even settled, Dinkins had announced that Brown would be the new commissioner. Simultaneous press conferences in New York and Houston were scheduled for nine A.M. Houston time, which gave me about three minutes to find Houston Police Headquarters. Leaving my Tandy at the *Chronicle*, I scribbled some directions and headed across town, running, walking, running, trying to look as dignified as possible, but acting like I was in the middle of a Laurel and Hardy skit. The whole day turned into a slapstick comedy filled with rookie errors and miscues. It didn't seem so funny at the time.

Trying to write 1,500 words on the Tandy scared me half to death. I kept telling myself it was just three 500-word stories. Or five 300-word stories. Or four 400-word stories minus 100 words. Muttering and typing and calling around Houston for comments was making me nuts. At the same time, I was trying to get an interview with Brown through the public information office down there. That's why I'd been flown to Houston, and if I couldn't come through, I'd feel worthless.

At two o'clock Houston time, the phone rang. Forst was on the speaker phone, calling from the four o'clock news meeting back home.

"What do you have?" he asked.

"We've got an exclusive with Brown, lots of good stuff on his background. He's a rags-to-riches story," I said. "The guy started out in Wewoka, Oklahoma, and now he's going to New York."

"Have you talked to him yet?"

"Will in a few minutes," I said. Lying is easier when you're two thousand miles away. "I have to go over there, now."

"All right. Thank you."

Click. I was close to panic and nearly hyperventilating. Brown had told me at a press conference that morning that he'd give me an interview, but I'd just promised something and had no idea whether I'd be able to deliver it. The Tandy wasn't helping me any either. The screen showed only a few lines at a time, which was like trying to write a novel on a napkin. And I wasn't even sure the photographer I'd lined up could focus a camera. I started typing like a madman, one hand on the keyboard, another holding the phone between my left ear and neck. In New York, the editors already had a front-page headline—NEW TOP COP: THE MAN BEHIND THE BADGE—and the paper's public relations team was sending a press release to local radio stations about our Brown exclusive. But down in Texas, I didn't have diddley.

The fellow I was talking to at Houston police public information was named Sergeant Joe Bob or something. He had a good-old-boy drawl and kept saying he'd get back to me, but never did. When I called again, his secretary would say, "Ah'm sorry, Sergeant Joe Bob's in with the chief raight now. Can ah take a message for 'im?" Finally, I barged into Sergeant Joe Bob's office and told him Brown had promised me an interview.

A few minutes before five P.M. in Houston, Brown was ready to meet the media. Sergeant Joe Bob said the commissioner had to do a live television feed for local news before he could get to me. I could hardly stand still knowing I had a Tandy I could barely write on halfway across town and a desk full of editors in New York holding back deadline for the lead story. When Brown finished the television spots, I bounced up the stairs next to him and poked a tape recorder in his face. Brown is about six three, and I had to reach up with the microphone. As Brown talked, I checked my watch. After my last question, I mumbled a thank-you and raced back to the *Chronicle* and finished putting my story together.

Then it was time for a new fear: What if I couldn't get the modem to work? I'd heard horror stories about them only functioning properly about 40 percent of the time. My story was fifteen hundred words, which was about twelve hundred too many to dictate on deadline. It had to work. But it looked like I wasn't ever going to find out, because I didn't know what numbers to dial to connect with the paper's computer system. Finally, I reached one of the paper's computer guys at home and he gave me the access phone number. I dialed. The phone line beeped. I put the modem's telephone muffs on the receiver and waited. The story flashed on the Tandy. Somehow, by the grace of the guiding light of computer chipdom, the story made it. The desk received all fifteen hundred words. We would be the only paper in the city with a story on Brown that had a Houston dateline.

When I got back to the hotel, I tried calling Esposito at home but got his message machine. Not only did he return the call but so did his wife, Debbie. A few weeks before, I'd helped her put together a guest list for a surprise party for his thirty-fifth birthday. The party was December 29 and she was supposed to drop off invitations that day for me to distribute at the office. With me out of town, we arranged to have Rose deliver the invitations.

The next day, I filed a few sidebars from Houston that rounded out our coverage, and I ate some great Mexican food. Then I remembered Uncle Abe's motto—"Bring a small pumpkin pie and the hell with 'em" —and found the Texas equivalent on my way to the airport. I picked up a couple of cowboy hats and armadillo key chains for the editors, some Armadillo Droppings (praline cluster cookies) to bring to the Shack, and I LOVE HOUSTON coffee mugs for some of the cops in DCPI.

Mayronne beamed when I gave him the coffee mug. He raised it to his chest and boasted that he was going to use it to taunt Chief of Department Robert J. Johnston. Johnston, an old-time city cop who ran the operations end of the department like he was General Patton, was scared shitless about what his new boss was going to do to the department. Mayronne was going to use the I LOVE HOUSTON mug to bust the four-star chief's balls. I enjoyed seeing them sweat a little. Yet, for the first time, I felt a little clubby with these characters and shared their nervous laughter. Information was influence and almost everything they knew about Brown they'd learned from the article I filed from Houston. I knew him better than they did. Before Mayronne headed across the hall, he summed up the department brass's impression of Brown. "This guy pisses ice water," Mayronne said. "I wouldn't want to play poker with him."

Certainly, big changes would take place when Brown moved into the commissioner's office. For one, he'd have to pick a new first deputy, because Alice McGillion was taking a job in public relations for Philip Morris, the cigarette makers. In the Shack, many of us thought that it was a logical career move for her to go to the tobacco industry. We had a laugh over it, but not for long. It was time to let A.M. rest in peace.

When Brown came to New York the next day, I was the only local reporter he knew by sight. For some reason this gave me a confidence during a press conference that I hadn't had before. I don't think Brown even recognized me in the rows and rows of reporters, but it was fun thinking I had some advantage over the others.

I took Christmas off and spent the holiday in Washington, D.C., with Rose and her family. We opened presents and enjoyed a quiet day with her parents, two brothers and a cute little niece, Elaina, whose baptism we'd attended a few months back. I gave Rose a gift certificate to get some fishes she wanted for her aquarium, and she gave me a leather jacket that she said would improve my street credibility and newsroom style.

On December 28, Esposito wanted a year-end crime story. Based on figures through the first of December, the city was ahead of 1988's record homicide count. Another reporter and I rounded up the obligatory quotes from criminologists and found out that 250 guns and 2,100 other weapons had been taken from kids in schools.

To broaden the article's scope, I phoned Dr. Clarke. He had recently appeared on several television panels and his *New York Times* Op-Ed piece was selected for a collection of articles on drug legalization. That morning, he was still incensed at the government's refusal to consider legalization as a policy option. "The politicians won't come around until the blood of their children flows in the gutters of the suburbs," he said. I had come to believe he was probably right.

Clarke's thoughts on how drug violence was hurting the hospitals helped give context to our year-in-crime wrap-up. But the story still needed live detectives, so I called the 34th Precinct squad in Washington Heights. They had recorded ninety-nine murders and were running corpse-and-corpse with the Seven-five as the highest precinct in the city.

One of the detectives picked up the phone. "Three-four. Detective Montuori," he said.

"Detective Montuori. This is Reporter Gelman. How's things in the Three-four?" I said.

"Busy," he said.

The key to talking with detectives was hooking their ego early. Otherwise, they'd tell you to call DCPI.

"You guys have had a hell of a year."

"It's not over yet."

"How's the holidays treating you?"

"Not bad. We've been quiet the last few days. We've got our tree up and our candles going."

"Hanukkah candles?"

"No," he said. "The Santería kind."

"You mean that voodoo stuff?" I asked.

"We'll try anything," he said.

"Are the candles working?"

"As good as anything else," he said.

I knew things were bad out there, but now the detectives in the largest municipal police force in the capitalist world were burning Santería candles in the middle of the squad room. I called the desk and told Esposito.

"They're what?" he said.

I repeated the stuff about the candles. "It's that bad," I said.

"That's great! That's a separate," he said. I could tell by the speed of his voice he liked the story. "Bang out the main and give me a five-hundred word sidebar on the cops and the candles. Get in all the details."

Despite death's spirits marching on in the Three-four, that afternoon was not without its levity. One sheet showed a burglary suspect who'd gotten stuck in a chimney while trying to break into a Bronx grocery store. Somehow, the lead I wrote—HO, HO, HO, HELP!—actually made it through the copy desk and into the paper. It was my favorite of the year.

On the morning of Esposito's surprise party, it was slow at the Shack so I went to the paper's midtown office and picked through my mail. Esposito offered to take me to Brooks Brothers. He said he was going to help me look like a journalist now that I was starting to report like one. We hustled down Madison Avenue and talked about the paper and women and stuff guys talk about. It was a Friday and he asked me what I was doing over the weekend. I made up something about going upstate and asked if I could leave early to get a jump on traffic. I didn't want to blow the surprise.

At Brooks Brothers, I fell in love with a soft brown sport coat with flecks of gray and two shades of blue in the weave. It cost nearly a week's salary. As the tailor snapped chalk marks on the cuffs and mumbled about taking in the waist and letting out the shoulders, my beeper went off. It was Tom Curran.

A Con Edison gas main had exploded in the Bronx. The power was out, the subways were down, and the fire was still raging. Esposito went back to the newsroom, and I went to the fire. Driving across the Willis Avenue Bridge, I saw a fireball rising like a bright orange mushroom cloud hundreds of feet into the sky.

The explosion had melted the paint off of parked cars and had killed two people. The Coast Guard fished a teenager's body from the river half a block away, and a Con Ed worker's charred body remained by the backhoe he was using to dig up the street when it struck the main. I filed the details on the blast, and waited for the rampaging to begin. With the power out, no one knew what would happen.

As it got dark, store owners shuttered their shops and people who'd been let out of work early scurried home with bundles of candles and canned food in their arms. The streets were eerie, with the only light coming from the headlights of passing cars. Cops stood sentry at major intersections. Buses were the only public transportation running and there were lines of people at stops, pushing their way through crowded doors.

I got two beeper calls as I was driving around Mott Haven watching this prelude to a possible disaster. The first was Esposito, who wanted to know what was going on, and the second was his wife, Debbie, who wanted to know whether Richie was going to be stuck at the office along with every reporter she'd invited to his party. There was still time, I reassured her. But unless Con Ed got the power back on soon, it could be a long night.

At six twenty-four P.M., the first streetlight flickered, and a few minutes later, they were all on. There'd be no rioting in the Bronx that night, and the party would go on.

I went back to the office and found Forst sitting on the desk between Esposito and Curran. The tabloid promise of the explosion hadn't been fulfilled, but Forst was going to squeeze every inch of copy out of the story. He told me to do a tick-tock—a chronology starting from the minute the hoe hit the main—and four hundred words on the fear on the Bronx streets. This was the first time Forst had assigned me breaking news.

The stories would be easy enough to deliver. Other reporters had already compiled most of the chronology, and the street scenes were still in my mind. But sitting down to write, I remembered the morning Forst interviewed me for the researcher job. He and my father knew each other, and my father must have talked about his son. Forst looked at me and said, "You're the athlete." I hadn't hit a curve ball since college and told him that was once true, but not anymore. "Right now," I said, "I'm just unemployed." After a few innocuous questions, he asked me what I wanted to be doing in three years. I told him I hadn't thought about the future much but hoped I'd be a reporter at his newspaper. Three years later, I realized how close that future had been, and how little I'd understood about what it would be like to get there.

By eight o'clock, the subways were running and the stories were in. I headed downtown and joined Rose for dinner before the party. When

Esposito walked into the Palladium, he was genuinely surprised. "You keep a good secret," he told me later, which in the world of Italian Rules was not something to be taken lightly. It was a great party with everyone there. McAlary and Drury hung out by the bar, and Hap Hairston was talking with a *Daily News* reporter in the corner. A few of the cops from DCPI showed up, along with Rich Galant, Barbara Strauch, Stutman from the DEA and a lawyer representing one of the Bensonhurst defendants. A few editors and reporters from the *Post* and *Times* also came. Looking around, the year scrolled through my mind, each face linked to a time, a place and a story.

A few minutes after midnight, my beeper went off. I had forgotten that I was doing a radio call-in show that night. *The Barry Gray Show* had asked me to talk about the year in crime, and I'd told the producer to beep me ten minutes before we had to go on the air. I'd been drinking beer and Irish whiskey all night, so I stumbled into the bathroom and slapped cold water on my face. I didn't want to make a fool of myself.

I used to listen to talk-radio shows when I was a kid in the city and got a big kick out of being on them. I pressed the phone to my ear so I could hear over the noise of the party. Gray and his listeners wanted to know what we could do about crime. They wanted solutions! Gray advocated stiffer sentences and more jail cells. One caller wanted anyone caught with a gun to be put away for life, and another argued for legalizing drugs. The final caller said the key was reaching kids early enough to prevent them from becoming crack dealers or addicts.

As he was wrapping up, Gray asked me if I had any last thoughts. At first, I didn't recognize my own voice. I hadn't spoken like this for a while. I was saying the problems were daunting but not insurmountable, that we couldn't trust politicians or police officers to stop violence or get rid of drugs, but that New Yorkers had good judgment and wouldn't self-destruct. That, I said, was how we'd survive the crime scourge and come through together in the end. I'm not sure I actually believed what I was saying, but that didn't really matter. I was saying it! The lift in my voice recalled an idealism I was startled to hear. It proved the cynicism that had stalked me all year hadn't completely taken me over and crushed my spirit.

Most of the guests had cleared the club by two A.M. when Rose and I picked up our coats and drifted down the stairs with a few others. A light snow had fallen. Flakes clustered in the sky and floated to the ground as we drove across town to the Lion's Head.

Entering the saloon, I passed the jukebox and gazed over at the book covers on the wall. I saw the Pete Hamill column near the kitchen, the same one I'd seen hanging over Esposito's desk my first day at the Shack. The column was about a winter night just like this one, the snow falling outside while a group of reporters huddled around the bar.

Shortly past four o'clock, when we left, the snow was piling up on Christopher Street. The whiskey warmed my stomach and blended with the snow that hit my tongue as Rose and I stepped playfully toward the car. It was a moment when everything seemed possible. For the first time all year, I reached down to my belt and turned off my beeper.

Epilogue

The dog story was the one that convinced me it was time to leave the police beat.

An off-duty cop was taking his two young children to a wake on June 16, 1991, when a dog started barking at them. The cop said he shot the golden Labrador retriever to stop it from attacking his kids. The dog's owner said the dog loved children and was yapping only because the officer was scolding his children. I recounted the dog's final moments: *Whimpering and bleeding, Sandy limped into the store, lay down, yelped once and died.* I didn't forget a picture of the dog this time and Don Forst wrote a front-page headline: SANDY'S LAST BARK. The next morning, a friend told me he couldn't believe we'd actually run that story on page one.

"What are you talking about?" I said. "Sandy made the ultimate sacrifice. He gave his life for a headline."

It was definitely time to go.

A lot had happened since Lee Brown settled in as police commissioner in January 1990. Richie Esposito was named city editor, Tom Curran was made a top editor on the investigations team, and the faces changed in the Shack. My former bureaumates, Elaine Rivera, Alison Carper and Chapin Wright, all went on to new assignments and were replaced by other reporters. Oddly enough, with those three gone and Esposito now running the desk, I had the most seniority in the bureau.

When I received the Nellie Bly Cub Reporter award from the New York Press Club for stories I worte in 1989, the ribbing I got proved that the people might change but the Cop Shop was the same old place. Anne Murray of the *Post* was the first to congratulate me. "Hey, here's Nellie Bly," she said, referring to the legendary female reporter. "Does this mean you're going to wear a skirt to work from now on?" This was Anne's revenge for all the cookies I'd taken. The best surprise we got all year was when Joe Cotter actually kept his promise to return to work. He came back to his old morning shift and kept at it for a few months before retiring after forty-two years on the beat.

The Bensonhurst trials started that spring, and on May 17, a Brooklyn jury found Joey Fama guilty of second-degree murder for killing Yusuf Hawkins. Rose was covering the trials for the paper. We had stopped dating, but were still good friends and worked well together. She wrote about the Fama verdict and about Keith Mondello's conviction for first-degree riot the next day. Russell Gibbons's friend, Charles Stressler, was acquitted on all charges. Of the five other white youths accused in the Bensonhurst incident, two were acquitted of all charges, two were given probation and one was sentenced to a short jail term.

I had become comfortable in the Cop Shop, but some days covering the police beat got me so down that I just sat at my desk and tossed a baseball against the metal wall waiting for another homicide to come over the hotline. The death toll had gone up in 1989, and 1990 was ahead of the pace. After a nine-month-old boy was shot through the door of his Bronx apartment while he was sitting in a walker— the latest of four children slain in eight days—I did a story tracing the history of the gun that killed him. It had been made in Brazil and purchased over the counter at a sporting-goods store in Petersburg, Virginia, by a former mental patient for $379 plus 4.5 percent sales tax. It was then smuggled into the city, where police said it was sold on the streets for about a thousand dollars. The gun was one of tens of thousands in the hands of criminals. Esposito and I tried to come up with themes that would dramatize the killings for readers. When Mayor David Dinkins said that New York was not Dodge City, we ran a front page that said, IT'S NOT DODGE CITY, BUT ... Inside was a package of stories comparing New York of 1990 to Dodge City, Kansas, of 1878, when Wyatt Earp was sheriff. Dodge City may have had a higher per-capita murder rate, but New York still seemed more and more like a lawless frontier town.

Once in awhile there was some good news, like the first birthday party for Grace Ann Machate's baby, Nicole Marie. I had stayed in contact with the family, and Bobby's father, Robert Machate, Sr., invited me to the party. There were balloons and a clown, but Robert Sr. wasn't having a good time. More than a year after his son's death, he still hadn't gotten over it and told me he was planning to move to Florida.

Another person still adjusting was Lori Gunn, who still visited Billy twice a week. She had him moved to a nursing home half an hour from her house and went to see him on Sundays and once during the week while Jennifer was in nursery school. His condition was unchanged, but he had a modern room with a wall covered with photographs of Jennifer, who was growing up without him. Lori had been through three therapists until she found a fourth whom she felt comfortable with. He helped her deal with her stress and convinced her that after what she'd been through, there was nothing she couldn't handle. Lori started to exercise regularly and enrolled in English and psychology classes at Nassau Community College. At first she thought school would be just a place to train her mind, but the next semester, she started thinking about going to college full-time and getting the degree she'd given up on years earlier.

Toward the middle of 1991, Jennifer began asking a lot of questions about Billy, even having dreams about him.

One morning, she told Lori, "I dreamed about you and Daddy last night."

"Was he lying down or walking and talking?" Lori asked.

"Walking and talking," Jennifer said.

Lori believed that Jennifer's curiosity was a sign she was beginning to understand what had happened. That pleased Lori, and she was careful to answer Jennifer's questions honestly. When her daughter asked what had happened to the man who hurt Billy, Lori said, "Daddy got the bad man so he can't hurt anyone else." That didn't satisfy Jennifer. "If Daddy hurt the bad man, how did the bad man hurt

Daddy?" she asked. Not the usual questions of a four-year-old. Still, Lori was confident she'd be able to raise Jennifer and get her own life back on track at the same time.

Lori wanted to meet more people and maybe join a tennis club. But she was being patient with herself. She was still working on becoming a whole person again. More than two years after Billy's shooting, Lori continued to get by minute to minute, even though she had begun to live day by day.

Over the summer of 1991, I began talking to Esposito about what I should do next. I was burned out on covering cops but didn't know where I should go from there. Then, oddly enough, the answer developed out of the biggest crime story of 1991.

A car driven by a Hasidic Jew in the Crown Heights section of Brooklyn went out of control on August 19 and struck and killed a young black boy. A few hours later, hundreds of blacks in the neighborhood took to the streets and one roving mob attacked the first Hasidic man they saw. They singled out Yankel Rosenbaum, a twenty-nine-year-old visiting scholar from Australia, and one of the teenagers stabbed him four times. Rosenbaum was taken to Kings County Hospital, where he died early the next morning. This led to a confrontation between cops and robbers for the next three nights that Jews compared to Kristallnacht and blacks likened to the way police rounded up protesters in the old South. Once again the city seemed to be on the brink of a race war; it was a tense situation, but eventually the police regained control.

On August 29, Kildare Clarke called me at home with a tip I didn't believe at first. Clarke said that Rosenbaum never should have died, and he put me in touch with another doctor, who confirmed that the doctors in the emergency room had missed one of Rosenbaum's most serious wounds. The second doctor said that Rosenbaum drowned in his own blood while lying on a stretcher in the trauma unit. The emergency room doctors on duty that night apparently were diverted by two other crime victims—one with a gunshot wound and another who'd been slashed—and didn't give Rosenbaum enough attention. I wrote the story for the paper the next day, and the New York State Department of Health opened an investigation into the case. A few weeks later, they issued a report faulting the care Rosenbaum had received.

My relationship with Clarke had paid off in a way that I'd never imagined it could. His tip and the paper's reporting helped focus more attention on the city's hospital system than there had been in twenty years. Dinkins appointed a special counsel to review the Rosenbaum case, and then named a commission to review the city's overall health-care network. Health and hospitals became a topic of growing interest. It was also an area that *Newsday* wanted to pay more attention to. Esposito asked if I'd be interested in covering it. I said that I would. My new beat wouldn't start till January, so I continued to cover cops through the end of 1991.

In the three and a half years I covered the police beat, 7,368 people were slain in New York City, more than twice the number killed during the 1950s—nearly one every four hours. It was odd to feel sentimental about a place that concerned itself with statistics like that, but I would miss the Shack. I'd done a lot of growing up there. The place was like a childhood home. On my last day there, I deliberately left some things so I'd have an excuse to return. But when I went back a few weeks later to get those files and notebooks, it seemed a lot smaller than it had on my first day, when I had felt like I was stepping up to the plate at Shea Stadium. Police reporting was a great thing to have done, in many ways an adventure. But 1,100 stories—and twice as many beeps —later, it was time to move on.

February 1992
New York City

Acknowledgments

In many ways, this book is a collaboration, and I am indebted to everyone whose path crossed mine during the period it covers. Hundreds of people were generous with their time, expertise and emotions. But there are some to whom I owe special thanks.

I have benefited tremendously from the patience of my editors at *New York Newsday*, especially Dee Murphy, Barbara Strauch, Tom Curran, Debbie Henley, Laura Durkin, Jackie Jones, Kristen Kelch, Kate Phillips, Joe Gambardello, Joe Demma and Clem Richardson. I am grateful to Tom Plate, Ben Gerson and Ernest Tollerson for their guidance; to Rich Galant and Richard Esposito for giving me time to work on this project; and particularly to Don Forst, the creator of *New York Newsday*, who gave me a job and a chance to see what I could do.

I appreciate the support of my partners in the Shack, Russell Ben-Ali, Peg Tyre, Curtis Taylor, Curtis Rist, Elaine Rivera, Alison Carper, Chapin Wright, Mike Koleniak, Anne Murray, Ginny Byrne, Chris Olert, George James, Jim McKinley, Patrice O'Shaughnessy, Larry Celona, Don Terry, Donatella Lorch and Denise Barricklow. And I am lucky to have friends and colleagues like Manuel Perez-Rivas, Bob Liff, Chris Hatch, Ed Quinn, Ken Sawchuck, Jon Naso, Donna Dietrich, Dave Herndon, Julio Laboy, Paul Marinaccio, Scott Ladd, Jim Dwyer, Phil Messing, Andy Furrillo, Len Levitt, Denis Hamill, Jeff Goodell, Joanne

Wasserman, Rita Giordano, Julie Shpiesel, Kirsten Hamilton, Yolanda Edwards, Kim Schaye, Sharon Epel, Ken Yamada, Jim Nolan, Jim Ledbetter, Lyle Harris, Mark Lowery, Peter Moses, Bob Gearty, Bill Douglas, Sheldon Ito, Jeff Silverman, Ken Sanzel, Helmuth Ruppe, Scott Snyder, Tom Feuer, Mike Robin, Eric Spillman, Christine Baird, Karen Van Rossem, Teresa Moore, Tom Goldstein, Mary Cronin, Bonnie Angelo, Gillian Shreiber, Giselle Benatar, Yeo Lay Hwee, the Sandlers, the Buxbaums, the Masons, the Friedmans, Jerry Migliore, Jack Walsh and Mike Race, and others who offered experience, advice and encouragement.

I'm also thankful for the many kindnesses of Mireya Navarro, Joe Queen, Regina Taylor, Marshall Hennington, David Kocieniewski and Willie Rashbaum, who were never too busy to listen.

In addition, Bob Cividanes, Al O'Leary, Bob Valentino, Bob Nardoza, Joe Gallagher, Tom Fahey, Pete Berry, Pete Sweeney, Nick Vreeland, Ray O'Donnell, Suzanne Trazoff and Lynn Shulman are all good people in tough jobs. I also value the loyalty and integrity of numerous transit and city police officers who would only get in trouble if I mentioned them here, but who know who they are.

This book would not have been possible without the talents of David Black, who honed an idea into a proposal, and Henry Ferris, who used a sharp mind, and an even sharper No. 2 pencil. I am also grateful to Timothy Murphy, who helped take it the rest of the way.

Thanks, as well, to Frances Golden, Rita Golden Gelman, Jan Gelman and Steve Gelman for giving me attention and solitude: whatever was needed whenever I needed it.

I am, of course, fortunate that Dr. Kildare Clarke took me into his confidence during a turbulent year.

But no one gave more to this book—or asked less from it—than Lori Gunn. To her and her family, I will always be grateful.

Above all, there is one person whose energy and companionship helped make 1989 a year to remember, and for that and much more, Rose Marie Arce has my gratitude and trust.

About the Author

MITCH GELMAN was part of the *New York Newsday* team that received a Pulitzer Prize for its coverage of a subway crash in 1991. He worked in the police bureau from 1988 to 1992, and currently covers crime, health and urban affairs for *New York Newsday*. He is the author of seven children's sports books. He lives in Brooklyn, New York.